The Vinyl Dialogues
Volume III

"Stacks of Wax"

Mike Morsch

Copyright©2016 Mike Morsch

Cover photo and design by Ron Dacanay.

Editing by Frank D. Quattrone and Gemini Wordsmiths: Ruth Littner and Ann Stolinsky.

ISBN: 978-1-62249-352-4

Published by Biblio Publishing
BiblioPublishing.com

Table of Contents

Introduction
1

Watching the Beatles take America by snowstorm
Sands of Time
Jay and the Americans
3

Standing out while . . .
Sittin' In
Loggins and Messina
15

Stretching right up and touching the sky
Electronically Tested
Mungo Jerry
29

Kicks just kept getting harder to find
Indian Reservation
The Raiders
39

The bluesman and the bad boys
Hooker 'n Heat
John Lee Hooker and Canned Heat
49

Mike Morsch

A wolf in simple clothing
Of a Simple Man
Lobo
57

People all over the world get on board
Back Stabbers
The O'Jays
67

A new Cadillac for the guy who couldn't even drive
Spinners
The Spinners
79

It was a movement, not a rock band
Wovoka
Redbone
91

A worn-out, ragtag bunch of musicians
Bloodshot
J. Geils Band
99

They don't know you, but they know these people
Friends and Legends
Michael Stanley
109

A vintage look with a different sound
Self-titled
The Pointer Sisters
121

Failing at something long enough to be a legend
Sold American
Kinky Friedman
131

Re-launching a career with help from the Rocket Man
Sedaka's Back
Neil Sedaka
139

Wacky cover photo, cool music inside
Daryl Hall and John Oates (The Silver Album)
Hall & Oates
149

A 'reunion' song for two different solo albums
Breakaway
Art Garfunkel
165

Blown away by her own voice on a boom box
Inseparable
Natalie Cole
177

Mike Morsch

Surviving the stranglehold of a big psychological mess
Self-titled
Ted Nugent
187

Encouraging the booty shakers
Part 3
KC and The Sunshine Band
197

Avoiding the electric fan in favor of spiders and snakes
Let Your Love Flow
The Bellamy Brothers
205

Movin' up to the big time with *'Movin' Out'*
The Stranger
Billy Joel
213

Building the brick house wasn't so easy
Self-titled
Commodores
223

Two tickets to rock stardom
Self-titled
Eddie Money
233

They wanted to see the old card trick first
Works Volume I
Emerson, Lake and Palmer
241

The hush surrounding a blond-haired soul brother
Self-titled
Bobby Caldwell
251

A bottle of Jack to complement *My Fair Lady*
Kenny
Kenny Rogers
261

The success just spread like wildfire
Lost in Love
Air Supply
271

Finding the lost skins and laying the foundation
On Through the Night
Def Leppard
279

Acknowledgements
289

Sources
293

**About the Author
297**

**Index
299**

Introduction

Natalie Cole gave me the impression that she really didn't want to talk. Sometimes that happens. A veteran artist gives many interviews over the course of a career, and answering the same questions over and over can be tedious.

I had requested an interview with Ms. Cole for a story that would advance a show she was doing in New Brunswick, New Jersey in March 2015. She didn't agree to the interview until late in the process, but still in time to make my deadline for *Time Off*, the entertainment section of Packet Media LLC, the company for which I work.

But it was apparent to me from the get-go that she would have preferred to be somewhere else besides on the phone, talking to me.

Ms. Cole wasn't impolite or evasive, just uninterested. In fact, she sounded a bit run-down — fragile even — so much so that I inquired about her health. She had experienced health issues in the past, announcing in 2008 that she had been diagnosed with hepatitis C, which she attributed to intravenous drug use. That eventually led to her having a kidney transplant in 2009. But she assured me that she was fine.

Ten months later, on December 31, 2015, Natalie Cole died.

Her death on the last day of 2015 seemed to usher in a rough start to 2016. Just 11 days later, David Bowie died. And six days after that, Glenn Frey, founder of the Eagles, died. Then in another 10 days, Paul Kantner of Jefferson Airplane died.

And the list continued to grow in the first half of the year. Maurice White of Earth, Wind and Fire died in

Mike Morsch

February; Beatles producer Sir George Martin, and Keith Emerson of Emerson, Lake and Palmer both died in March; Country music legend Merle Haggard died in April, as did Prince.

The Vinyl Dialogues series has, from the beginning, been about accurately documenting the recollections and perspectives of the artists who made the music that is the soundtrack of my generation, specifically the 1960s and 1970s.

But there seems to be a sense of urgency now. The artists who crafted he soundtrack of our lives are getting older, and some of them are "moving on." And with them go those stories about the making of the music.

The Vinyl Dialogues Volume III: Wax On continues the tradition of documenting those stories. It's a lot of fun to talk with the people I listened to on the radio of my dad's 1975 Chevy Impala — the one with the bench seat that allowed my girlfriend to slide over and sit right next to me while I drove.

And that's the other thing about *The Vinyl Dialogues* series that's always been a huge kick — many of the albums and songs remind me of a simpler time when I was younger, growing up in the 1970s. My hope is that it does the same for you.

So sit back, put some wax on the turntable, and relive those times with these stories.

- **Mike Morsch**

Watching the Beatles take America by snowstorm
Sands of Time
Jay and the Americans

Jay and the Americans didn't just do cover songs on their "Sands of Time" album, they acted like they had never heard the songs before and styled them after the way they did songs. (Photo by Mike Morsch)

In February 1964, a snowstorm had blasted the Northeast. The region was paralyzed and air travel was virtually shut down.

Sandy Yaguda waited out the storm at his home in Brooklyn.

Yaguda — stage name Sandy Deanne — was one of the original members of the group Jay and the Americans, which, by winter of 1964, had recorded a couple of hit songs, most notably "She Cried," which reached No. 5 on the Billboard Hot 100 chart in 1962.

And then the phone rang on February 10 at Yaguda's house. It was the band's manager.

"He called and said, 'Listen, you guys have to find a way to get to Washington, D.C. You're playing with the Beatles and the Righteous Brothers tomorrow night,'" said Yaguda.

The Beatles had taken America by a storm even bigger than the one that had rocked the Northeast that week. They had made their U.S. debut on the *Ed Sullivan Show* on February 9, 1964, in New York City, and their first live concert in the U.S. was scheduled just two days later, on February 11, at the Washington Coliseum in the nation's capital.

Because of the heavy snow blanketing the region, all flights had been canceled and the Beatles had taken a train to D.C. for the gig. Originally scheduled to appear with the Beatles at the Coliseum were the Chiffons, an all-girl group from the Bronx who had the hits "He's So Fine" and "Will You Still Love Me Tomorrow" in 1963; and Tommy Roe, who had a No. 1 hit with "Sheila" in 1962.

But because of the storm, neither the Chiffons nor Roe could make it to D.C. Instead, the call went out to the Righteous Brothers and Jay and the Americans to fill the bill.

"We had seen the newsreels of the Beatles, with girls screaming and fainting in Germany. The hype was on but they hadn't really been here yet. They were just starting," said Yaguda.

Jay and the Americans made it safely to D.C. the day of the show and upon arrival were immediately greeted by the marquee on the outside of the Coliseum that read, "The Beatles . . . and others."

That didn't sit too well with Jay Black, the lead singer for Jay and the Americans.

"Fuck this! Turn the car around! We're leaving!" Yaguda recalled Black saying.

"And me being the voice of reason — the Ringo of the group — I said we can't do that, we signed a contract, we'll get sued for twice the money. We have to play the show," said Yaguda.

Black calmed down and the group unloaded the car and went inside the Coliseum.

A pre-show press conference with the Beatles was about to start and the members of Jay and the Americans wanted to see what all the fuss was about. So they sat in the grandstand of the Coliseum, close enough to hear what was going on between the reporters and the Beatles.

"One of the reporters said, 'How did you find America?' And Ringo said, 'We made a left at Greenland.' We all looked at each other, and we said you know what, these aren't silly little kids. These kids are sharper than they're getting credit for," said Yaguda.

The show itself was a madhouse. During the performance by the Righteous Brothers, the crowd of mostly young girls chanted "We want the Beatles!" so loudly that it nearly drowned out the opening act.

Once again, that wasn't acceptable to Black. When the crowd continued chanting "We want the Beatles!" during the Jay and the Americans set, Black reacted, but not in anger.

His instincts turned out to be right this time.

"Jay, being who is he, went out and said, 'Hey, man, I'm glad you all came out to see us tonight,'" said Yaguda. "And they all cracked up. That won them over, so they shut up and listened to us and when we were done, gave us a big round of applause."

When Jay and the Americans finished its set, the band members returned to their dressing rooms in the basement of the Coliseum.

Mike Morsch

Sandy Yaguda said that when the members of Jay and the Americans witnessed how Ringo Starr and the rest of the Beatles handled questions from the media before their first live concert in America, "We all looked at each other, and we said you know what, these aren't silly little kids. These kids are sharper than they're getting credit for." (Photo by Mike Morsch)

"About three minutes later, a noise went up the likes of which I've never heard in my life, not when the Yankees won the World Series, not when Elvis performed. Because it was an enclosed building, the sound couldn't escape; it just kept reverberating," said Yaguda.

The Beatles had taken the stage.

"It didn't die down. It was continuous. We all had to cover our ears with our hands and we just looked at each other in amazement," said Yaguda.

"When it finally stopped, we said to each other, 'Something just happened.' We saw Elvis and we played with Roy Orbison; we played with a lot of people. And we've seen great ovations and we've gotten great ovations. This was something entirely different. This was mass hysteria. And we knew without even seeing it. We heard it and we knew it," said Yaguda.

It would be the only time Jay and the Americans would share the bill with the Beatles.

But it wasn't always fame and fortune for Jay and the Americans. They were first "discovered" in the late 1950s. The original group consisted of John "Jay" Traynor, Howard Kane (Kirschenbaum), Kenny Vance (Rosenberg) and Sandy Deanne (Yaguda).

Three of the four members had assumed stage names early, something that was necessary when the band started getting some attention in the New York area.

In the early 1960s, households rarely had unlisted telephone numbers, according to Yaguda. He was still living at home with his parents in Brooklyn and it was easy enough to look up the rather unique name of "Yaguda" in the phone book.

"The phone would ring at three in the morning with girls giggling on the other end of the line and it would wake my mother," said Yaguda. "And my father would say 'I'm gonna break your legs if you don't do something about this.' My father was a big guy, so we said, 'Let's get stage names.' That's how simple it was. We just made up names. I didn't like Sandy Beach, so you know, I became Sandy Deanne."

The group eventually attracted the attention of Jerry Leiber and Mike Stoller, songwriting and record producing partners who had written hits for Elvis Presley, including "Jailhouse Rock."

Leiber and Stoller had a production deal with United Artists and they signed Jay and the Americans to a contract.

The first record Jay and the Americans did for Leiber and Stoller was "Tonight" from the movie *West Side Story*. It didn't chart. The second record had the single "Dawning" on the A side and a song called "She Cried" on the B side. As was sometimes the case in the 1960s, disc jockeys flipped the record over and played the B side, thinking that "She Cried" would be more popular with radio audiences.

"She Cried" was indeed more popular. It reached No. 5 on the Billboard Hot 100 Singles chart in 1962, and became the first big hit for Jay and the Americans.

But that success didn't carry over into the next two singles released by the group, and a dejected Jay Traynor, who was also suffering the strain of the constant travel by the band, decided to leave the group and pursue a solo career.

Enter Dave Blatt, who became the group's next lead singer as "Jay Black" or "Jay No. Two."

With Black singing lead, Jay and the Americans started appearing regularly on the U.S. record charts. Between 1964 and 1966, the band charted six Top 20 hits on the Billboard Hot 100 Singles chart, including "Come a Little Bit Closer" at No. 3; "Let's Lock the Door (And Throw Away the Key)" at No. 11; "Cara Mia" at No. 4; "Some Enchanted Evening" at No. 13; "Sunday and Me" at No. 18; and "Crying" at No. 25.

By 1968, Jay and the Americans had earned the right to start producing their own albums. They formed their own production company and named it JATA (for Jay and the Americans) and signed a production deal with their label, United Artists.

"They gave us a big chunk of money and said, 'Go ahead; go make some records.' It was like giving a little kid a loaded gun," said Yaguda.

But the band members were more performers than they were songwriters. Because Leiber and Stoller were big-time songwriters — and very successful ones by the mid-1960s — the band members were a little self-conscious about showing Leiber and Stoller some of the songs they had written.

It might not have mattered much anyway. Leiber and Stoller were having too much success with other artists who they were working with at the time — for example, Peggy Lee, who recorded the Leiber and Stoller hit, "Is That All

There Is" in 1969 — and Jay and the Americans had been relegated to the back bench.

In addition, none of the other hot songwriters of the era were submitting songs to the band to record.

"They were submitting them to hotter artists. We were singers, and really good singers and vocalists. But we needed to find material. We couldn't find enough songs to do a whole album," said Yaguda.

So the band members decided to go a different route. Each of them made a list of 10 songs that they loved that had already been recorded by other artists, songs that had made each member of Jay and the Americans want to become singers in the first place. From those lists, they would choose which songs they wanted to record for an album.

They would call the album *Sands of Time*, and one of the songs they chose was "This Magic Moment," written by Doc Pomus and Mort Shuman. The song, which had been recorded in 1960 by the Drifters, with Ben E. King as the lead vocalist.

"We did 'This Magic Moment' because we always wanted to be the white Drifters. That's why we went to Leiber and Stoller to begin with," said Yaguda. "And when we finished it, we knew we did it good. But we didn't think that we did a better job with it than the Drifters did. As far as we were concerned, the Drifters' song was the hit. This was just our tribute to how good we thought they were. That's all it was."

According to Yaguda, though, the songs on the *Sands of Time* album weren't just covers done by Jay and the Americans.

"We didn't just copy the songs and their arrangements. We attacked each song on that album like it was a brand-new song that somebody had brought to us. We acted like we'd never heard it before and styled it after our way of doing the song," said Yaguda.

Mike Morsch

In addition to "This Magic Moment," Jay and the Americans recorded a song called "Gypsy Woman" by Curtis Mayfield for the album, even though Black wasn't a blues singer and Mayfield was.

"Jay wasn't the easiest guy to work with. He had to do forty-five takes on some things. And he would get pissed off because he wasn't at the track," said Yaguda. "Jay Number Two is more like Mario Lanza — he's that kind of a singer. It's all about power. I started yelling at him, 'Listen man, we need this song to have some soul, like an R and B artist.' I had to piece together a whole bunch of different takes."

But Black pulled it off with "Gypsy Woman," and the other songs on the album.

"When I listen to that record now, Jay just sang his ass off. If I didn't know that was Jay and the Americans, I'd think it was an Impressions record. It's a great performance.

"Also, we had been singing together for a very long time and I think at that point, Jay Black was at his finest vocally. There was nothing he couldn't do. He was effortless and easy. He was better than anybody else at the time. He was that good."

The album includes the song "Hushabye," also written by Pomus and Shuman, which the Mystics had taken to No. 20 in 1959.

Disc jockey Alan Freed, who had become internationally known in the radio business in the 1950s for promoting a mix of blues, country, and rhythm and blues songs and calling it "rock and roll," had used "Hushabye" as the closing song on his televised "Big Beat Show." The Beach Boys had also recorded a version of the song for their 1964 album *All Summer Long*.

When *Sands of Time* was released in 1969, it became the highest-charting album for Jay and the Americans, reaching No. 51 on the Billboard Hot 200 Albums chart and No. 30 on the Cashbox chart. "This Magic Moment" shot to No. 6 on the Billboard Hot 100 singles and "Hushabye" charted at No. 62 on the same chart.

Yaguda calls *Sands of Time*, and the group's follow-up album *Wax Museum* in 1970, his and the group's "finest hour."

"We put our hearts and souls into those albums. We got great performances out of Jay Number Two and the rest of it we took care of ourselves. Those records are heartfelt—the choices, the arrangements, the recording techniques, the time spent mixing them and getting them to sound good...," said Yaguda.

Sands of Time would go on to be considered "the first rock and roll revival" album of its time, according to Yaguda. And as a tribute to Freed, the band included his final radio sign-off at the end of the album.

"To be honest, there are two words in show business: 'show' and 'business.' Had we been on a record label like Capitol or Columbia, it would have been an entirely different story for our careers," said Yaguda.

"The Beach Boys were on Capitol and the people at Columbia, they knew how to promote records. United Artists didn't promote our records. Their record label was simply a write-off for their film company. They just wanted to put out songs that were going to be in movies to get Academy Awards. That's what that was about. And we were caught in the middle. So had the distribution been better, I don't think that it would have ever stopped for us," said Yaguda.

But it did stop. By 1973, the band had split and the members moved on to solo careers. Black continued to perform under the name "Jay and the Americans" until 2006, when he filed for bankruptcy because of unpaid gambling debts.

At an auction, a federal judge awarded the name "Jay and the Americans" to Yaguda and his son, Todd. Also bidding on the name, but failing to get it, was a guy named Jay Reincke. At Yaguda's invitation, he became "Jay No.

Three," the lead singer for today's version of Jay and the Americans.

"We had no game plan. And it's turned into a fifty-five year career," said Yaguda, who was still performing with Jay and the Americans in 2015.

"We consider it a gift to be able to do what we do. It's an honor and a privilege to go out and do something you love to do and actually get paid for it. That's how we look at it. Because I would be doing it for nothing, anyway," he said.

Discography

"Sands of Time"
Jay and the Americans
March 15, 1969

"This Magic Moment" (Doc Pomus, Mort Shuman) 2:50

"Pledging My Love" (Ferdinand Washington, Don Robey) 2:45

"Can't We Be Sweethearts" (J. Herbert Cox, Morris Levy)...... 2:32

"My Prayer" (Georges Boulanger, Jimmy Kennedy)................. 2:43

"So Much in Love" (George Williams, Bill Jackson, Roy 2:23
Straigis)

"Since I Don't Have You" (Joseph Rock, James Beaumont) 4:20

"Gypsy Woman" (Curtis Mayfield)... 3:15

"Hushabye" (Doc Pomus, Mort Shuman).....................................2:57

"When You Dance" (Andrew Jones, Jr.)......................................2:52

"Life Is But a Dream" (Raoul Cita, Hy Weiss, Sam Weiss)....... 2:32

"Mean Woman Blues" (Claude Demetrius)............................... 3:00

"Goodnight My Love" (George Motola, John Marascalco)....... 2:38

Standing out while . . .
Sittin' In
Loggins and Messina

Jim Messina had spent some time in the late 1960s getting a first-hand look at what he called the "chaos" of being a member of Buffalo Springfield, a band whose short, two-year existence was plagued by drug busts, lineup changes and the creative bickering between Neil Young and Stephen Stills.

After the Buffalo Springfield disbanded in 1968, Messina and band mate Richie Furay formed the country-rock band Poco. But by 1970, Messina was newly married and just didn't want to be on the road anymore with Poco. As soon as his final album and tour commitments with the band were completed, Messina planned to settle back into being a record producer, which he had done before becoming a member of Buffalo Springfield.

He had hooked up with Columbia Records as an independent contractor. In that role, Messina met Don Ellis, who also just started working for the company in artist development. Ellis had an artist he wanted to sign to Columbia, the little brother of one of his friends.

His name was Kenny Loggins.

"I said the best thing to do is have him contact me, get a tape, and I'll meet him after October," Messina recalled telling Ellis. Messina's last tour date with Poco was scheduled for October 31, 1970.

Just a few weeks later, in early December, Loggins called Messina to plan the meeting. Messina invited Loggins over to his house for dinner.

"He showed up and he came in and he was very tall and kind of lanky and he had a funny beard. He was quite different than what I expected," said Messina.

The two chatted for a while.

"I said, 'Did you bring a tape?' And he said, 'Well, I don't really have a tape of my songs.' So I said, 'Did you bring a guitar?' And he said, 'Well, I don't really own one,'" said Messina. "I wasn't sure what to think."

Messina had a tape recorder set up in his house that he recorded into, so he grabbed a microphone out of a closet, plugged it into the recorder and handed Loggins a guitar.

"I said, 'Press the "Record" button and sing your songs,'" said Messina.

Loggins ended up singing five or six songs for Messina that evening. Among those were tunes called "Danny's Song" and "House at Pooh Corner."

Afterward, Messina, his wife, actress Jenny Sullivan, and Loggins ate dinner. And then Loggins left.

"Well, what do you think?" Messina recalled Sullivan asking him after Loggins departed.

"I said, 'I don't know what to think.' I was surprised that he didn't own a guitar and I was surprised he didn't come prepared with any tunes for me to listen to," said Messina. "But I was also surprised by the fact that he was able to sit down and just do those songs live, which took a lot of courage. Also, there was quite a bit of enthusiasm in his performance. But I was going to need to think about producing an album for him because most of his songs were folk songs and we were moving away from folk music at the time."

So Messina thought about it. And he came back around to the idea, after listening to the tapes that Loggins had recorded that evening, that he really liked Loggins' voice.

"I liked the fact that he had some versatility in his voice. And perhaps, from what I gathered, he might be able to sing something other than folk songs," said Messina.

Stacks of Wax

The two continued to hang out and Messina eventually showed some of his own songs to Loggins. They sang together and did some more recordings there in Messina's house.

"I wanted to see how inspired he was as a musician. It took a little bit of time, a couple of months, but I finally felt confident that Kenny certainly had the vocal abilities. But the question was, could I move him into more of a rock and roll direction?" said Messina.

As their musical relationship continued to evolve, Messina learned that Loggins was more diverse than he first thought, and that Loggins enjoyed doing different types of material.

"My feeling was that in order to be successful in the music business, you had to have diversity. And perhaps Kenny might just be that one artist in a handful that could pull that off," said Messina. "And I began to be inspired by his energy and his enthusiasm and his real innocence in certain ways. He wasn't jaded and hadn't quite been bitten by the serpent of fame yet."

Messina was not that far removed from working with the likes of Stills, Young, and Furay, all artists who were set in their ways as well as in the directions they wanted to go with their music.

"It was a lot more refreshing to feel that perhaps I could really help this artist," said Messina.

With his independent production deal, Messina was committed to producing six albums a year for Columbia Records, and in return the company would deliver artists to Messina to produce.

One of the first was Andy Williams, who had joined Columbia in 1961 and had a great run of successful albums throughout the decade, all produced by Robert Mersey.

But by 1970, Williams, already a well-established star, had aspirations of appealing to a younger, more modern audience, so Columbia wanted to pair him with a producer who could help do that. And Columbia thought that Messina was the man for the job.

But Messina balked.

"The artists Columbia delivered to me I didn't feel were best for me or the artists," said Messina. "They gave me Andy Williams, who was a wonderful artist, one of my favorite singers at the time. But there was such a gap in our realities in terms of what music and age was. I didn't think it was a good move for him and certainly not a good move for me. So I turned that down. And Kenny was sort of still in my back pocket."

Loggins and Messina continued to work together and Messina convinced Loggins that he not only needed to be a recording artist, but also a performing artist. Loggins agreed.

The first thing they needed to do was put together a band. So Messina started looking for musicians who were available and who didn't — or couldn't — demand a lot of money.

The first two who joined were bassist Larry Sims and drummer Merel Bregante. Saxophonist Lester "Al" Garth, who played a little violin as well, joined next.

When Buffalo Springfield disbanded, the band didn't have enough money to pay everybody. So Messina was offered some amplifiers in lieu of cash payment. Messina had those in storage.

Once the band had been formed, Messina asked his father-in-law if it could rehearse at the pool house at his place on Mulholland Drive in Beverly Hills.

"I took all the equipment up there and we set the drums up and started just playing and getting a sense of what we had. Kenny was borrowing my guitars at the time and it was really starting to come together," said Messina. "The problem for me as the producer was that I needed more material from Kenny in order to create that diversification that I thought was really needed."

All the pieces were starting to fall into place, but Messina thought the band hadn't quite coagulated.

"Somewhere in there I talked to Kenny about the idea of perhaps maybe for the first album, I would be kind of sitting in. That way, I could get things rolling for him, I could help with the direction of the band," said Messina. "It was just a one-off thing in my mind. To be honest, I was tired of touring, I was tired of being on the road with Poco and Buffalo Springfield.

"But at the same time — and part of this is an ego thing — I just couldn't have my first artist as an independent producer come out and fail because I couldn't fill in the gaps to help him out.

"My thought was, 'Let's do this as a one-off and I'll just sit in on this first record. I'll give Kenny some of my material if he wanted to sing it. I'd do some of the tunes so there was some credibility to it. But the focus would be on Kenny,'" said Messina.

By mid-1971, it was time to offer tapes of Loggins and the band to Clive Davis, president of Columbia Records. Davis liked what he heard, but what he heard was too much of Jim Messina on the tapes.

"I thought you wanted to get off the road?" Messina recalled Davis saying. "I said I did, and I do, but I don't feel like it's good to put Kenny out there with the wolves his first time. I was afraid that the album wouldn't have the opportunity to have the success and the attention that it needed.

"I hear you," Messina recalled Davis saying. "But why would I want to invest in a band that's going to break up the moment the album is out? I've had too many of those already."

"I said, 'I think you need to consider the fact that I'm still going to be there, I'm still going to be producing Kenny's records. And that the band is his band and I'm just sitting in. What we want people to know is that there is a new artist out here, he's great, and I'm here sitting in and supporting him and he has a great career ahead of him,'" said Messina.

Davis reluctantly agreed. That first album would be called *Kenny Loggins with Jim Messina Sittin' In*.

Although the material for the album was well rehearsed, Messina wanted Loggins and the band to do some live performances to further hone and sequence the material before it was recorded.

The first professional performance for Loggins and the band was in mid-1971 at the famous Troubadour on Santa Monica Boulevard in West Hollywood. It was well received by the audience. Loggins came out to start the show by himself and did a few of his folk songs. The band eventually joined in and moved into more rock and roll material.

About three weeks later, Loggins and the band got another opportunity to perform at the Troubadour. Curtis Mayfield was due to headline one evening but his opener canceled.

Mayfield, a soul, R&B, and funk singer-songwriter, had started his career in 1956 as a member of the Impressions, a doo-wop, gospel, and soul group. But by 1970, he had embarked on a solo career and had a loyal and knowledgeable Black fan base.

Loggins and the band were offered the spot opening for Mayfield at the Troubadour. The evening would provide more valuable experience performing live for Loggins, and it would offer an example of a new artist learning his craft and his audience.

"When we first started, Kenny would come out and he would do the first three or four tunes. He'd sing 'Danny's Song' and 'House at Pooh Corner,'" said Messina. "So he's onstage and opening up for Curtis Mayfield and there are these two beautiful young Black women sitting right down in front of Kenny, looking up at him. One of the girls started shouting, 'Get down, man! Get down!' And Kenny's energy level started to move up."

Messina was off to the side of the stage and had observed the entire exchange. After the show, Loggins approached Messina and wanted to talk about the two women down in front of the stage.

"I can't believe it. Those two girls up front were so beautiful and were telling me to get down," Messina recalled Loggins saying.

"I said, 'Kenny, they were laughing. They were telling you to get off the stage.' He said, 'Oh, no. I'm glad I didn't know that because I would have never been able to finish the set.' But Kenny eventually had gotten their respect with his music and his performance. It was a hard audience to be put in front of, but it turned out to be fabulous," said Messina.

By the time Loggins had signed a record deal with Columbia, the material for the first album was pretty much arranged and ready to be recorded. And it was a different and refreshing experience for Messina.

"I just had a different experience of how quickly the stuff can go and how it should go. When the players are really proficient at what they do, the magic happens very quickly," said Messina. "But having worked with Buffalo Springfield, they were very labored. That was never a lot of fun for me as an engineer."

For the *Sittin' In* recording sessions, Messina brought in Alex Kazanegras as the engineer, and he added percussionist Milt Holland, with whom he had worked while with Poco.

"Everything was cut live. In the first week, we cut all the tracks. If there were any mistakes made on chords, I would just pick them up as soon as the tape was finished. I'd roll them back and say 'Gentlemen, we need to hit that B-flat note a little tighter on that part.' Boom-boom-boom-boom, done. Next song," said Messina.

The second week was devoted to the vocals and anything that wasn't cut live. The third week was for mixing.

And by the end of the third week, *Sittin' In* was ready to be mastered and released.

"That's pretty much how I made every Loggins and Messina record," said Messina.

Sittin' In was released in November 1971. It reached No. 70 on the Billboard Pop Albums chart in 1972. Although none of the singles from the album were Top 40 radio hits, two of the songs that Loggins sang for Messina the first time they met in Messina's house in 1970 ended up on the album, and would go on to become Loggins and Messina's best-known songs.

"House at Pooh Corner" appeared first on a 1970 album called *Uncle Charlie and His Dog Teddy* by the Nitty Gritty Dirt Band before being recorded for *Sittin' In*.

And "Danny's Song" first appeared on an album by a band called Gator Creek in 1970 before being recorded for *Sittin' In*. Canadian singer Anne Murray did a cover of the song in 1972 and had a hit with it, reaching the Top 10 on three Billboard charts in 1973.

The album cover of *Sittin' In* features Loggins and Messina dressed in Western-type garb, sitting at a poker table playing cards.

Messina's actress wife was shooting a movie in mid-1971 called *The Other* in Murphys, California, a mining town up the central coast in what is referred to as "Gold Country."

"While she was on the shoot I would walk around town. I was looking at this little town, the smells and the colors and the shops and the little ice cream store. It had such a feel to it," said Messina. "I wanted our album to have an appearance of the late 1930s, early 1940s, and to tie our music and our images into this little town."

Stacks of Wax

On the "Sittin' In" album, Jim Messina, right, believed he got the diversification he desired from Kenny Loggins, who was able to show his skills as what Messina called "a soulful singer with peace of mind." (Photo courtesy of Jim Messina)

Messina ran the idea by Columbia Records executives and the company eventually sent a photographer back to Murphys with the band members for the shoot.

"I told the photographer that the album was going to be called *Sittin' In* with Kenny Loggins.' I asked him, 'How can we get a 'sittin' in' vibe, visually?'" said Messina. "As we walked around town, I went into this old hotel and there was a poker table sitting over in the corner. And I thought, 'perfect.' We're all gambling that this is going to work and the idea of sittin' in with Kenny at this poker game might just have the right metaphor that I wanted to get. So we shot the cover there."

Loggins and Messina are even wearing their own clothes on the cover of *Sittin' In*.

In the end, Messina believes he and Loggins made the album they wanted to make with their debut record.

"One has to have an ego in order to have some skin in the game, so to speak. But at the same time, for me, my intention was to make the best record that I could with the components that I was given. I believed in the songs that we were doing; I believed in the musicians. I believed in the people we were working with, Columbia Records and Clive Davis. These were all hardworking, devoted people.

"For me, the idea was to get the best songs I could get together and get them sequenced right. My goal was to make albums in those days that people could put on the turntable, sit down and have a glass a wine or whatever it was that got their heads straight, and listen and enjoy it, like going to a concert," said Messina.

"And that's how that album was received. When people did go to a concert, they had the same experience because they had been home and listened to it. When they saw us perform, I believe we met their expectations.

"From that standpoint, that's what I was hoping would be the outcome. No one can ever know how something is going to be received. This was about creating a performance, about creating a performance artist, about supporting that performing artist, both as a producer and as an artist, putting all those components together and staying focused, which was my job.

"That was my intent. And after it was done, I thought that I had completed that, more so than anything I had ever done," said Messina.

Messina also believes he got the diversification he desired from Loggins, who was able to show his skills as what Messina called "a soulful singer with peace of mind."

As far as what was going on in the music scene in the early 1970s, Messina said he wasn't necessarily aware, nor did he concern himself, with where a new artist like Kenny

Stacks of Wax

Loggins, and the band Loggins and Messina, would fit into the mix.

"When you do that, you become a follower. I've learned over the years — and it's not a recipe for success; if anything, it could be one for failure — if you're different enough and you do not necessarily fit in and people take a liking to you, you've got a better chance of eventually rising above the masses," said Messina.

"In the case of Loggins and Messina, I knew that a lot of my competition was people that I had worked with, whether it be Crosby, Stills and Nash, Neil Young or Stephen Stills, or even Richie Furay with Poco. I knew we had to do what we did and I knew we needed to do it as differently and as interestingly and be more diversified than anyone else. And that's what I went for," he said.

Sittin' In would be the first of six studio albums and two live albums that Loggins and Messina would record from 1971 to 1977. Five of those albums would be in the Top 20 of the Billboard U.S. Top 200 Albums chart. The duo's highest charting single would be "Your Mama Don't Dance" off their 1974 self-titled second album, *Loggins and Messina*.

The two amicably parted ways in 1976 before what was called a Columbia corporate 1977 release of *Finale*, a live double album. Both went on to pursue solo careers, with Loggins recording several hits in the 1980s, including "I'm Alright" in 1980, which served as the theme song for the film *Caddyshack* and reached No. 7 on the Billboard Hot 100 chart; and the title track for the 1984 film *Footloose*, which was No. 1 on the Billboard Hot 100 Singles chart.

Messina calls his years with Loggins and Messina among his best in the music business and characterizes *Sittin' In* as one of the highlights of his career.

"I think it's one of my greatest accomplishments, although I feel that way about all those albums with Loggins and Messina," he said.

The first time that Jim Messina met Kenny Loggins, he was surprised that Loggins didn't own a guitar. (Photo courtesy of Jim Messina)

Discography

"Sittin' In"
Loggins and Messina
November 1971

"Nobody But You" (Jim Messina) 3:00
"Danny's Song" (Kenny Loggins) 4:16
"Vahevala" (Dan Loggins, Dann Lottermoser) 4:47
"Trilogy: 11:13
I. Lovin' Me (Messina, Murray MacLeod)
II. To Make a Woman Feel Wanted (Loggins, Messina)
III. Peace of Mind" (Messina)
"Back to Georgia" (Loggins) 3:19
"House at Pooh Corner" (Loggins) 4:25
"Listen to a Country Song" (Messina, Al Garth)
"Same Old Wine" (Messina) 8:17
"Rock 'n' Roll Mood" (Loggins, Michael Omartian) 3:04

Stretching right up and touching the sky
Electronically Tested
Mungo Jerry

The motorcycle sound that one hears in the song "In the Summertime" isn't really a motorcycle. And it wasn't put into the song for any artistic reason; it's there just to make the song more than three minutes long.

In 1970, Ray Dorset, founder of the band Mungo Jerry, picked up his secondhand Stratocaster guitar one evening and started "messing around," eventually coming up with the melody of a song.

"The next morning I went and sat at my desk and I had these words buggering around in my head. So I picked up a notepad and just wrote down the lyrics. Just like that," said Dorset.

"In the Summertime" was written in about 10 minutes.

"I just wrote songs for my own personal enjoyment to play with my band. I wasn't trying to write a hit song; it was just one of those things that I happened to write."

Mungo Jerry wasn't called Mungo Jerry at that point in 1970. The band, originally called the Good Earth, had experienced some lineup changes in the late 1960s, with Dorset and Colin Earl being the constants.

Record producer Barry Murray had formed a management firm and had gotten the band a gig at the Hollywood Festival in Newcastle-under-Lyme, Staffordshire, England. The festival was held May 23-24, 1970 on a pig farm, and was notable because it included the first performance of the Grateful Dead in the United Kingdom.

The festival lineup also included Black Sabbath, Traffic and Ginger Baker's Air Force, among others.

But Murray wanted the band to change its name to something different from the Good Earth before the festival appearance.

"We were going to be put on the bill as well. We thought, cool, that's great. But we couldn't agree on a name. So we said, 'Whatever we pick out of a hat, that's what we're going to be.' So Mungo Jerry was the name that got picked out of the hat," said Dorset.

The name "Mungo Jerry" itself actually comes from the 1939 collection of poems by T.S. Eliot titled *Old Possum's Book of Practical Cats*, in which one of the cats is named "Mungojerrie." The band took that name, made it two words, changed the spelling of the second word to "Jerry" and dropped that name into the hat.

The new name and the Hollywood Festival gig were a success, as was the release of the single "In the Summertime" right around the same time.

When it came time to record an album, the band included lead singer and guitarist Dorset, vocalist and guitarist Paul King, pianist Colin Earl, and Mike Cole on bass.

The self-titled debut album *Mungo Jerry* was released in 1970, just after the Hollywood Festival gig. But that album, and a subsequent summer tour in the United States, did little to create any buzz around the band, despite the album reaching No. 14 on the albums chart in the United Kingdom. And "In the Summertime" was not included on that album.

The band kept Murray as producer for its second album, but changed labels to Dawn Records, a subsidiary of Pye Records, replaced Cole on bass with John Godfrey, and headed back into the studio in late 1970.

The second album would be called *Electronically Tested*. The band recorded 17 tracks for consideration on the album, which this time would include "In the Summertime." Recording began in Studio One at the Pye Recording Studios in London. Studio One was the biggest on the lot, and featured eight-track recording equipment.

For another song on the album titled "Baby Jump," chosen as the follow-up single to "In the Summertime," the band had switched over to a refurbished Studio Two, which featured upgraded 16-track recording equipment.

But when producer Murray mixed "Baby Jump," Dorset didn't like the way the song sounded. The reason was the difference in the eight-track equipment in Studio One, where the vocals were put down, and the 16-track equipment in Studio Two, where the music was recorded.

It just didn't sound right in the mix. So Dorset and Murray decided to record all the rest of the cuts for *Electronically Tested* on eight-track in Studio One, with Howard Barry as chief engineer.

It was Barry who would ultimately be responsible for the distinctive "motorcycle" sound on "In the Summertime."

At that time, artists got what was informally called "double performance money" if a song that was being played on the radio was more than three minutes long. When "In the Summertime" was first recorded, it came in at just under three minutes.

"So Barry [Murray] said, 'How can we make this track longer?' I said, 'Let's get a motorbike sound, stick it in the middle, and then stick it on the end as well,'" said Dorset. "But we couldn't find a decent sounding motorbike in the [music] library. So we rigged up two microphones and put them into the street. And Howard [Barry] revved up his Triumph sports car and drove past the studio while we recorded it."

Dorset said after the sound of the Triumph was captured, Barry then edited it into two parts, which he then added into the song to make the final running time 3:30.

"And the second part is a slightly different mix than the first part. It was quite a technical feat. That is why if you try and count — you know when you're performing on TV and they ask you to lip sync for the playback — I could never come in on time after that car. You can't do it. There's no method to it. It doesn't make any sense, but it worked," said Dorset.

Murray, who had decided against putting "In the Summertime" on the band's first album even after it was released as a single, was certain from the first time he heard the song that it was going to be a hit.

But the band members weren't as certain. They had been playing a song titled "Mighty Man" in their live show that they thought had a better chance to be a hit.

"The audience used to go absolutely wild for 'Mighty Man.' All of us in the band thought we should release that one as a single," said Dorset. Eventually, the decision was made to release "In the Summertime" as the A side of the single, and "Mighty Man" as the B side.

Murray and the band also decided on another unique approach for the single: It would be released as what was called a "maxi-single," which was played at 33 1/3 rpm on a record player, rather than the standard 45 rpm at which single vinyls were played. Rather than just two songs, though, a maxi-single included three songs. For this record, "In the Summertime" and a cover of the Woodie Guthrie song "Dust Pneumonia Blues" would be on the A side, with "Mighty Man" on the B side. It was considered at the time to be more of a music value for the same price as a single.

When it came time to name the album, Dorset had yet another idea. Although "In the Summertime" had established itself as a bona fide hit, the naming of the album would have nothing to do with any of the songs that would appear on it.

No, Dorset's idea involved a company that made condoms.

Durex was the name of a brand of condoms made by SSL International, a British manufacturer of healthcare products. The Durex brand included nine varieties of latex condoms, and on each package the words "electronically tested" were written.

"It was my idea, but everyone thought it was a good idea," said Dorset. "So I thought that was a good idea to call the album that. That's the story."

Dorset believes that the photo on the cover of *Electronically Tested* is one taken from behind the band overlooking a sea of people attending the Weeley Festival in Essex, England, in August 1971. Among the artists who performed at that festival were the Faces featuring Rod Stewart, T-Rex featuring Marc Bolan, Mott the Hoople, and King Crimson.

"We would have liked it to have been photos from the Hollywood Festival, but the record company never got any photos, or any decent ones," said Dorset.

"In the Summertime" did become a big hit for Mungo Jerry when it was released. It reached No. 1 in the United Kingdom and many other countries while checking in at No. 2 on the U.S. Cash Box chart, and No. 3 on the U.S. Billboard Hot 100 Singles chart.

Off the *Electronically Tested* album, the single "Baby Jump" also reached No. 1 on the UK Singles chart. Like "In the Summertime," it was released as a maxi-single on the A side, and also featured a Paul King song titled "The Man Behind the Piano," which was not one of the songs on *Electronically Tested,*. The B side was 9:50 long and featured live recordings of "Mighty Man," a cover of a traditional folk song called "Midnight Special" and an excerpt of a song titled "Maggie" recorded during Mungo Jerry's Hollywood Festival appearance.

Despite the strength of "In the Summertime," the *Electronically Tested* album did not chart in the U.S., but did reach No. 13 in the U.K.

Dorset believes that during that early 1970s time period, Mungo Jerry struggled to find its niche.

"We didn't fit in anywhere, to be quite honest. I liked so many different genres of music. When Mungo Jerry came onto the scene as a band, I had been right in the center of all this psychedelic hippie stuff," said Dorset.

The demographic audience for a song like "In the Summertime," didn't necessarily match up with the demographics of bands like Pink Floyd, Santana, or Johnny Winter, which were among the bands for which Mungo Jerry served as an opener.

"'In the Summertime' became a children's favorite on the radio. All age groups from all walks of life dug that record," said Dorset. "But toward the end of 1971, Mungo Jerry as a band started to become a bit uncool. We didn't see it that much, because it was retrospective of our story."

Dorset thought the blues and jug band repertoire of Mungo Jerry was somewhat restrictive and to stretch his creative chops a bit, he released a solo album titled *Cold Blue Excursion* in March 1972. It was designed to showcase his versatility as a songwriter and to prove that he wasn't confined to just the sound that Mungo Jerry had developed.

The attempt by Dorset to broaden the Mungo Jerry appeal with more diverse music coincided with an eight-week tour of the Far East in 1972 — which included gigs in Japan and Australia. It hit a snag, though — when the band returned to the U.S. after the tour, Dorset was "fired" by Colin Earl and Paul King, who had decided to become Mungo Jerry.

Record company officials, however, disagreed with the decision by Earl and King.

"The record company management said, 'Hang on a minute. If you go to a gig, the promoter is going to say,

"Where's Mungo?"' I was writing all the songs and I was the front man. So the record company said, 'You're Mungo Jerry the performer and Ray Dorset the songwriter,'" said Dorset. "The thing was, I didn't realize what a good thing it was until a long time after that. I kind of thought at the time that I didn't want to be called 'Mungo.' It doesn't sound as sexy as Elvis, does it? For some reason, I thought it was a name from a Boris Karloff movie, some kind of monster in chains in a dungeon. Mungo. Mungo. I didn't realize it was a good thing."

It all worked out for the best, though. Dorset still performs today as Mungo Jerry.

As for *Electronically Tested*, Dorset believes history has shown that some of the songs from that album have stood the test of time.

"At the time, I thought it was far superior to our first album," said Dorset of *Electronically Tested*. "There was a time when people would go into the studio and they'd spend about a year making an album, a phenomenal work of art. Or three years. Whereas my heroes, like Fats Domino, Jerry Lee Lewis, Elvis, Bob Dylan — they just went into the studio and captured the performance. Neil Young did that on his first few albums. There is nothing like a group of musicians and performers creating something really special that's captured in a sound recording. Then you've got a piece of art."

"In the Summertime" continues to be in the regular rotation on classic rock radio stations to this day.

"It didn't actually cross my mind at the time, but what has been said over the years — and it's true — if you write a song and it stands up in its own right, and people sit around and play it around the campfire, it's like folksong history," said Dorset.

"Oh, I loved 'In the Summertime' when it became popular. The thing is, when you write something quickly, it sometimes comes down to intuition without you sometimes realizing it. And even today, forty-five years after, 'In the Summertime' goes on and on and on," he said. "If you look at it line by line, every line has got some kind of a meaning. Sometimes it's got a double meaning. It's a celebration of life. It's a very spiritual kind of track.

"I didn't expect to still be talking about this album now, but it doesn't surprise me that some people have picked up on some of my songs," he said.

Discography

"Electronically Tested"
Mungo Jerry
March 1971
(All songs written by Ray Dorset except where noted)

"She Rowed" 3:15
"I Just Wanna Make Love to You" (Willie Dixon) 9:01
"In the Summertime" 3:30
"Somebody Stole My Wife" 2:53
"Baby Jump" 4:09
"Follow Me Down" 3:17
"Memoirs of a Stockbroker" 4:00
"You Better Leave That Whisky Alone" 3:55
"Coming Back to You When the Time Comes" 3:38

Kicks just kept getting harder to find
Indian Reservation
The Raiders

It didn't crack the U.S. Billboard Hot 100 Singles chart, but recording a version of the single "Louie Louie" in April 1963 proved to be the break that Paul Revere and the Raiders had been looking for, because it got them noticed by officials at Columbia Records.

And they got a record deal out of it.

While the band was in California to sign the deal in October 1963, the suits at Columbia thought it would be a good idea for the members of Paul Revere and the Raiders to meet their new producers: Terry Melcher, son of screen and music legend Doris Day, and Bruce Johnston, who had not yet joined the Beach Boys.

At the time, Melcher and Johnston were co-producing a band called the Rip Chords. Not only that, but the co-producers were also lending their vocals to a song that they hoped would be the Rip Chords' next hit, a single called "Hey Little Cobra."

Mark Lindsay, lead singer for Paul Revere and the Raiders, first met Melcher and Johnston when Melcher and Johnston were in the recording studio finishing the vocal overdubs on "Hey Little Cobra."

"Bruce was in the studio with a wastebasket over his head and an RCA 44 microphone in there with him. And he was going, 'Shut 'em down, shut 'em down.' The wastebasket was there for the resonance, I guess," said Lindsay.

"Terry was in the control booth and he called me in and said, 'Listen to this.' I thought it was great. It sounded like a hit. That was my first introduction to Bruce and Terry," said Lindsay.

(Author's note: More than 50 years later, Johnston confirmed the wastebasket story, with one slight change: "Great, true story, except the large and deep Rubbermaid wastebasket overdub microphone was a Neumann U48 and not an RCA 44. And yes, I really did use the wastebasket for the 'Shut 'em down, shut 'em down' pretend bass voice vocal part that I sung.")

Lindsay was right, though, and "Hey Little Cobra" was a hit for the Rip Chords. It peaked at No. 4 on the Billboard Hot 100 Singles chart in February 1964, right about the same time the Beatles arrived in New York to begin what is now known as the British Invasion.

Paul Revere and the Raiders recorded their first album, *Steppin' Out*, in 1965 with Melcher and Johnston at the helm. Sort of.

"Terry didn't know what to do with us, so he palmed us off on Bruce, who cut the first half of our album, which was a live repertoire of what we were doing on our dance circuit," said Lindsay. "And then Bruce played on a couple of cuts with the Raiders, and was involved on the background vocals on *Steppin' Out*. He was actually working with the Beach Boys by this time and he had to run across town to the studio to help us do our album. He was there off and on."

While Johnston went on to join the Beach Boys fulltime by 1966, Melcher continued his relationship with the band through the end of the 1960s. The band had some success with charting songs on the U.S. Billboard Hot 100 Singles chart: "Kicks" was No. 4, "Hungry" was No. 6, and "Good Thing" was No. 4 in 1966; and "Him or Me, What's It Gonna Be" made it to No. 5 in 1967.

And the band had three consecutive Top 10 albums in 1966 all under the direction of Melcher: *Just Like Us!* was No. 5, and *Midnight Ride* and *The Spirit of '67* both made it to No. 9.

Paul Revere and the Raiders also gained some attention with several appearances on the Dick Clark-produced television show *Happening '68*, a weekly rock and roll variety television show on ABC that followed Clark's *American Bandstand*.

But by the late 1960s, Paul Revere and the Raiders had experienced some lineup changes and creative differences among its members.

Despite those challenges, the best was yet to come for the band. Paul Revere and the Raiders — which had changed its name to The Raiders in 1970 — would have its first and only No. 1 hit that would anchor a Top 20 album as the new decade dawned.

Lindsay had mostly taken over the writing and producing duties for Paul Revere and the Raiders by 1968. But he and his band mates were exploring individual opportunities for themselves as well at the same time.

In November 1969, Lindsay had released a solo single called *Arizona*, produced by Jerry Fuller, which made it to No. 10 on the Billboard Hot 100 Singles chart, and No. 9 on the Cash Box Top 100 Singles chart in the U.S. The song did better north of the border, where it got as high as No. 4 on the Canadian RPM Top Singles chart.

For much of 1970, Lindsay was writing and planning to record a solo album. He was in the studio as often as he could be, cutting records that he thought might be hits.

"When I cut a song, I could usually predict where on the charts it would be, give or take five or ten spots," said Lindsay. "If I cut something and I didn't think it was going to be a Top Forty hit or better, I just went on and did another one."

Mike Morsch

One day, Jack Gold, the West Coast artist and repertoire director for CBS, parent company of Columbia Records, approached Lindsay with a suggestion on what Lindsay's next single should be. And he played Lindsay the song "Indian Reservation (The Lament of the Cherokee Reservation Indian)," a song written by John Loudermilk and first recorded in 1959 by Marvin Rainwater under the title "The Pale Faced Indian."

It had been covered again in 1968 by Don Fardon and had reached No. 20 on the U.S. Billboard Hot 100 chart, and had gotten all the way to No. 3 on UK Singles chart.

"I said, 'No Jack, Don Fardon had this out and it didn't even make it.' Gold said, 'Well, it made it big in England. I think you could sell this song. You're part Cherokee, aren't you?' I said, yes, a little. He said, 'Now is a good time for the song. I think it's a smash and I want you to cut it,'" said Lindsay.

Reluctantly, Lindsay agreed to record "Indian Reservation." He approached Fuller to see if he would produce it. But Fuller said no, he was in the middle of projects with both Gary Puckett and Johnny Mathis, and he didn't have time to cut the song with Lindsay.

Lindsay returned to Gold and told him that Fuller was too busy to produce the record. Gold suggested that Lindsay produce it himself.

"I produced The Raiders, but that was one step removed," said Lindsay. "I can't produce myself. That's too close to home."

Still, Gold insisted and Lindsay relented. He planned from the beginning for "Indian Reservation" to be a Mark Lindsay song and not a Paul Revere and the Raiders song. So he recorded it with studio musicians, among them keyboardist and arranger Artie Butler and Wrecking Crew drummer Hal Blaine.

"We cut the basic track and there are two stories here: At the end of the basic track, we cut it and it was over. That was it. It just ended," said Lindsay. "The musicians were leaving and Artie was still there listening to the playback. I said, 'Artie, this song has too abrupt of an ending. It needs a tag on it, something like that song from Janis Ian.'

"We were sitting outside the recording area listening to the playback through the speakers in the studio, and Artie said, 'You mean this one?' and he rips off the riff at the end of Janis Ian's 'Society's Child.' I said, 'Yes, something like that.' He said, 'Well I produced that record and that's me on that riff. That's my riff. If you want it, you've got it.' I didn't think we could have the same thing as Janis, but Artie said, 'Don't worry, you can't get sued, it's my riff.'

"We put it on the end and it became a real signature ending for the song. I think it put a wonderful coat on it," said Lindsay.

But despite his penchant for being able to sense when a song was a hit, Lindsay wasn't sure about "Indian Reservation."

"I didn't know. I could usually chart positions of our records and call them pretty accurately, but I had no idea on it," said Lindsay. "I loved the song; it was one of the best things I ever produced. But I wasn't sure whether I was in love with the song because I had done it and pulled it off, or whether it was really in the groove. I thought it could be the biggest hit we ever had or the biggest dud."

Lindsay kept delaying the release of the single, but he eventually couldn't put Gold off any longer. Gold had threatened that if Lindsay wasn't going to put "Indian Reservation" out as a solo single, then CBS would release it as a single for The Raiders.

"So we put it out as The Raiders and it was the biggest-selling single in the history of CBS, and the biggest record that The Raiders never played on," said Lindsay.

The song, released in February 1971, sold more than a million copies.

But now the pressure was on from CBS to have an album by The Raiders on which to put a single. Since he had been writing and recording on his own, Lindsay had enough songs for an album. Almost.

"I was on tour at the time with the Carpenters, but CBS said we had to have this out," said Lindsay. "I had two days off in Nashville and CBS had a studio in Nashville. So I went to that studio and we were mastering and finishing the cuts for the album. But we came up one cut short. We only had nine cuts and we needed ten. It was like, oh crap."

Lindsay decided to enlist the musicians from the tour — among them Tony Peluso, who had just started what would become an 11-year stint as lead guitarist for the Carpenters — to record one final song for the album.

The song would be called "The Turkey."

"The drummer had one half of a set of bongos and a high hat — that was the drum kit. I was beating on a cardboard box. There was a bass and guitar," said Lindsay. "I went out and adlibbed the song. It was just off the top of my head, like a rap. That became the final cut. We'd been up for two days because we were on tour, so the part where we all had to gobble, everybody fell down on the floor laughing. We did about fifteen takes on that. We were so zoned out."

The *Indian Reservation* album itself, which was released in the fall of 1971, was admittedly a bit of a mish-mash, according to Lindsay. In addition to the songs Lindsay wrote, the album included the tunes "The Shape of Things to Come," which was from the movie *The Wild Street*; "Eve of Destruction," the P.F. Sloan protest song that was a hit for Barry McGuire in 1965; Leon Russell's "Prince of Peace"; and "Heaven Help Us All" by Stevie Wonder, all songs that Lindsay was planning to cover as a solo artist at the time.

"I'll take the blame for part of that. When we did the other albums and Terry or I was producing, they were kind of concept albums. We always had some sort of theme in mind and more or less stuck to it," said Lindsay. "On this one, the various cuts were kind of all over the place. I was cutting the songs as singles; I wasn't worried about how they would fit together as a package. But it was all I had in the can and I was on tour. CBS said it had to have the album out now and that was it."

Despite its lack of cohesiveness, the *Indian Reservation* album made it to No. 19 on the U.S. Billboard 200 Albums chart.

The Raiders continued to release singles for the next few years, but by 1975, the band had mostly dissolved, and Lindsay had left to pursue a solo career.

"I left The Raiders because we were doing the same exact thing every night. There was no adlibbing at all allowed. You had a script and you had to stay with it. If you veered from the script, you got chastised," said Lindsay. "I really got tired of being that enclosed, that smothered. That was one of the reasons I left the group. That and I wanted to do my own thing."

Lindsay continued to release solo singles for the rest of the decade, but eventually retired from performing for a while to become head of A&R for United Artists Records.

"Unfortunately, by that time, Jerry Fuller wasn't producing for CBS anymore. I was still under contract to CBS, but they had no producer for me. So I had to do it myself. Looking back, I wasn't in the best position to call my own shots because I had no sounding board, nobody to tell me, no, don't do that," said Lindsay.

"So I was doing it all myself and I was kind of trying different directions. I got several singles out. Even though I had left The Raiders, I still had a lot of rock and roll left in me. And [then Columbia Records president] Clive Davis wanted me to become just a total ballad singer. He saw me as like a Barry Manilow-type. But I didn't want to do just all ballads. I still wanted to rock."

Mike Morsch

Lindsay looks back on the production of the *Indian Reservation* album now and assumes what he calls "blame" for how it sounded.

"I was so close to it I wasn't as objective as I should have been," he said. "It was heady but it was very confusing as well. Disco was rearing its head — I actually liked disco — and it was a transition time. I kind of got caught in the middle between the tail end of hard rock and the singer-songwriter ballad stuff and disco. I was lost in the maelstrom.

"Looking back, I suppose if I would have really concentrated on ballads, like Bobby Goldsboro or Gary Puckett or whatever, I might have done much better. But that's the way it went down."

Still, Lindsay looks back fondly on the music of the 1960s and the 1970s.

"I truly think it was one of the richest periods of music production and writing. The times, the Summer of Love, it was when things were just working and it was so positive. All the songs were really positive. And I think people would rather hear a positive song, especially today," he said.

Discography

"Indian Reservation"
"The Raiders"
1971

"Indian Reservation" (John D. Loudermilk) 2:52

"Shape of Things to Come" (Barry Mann / Cynthia Weil) 3:22

"Prince of Peace" (Greg Dempsey) 3:29

"Heaven Help Us All" (Ronald Miller)...3:23

"Take Me Home" (Terry Melcher)... 4:09

"Just Remember You're My Sunshine" (Mike Settle) 2:43

"Come in, You'll Get Pneumonia" (George Young,
Harry Vanda, Tony Cahill)...3:11

"Eve of Destruction" (P.F. Sloan) 3:17

"Birds of a Feather" (Joe South)... 2:51

"Turkey" (Mark Lindsay) 4:06

The bluesman and the bad boys
Hooker 'n Heat
John Lee Hooker and Canned Heat

In mid-1970, the members of Canned Heat had arrived at Portland International Airport on their way to a gig in Oregon. While in the baggage claim area waiting for their luggage, they noticed an African-American man at the next carousel, picking up his luggage, which included an old guitar case.

"We said, 'Man, who is that? He's picking up a guitar,'" said Fito de la Parra, the drummer for Canned Heat.

It was blues legend John Lee Hooker. And the members of Canned Heat were big fans of his music.

"We ran toward him. We wanted to shake his hand and meet him," said de la Parra. "We were famous already and he was barely making it. He was really not doing good at the time. The blues was not yet accepted as an American art form. It was for Blacks and a few beatnik Whites that liked it."

Canned Heat was indeed famous at that point. The band had performed at the Monterey Pop Festival in June 1967, and was developing a reputation as "the bad boys of rock" after an incident that same year in Denver, Colorado, where they were arrested and jailed for drug possession.

A personnel change in 1967 established what would become the classic lineup of Canned Heat that featured Bob "The Bear" Hite, Alan "Blind Owl" Wilson, Henry "The Sunflower" Vestine, Larry "The Mole" Taylor, and Adolfo "Fito" de la Parra.

The band continued to record and perform, and in November 1968, released its third studio album, *Living the Blues*, which was notable because it included the single "Going Up the Country," written by Wilson. It would reach No. 11 on the U.S. Billboard Hot 100 Singles chart in late 1968.

It was also the song the band chose to play at its Woodstock appearance in August 1969. In the 1970 film *Woodstock*, the Canned Heat spoken introduction to the song at the festival can be heard, and then the film cuts to a studio version of the song. The song would eventually be described by some as the "unofficial anthem" of Woodstock.

So Canned Heat's career was definitely on the upswing when they met Hooker in the Portland airport.

"We were like groupies. We shook his hand and said, 'We're Canned Heat and we love your music.' Alan and Bob, our founders, were musicologists and record collectors, so they had all of John Lee Hooker's stuff. And I had a couple of his records, too," said de la Parra.

Hooker had heard of Canned Heat as well.

"It was wonderful to shake his hand and meet him," said de la Parra. "And he said, 'Oh, the Canned Heat. I like the way you boys boogie.' It was a marriage that was made to happen."

Indeed it was. Right there in the airport, Hite suggested to Hooker that the bluesman hook up with the bad boys and record an album. And Hooker liked the idea.

After some negotiations between record label executives — Canned Heat was on Liberty Records (which eventually became United Artists Records) and Hooker recorded for Specialty Records, an independent R&B label — a deal was struck.

The album would be called *Hooker 'n Heat*.

For Canned Heat, being in the studio with Hooker was a real treat, although Hooker did by then, have his own way of doing things.

"One of the things with John was that he didn't want to do more than one take. And there was no rehearsing. You know, that's the purity of the blues, the purity of that kind of music. It's something that is spontaneous. And John Lee Hooker was the best at that," said de la Parra. "He was primitive and he was spontaneous and he continuously improvised and that's why it was almost impossible to rehearse and set up a song, because he never played a song the same way. In a way, that was a challenge for us. But since we were already blues players and pretty experienced by that time, we were aware of his style."

Hooker not wanting to do second takes was indeed an issue during the recording sessions.

"The times when we asked him to do a second take, he'd say, 'Well, I don't do no second takes.' We'd say, 'Well John, we had a problem here with this take, it broke or something.' So we would actually have to push him into doing a second take. He didn't want to do it," said de la Parra.

Skip Taylor, the band's manager, co-produced the album along with Hite. The goal was to have Hooker play some of his older songs, those that people weren't as aware of or familiar with, by himself. The producers then wanted to follow that with some duets of Hooker with Wilson on piano, and then the rest of the songs with Hooker backed by Canned Heat.

And to do that, the producers wanted to make Hooker comfortable by recreating the environment in which he recorded in the 1940s and 1950s.

"We got an old amp for his guitar and we also built him a little box, a little wooden box, almost like a place where he could sit down and tap his feet the way he did on those original songs," said de la Parra. "It was like a small stage so we could re-create the environment of those old Detroit sessions and have his foot tapping against the wooden floor, like the old boogie songs he did."

In the end, there was enough music for a double album, and it was recorded in just a couple of days at the Liberty Records studios in Los Angeles.

"When Skip asked him to do more songs by himself and with Alan on the piano, or something like that, John said, 'What, is this going to be a double album? Then I'm gonna want double the money,'" de la Parra recalled Hooker saying.

But all the good vibes associated with making the album were about to end. Soon after the original recording sessions were completed, Alan "Blind Owl" Wilson, who had suffered from depression, was reported to have attempted suicide by driving his van off the road near Hite's home in Topanga Canyon, in the Santa Monica Mountains. Although he survived that crash, just a few weeks later, Wilson died of a drug overdose.

"Alan was not at ease with people. He sometimes used to sing standing behind the drums. And he would sing to the harmonica mic," said de la Parra. "Alan couldn't deal with the fact of being famous and the interaction you need with the audiences. It was very difficult for him. And of course, it was devastating for us to lose this genius at that early point in our lives."

When it came time to shoot the album cover photo, the band wanted it to not only have a blues vibe, but to pay tribute to Wilson's death as well. For the photo shoot, the band rented an apartment from an elderly lady who lived on Spring Street in downtown Los Angeles.

"That is the background you see in the window. It's funky and it's dark. It reflects the blues music. We paid this lady some money to use her apartment, facing that area of Los Angeles, which used to be a pretty funky area. We also got a sign with the *Hooker 'n Heat* lettering and we plugged it in at the apartment," said de la Parra.

Henry Vistine missed the photo shoot. Some reports have manager/producer Skip Taylor standing in for Vistine in the photo, but de la Parra isn't certain of that. He believes it was either Taylor or one of the photographers on the shoot.

"Henry didn't make the session, for whatever reason. He might have been drunk or he might have forgotten about it. So we got one of the photographers to stand there and later on we cropped Henry's face in and put it on the photographer's body. It is possible that it is Skip, though. The main thing was that whoever was there, we later cut his face off and put Henry's face there," said de la Parra.

A nod to Wilson came in the form of a picture that was hung on the back wall, next to the window, in the upper right corner of the album cover, just above where Hooker is sitting in the photo.

"So we have his picture there on the wall. That's one of the reasons we wanted the cover to be dark — we were mourning Alan's death. We missed him. It was a very bluesy cover. It reflects how we felt and it reflected the blues," said de la Parra.

Hooker 'n Heat, released in January 1971, would become the first of Hooker's albums to reach the charts, checking in at No. 78 on the U.S. Billboard 200 Albums chart.

Canned Heat fell on hard times throughout the rest of the 1970s. There was a lot of infighting, several lineup changes, a change of record labels, and continued drug use among some of the band members. In 1981, Bob "The Bear" Hite collapsed during a show in Los Angeles from a heroin overdose and died shortly thereafter.

But the band has continued to perform, with de la Parra still manning the drum kit. Joining de la Parra in today's version of Canned Heat are Harvey Mandel on guitar, Dale Spalding on guitar, harmonica, and vocals, and Larry Taylor on bass.

"This band has been a tragic band, but it's been quite an adventure," said de la Parra. "There have been a lot of great events and a lot of great times but also a lot of tragedy. And when you see it all in retrospective now, after fifty years, it's been just great, despite the tragedies."

People still approach de la Parra with memories of Canned Heat and how the band affected their lives.

"It happens all the time — people who met and fell in love at one of our shows, people who took their first LSD or smoked their first joint at one of our shows. It's really funny," said de la Parra. "Those are the kinds of stories that we hear all the time. It's almost like a community, not necessarily fans: Those people who were touched by our music and records and live shows, and then they come back years later and share those experiences with us, which makes us feel real good, especially when the stories are funny."

And de la Parra said that nowadays, he's comfortable with the legacy of Canned Heat.

"To us, it was something we never expected. In those times, bands would get together to play music, to be compelling, to share some ideals and political ideas or environmental ideas — the ideals of the 1960s. We never really expected to become big and famous because we were really just a blues band," he said.

"There were three songs that were very much blues-influenced songs, and we were able to put those three songs in the Top 10 worldwide: "Going Up the Country," "On the Road Again," and "Let's Work Together." That was a thing we never expected. Then that also inspired us to try to make blues music palatable and be accepted by White audiences."

As for the *Hooker 'n Heat* album, it holds a special place in the Canned Heat legacy for de la Parra.

"I think that record is considered a classic. We enjoyed those sessions quite a lot," he said. "We were America's number one band in 1969 [after Woodstock]. If Alan and Bob had stayed alive, we probably would have been as big as Led Zeppelin."

Discography

"Hooker 'n Heat"
John Lee Hooked and Canned Heat
January 15, 1971
(All songs written by John Lee Hooker except where noted)

Side One
"Messin' with the Hook" 3:23
"The Feelin' Is Gone" 4:32
"Send Me Your Pillow" 4:48
"Sittin' Here Thinkin'" 4:07
"Meet Me in the Bottom" 3:34
Side Two
"Alimonia Blues" 4:31
"Drifter" 4:57
"You Talk Too Much" 3:16
"Burning Hell" (John Lee Hooker, Bernard Besman) 5:28
"Bottle Up and Go" 2:27
Side Three
"The World Today" 7:47
"I Got My Eyes on You" 4:26
"Whiskey and Wimmen'" 4:37
"Just You and Me" 7:42
Side Four
"Let's Make It" 4:06
"Peavine" 5:07
"Boogie Chillen No. 2" (John Lee Hooker, Bernard Besman)..11:33

A wolf in simple clothing
Of a Simple Man
Lobo

    Singer-songwriter Kent LaVoie had done a demo session in New York in mid-1970 and while he was there, his producer, Phil Gernhard, an executive with Big Tree Records, had introduced him to Billy Meshel, creative director for Famous Music, a music publishing company.
    Meshel was going to handle the publishing of LaVoie's records, and the two spent about an hour together, talking about the music business and various other current events at the turn of a new decade.
    Meshel described the state of the music business to LaVoie, saying it was something akin to a "you and me against the world" approach. What Meshel meant, LaVoie believed, was that young people, through the protests of the late 1960s and into the early 1970s, were starting to stand up for themselves and meet their challenges head-on.
    That phrase "you and me against the world" stuck with LaVoie, and he took it home to Florida with him.
    Soon after that trip to New York, LaVoie was at home during a songwriting session and was trying to build a song around that "you and me against the world" phrase.
    LaVoie ended up flipping the phrase around to "me and you against the world," but he couldn't find the right rhythm. He was looking for a word to rhyme with "you" and it just wasn't happening. Nothing was clicking in the creative process.
    At the end of the room in which LaVoie was working was a sliding glass door. As he continued to strum his guitar looking to create some words and music, his basset hound,

Blake, followed by six basset hound puppies, stationed themselves at the sliding glass door, looking in at what LaVoie and his guitar were doing. Just sitting there, staring in at him.

Soon thereafter, LaVoie's other dog, a German shepherd named Boo, joined the basset hounds at the sliding glass door to observe LaVoie, who was still struggling to come up with a word to rhyme with "you."

Me and you against the world. You. Boo. There it was.

LaVoie wrote the words, "Me and you and a dog named Boo."

"Everybody thinks I made that story up, but I'm telling you, that's the way it was. I couldn't make that up," said LaVoie.

The line ended up being the title of the song that LaVoie built around it, "Me and You and a Dog Named Boo," which would change his life when he recorded it in 1971 under his stage name, Lobo.

LaVoie took the song to Gernhard, and the producer liked it. The officials at Big Tree Records liked it. LaVoie recorded it and the record company put it out as Lobo's first single in March 1971.

Everybody smelled a hit record.

"Me and You and a Dog Named Boo" was getting some airplay on AM radio and it was starting to make some noise on the charts, but it couldn't quite get over the hump. It needed a bigger push.

Radio stations in that era could really help a record by putting it in their regular play rotation. Consequently, a radio station in a certain region of the United States that didn't choose to play a single could essentially kill the song in that region by not even allowing it to get into the ears of fans.

One afternoon soon after the song had been released, LaVoie got a phone call from Gernhard. It was good news.

"Phil said, 'It's a smash! WLS in Chicago started playing it a week ago and we got a record order today,'"

LaVoie recalled Gernhard saying. "I was thinking maybe 500 or 1,000 records. But Phil said the order was for 20,000 records. That statement changed my life."

WLS was an AM station in Chicago that was known as a Class A station, and it broadcast with 50,000 watts of power from what was called a non-directional tower. That meant that during the daytime, WLS could be heard primarily in northern Illinois, northern Indiana, and southern Wisconsin. But at night, especially on a clear weather night, the WLS signal could be heard throughout much of the United States and Canada.

An hour after the call from Gernhard with the news about the order of 20,000 records, LaVoie got into his car and headed toward St. Petersburg, Florida. It was just turning dark and LaVoie still had the heady feeling of getting big-time airplay for his record from one of the country's biggest radio stations rolling around in his brain.

So he decided to see if he could get WLS to come in on the car radio while he was on the road to St. Petersburg.

"They [radio stations] weren't playing it locally [in Florida] and I had yet to hear it on the radio," said LaVoie. "So I've got WLS on and I'm going down the road and it fades out. Aw, shit. I had about a half-hour drive. But it faded back in, and I heard the hook to the song, 'Me and You and a Dog Named Boo.' I just stopped beside the road and cried. It was the weirdest thing. That's the first time I ever heard it on the radio. And it was like, all of a sudden, everybody likes you."

"Me and You and a Dog Named Boo" made it to No. 5 on the U.S. Billboard Hot 100 Singles chart, reached the top spot as No. 1 on the U.S. Billboard Adult Contemporary chart, and got to No. 4 on the United Kingdom Singles chart.

The song would anchor Lobo's debut album, called *Introducing Lobo* later in 1971. The album itself only reached No. 178 on the U.S. Billboard 200 Albums chart.

In early 1972 Big Tree Records ordered a second Lobo album, but its distribution deal fell apart. The album, called *Closeup*, went unreleased.

"That album just went into space. It never was put out. I was charged for it, of course," said LaVoie.

Gernhard was in complete control of LaVoie's career at that point. Not only was Gernhard his producer, but he also owned LaVoie's publishing and production rights.

"So I did whatever I was told. That's how I got something done. I've talked to a lot of people over the years who couldn't figure out why they couldn't get things done. But if somebody else isn't making money off of you, you might as well stay home," said LaVoie.

Gernhard and Big Tree Records put a deal together with Atlantic Records for what would be Lobo's third album. The first two albums were recorded at Electric Lady Studios at 52 West Eighth Street, in Greenwich Village, New York.

Electric Lady Studios was relatively new at the time, having been built in 1970 and specifically designed for Jimi Hendrix. According to published reports at the time, the studio was designed to help Hendrix be comfortable and relaxed, the hope being that the atmosphere would encourage his creativity.

"Nobody ever believes me when I tell them this, but for those first two albums, we used Jimi Hendrix's studio in Greenwich Village," said LaVoie. "While I was there, Santana was in Studio A, just hammering it out. And there I was, singing my little songs in the next studio. It was surreal, it really was."

LaVoie said Gernhard had chosen Electric Lady Studios for the first two Lobo albums because Big Tree Records was located in New York and company officials — like Big Tree owner Doug Morris — could stick their noses in and see what was going on during recording sessions.

But for the third Lobo album, Gernhard decided that he didn't want to record in New York. So he contacted his friend, Bob Richardson, who owned Master Sound Studios in Atlanta, Georgia, and made arrangements to record there. Richardson would hire the best musicians in the Atlanta area to back LaVoie. It promised to be a completely different recording vibe for the third album.

Despite not having his second album released, LaVoie had continued to write songs because he was certain, through assurances from Gernhard, that another album deal was in the offing.

So LaVoie was prepared to go back into the studio with an armload of songs and cut the next album. Along with LaVoie in the studio this time was drummer Roy Yeager, bass player John Mulkey, and lead guitarist Barry Bailey, who had in 1971 joined Atlanta Rhythm Section.

"That was really the development of my sound," said LaVoie. "Phil was smart enough to not make me sound like everybody else. I think the uniqueness of it was what got me so much airplay, because I didn't sound like anybody else."

Four songs were cut in that first recording session in Atlanta for what would become Lobo's third album *Of a Simple Man*: the eponymous title track "Of a Simple Man," "Running Deer," "Gypsy and the Midnight Ghost," and "I'd Love You to Want Me."

"I'd Love You to Want Me" would become not only Lobo's next smash hit single, but it would also go on to become the biggest worldwide charting record of his career.

The song itself, according to LaVoie, was what he called a "constructed song."

"There's a couple of ways to write a song. One was you came up with a line and then you built on it. The other was that you just sat down with a guitar and started playing," said LaVoie.

"I had in mind to write a big ballad. And I had the hook, 'I'd love you to want me, the way I want you, the way that it should be.' I had this beautiful art teacher when I was in high school and I imagined that if we had connected, would she be as taken with me as I thought I was with her," he said.

Some of the other ballads at the time, specifically "Without You," written by Pete Ham and Tom Evans of Badfinger and released on the band's *No Dice* album in 1970; and the early 1972 hit "Baby, Don't Get Hooked on Me," written by Mac Davis and on his album of the same name, influenced the writing of "I'd Love You to Want Me."

"It wasn't copied after any one song; it was just sort of the format then of the way ballads were done," said LaVoie.

"The other thing with the song is that basically the chords and verses and the hook are the same. There is no bridge; it's just straight ahead. And it had a downbeat. That made it the real deal."

Another unique aspect about "I'd Love You to Want Me" emerged during the cutting and mixing of it. Gernhard had plans to release it as the first single from the *Of a Simple Man* album.

"But Phil kept saying it was too long. And so I said to him, let's cut the intro," said LaVoie. "It ended up being a real unique thing because disc jockeys couldn't talk in front of it. They had to announce it and then it came on. Most of the time, it would just come on the radio and they would talk about it on the way out. Once again, it wasn't done on purpose — it was to save time."

The rest of the recording sessions for *Of a Simple Man* had alternated between Atlanta and New York. LaVoie and the other musicians would track the songs in Atlanta, then LaVoie and Gernhard would return to New York and add strings and backing vocals from session singers Robert John, Michael Gately, Ellie Greenwich, Barbara Sipple, and Steve Tadanger.

"The song just kept getting bigger and bigger," said LaVoie. "I think it was because we had heard it so much that it sounded like a hit. And it was."

"I'd Love You to Want Me" was No. 1 on both the Billboard Easy Listening and Cash Box Top 100 charts, and No. 2 on the Billboard Hot 100 singles chart.

Gernhard had released the title track, "Of a Simple Man," as the follow-up single to "I'd Love You to Want Me." But it only reached No. 56 on the Billboard Top 100 Singles chart.

As it turned out, though, there was another hit single on the album. As was often the case, it was on the flipside of an already released single. A radio station disc jockey in St. Louis decided to flip over the single "Of a Simple Man" and found "Don't Expect Me to Be Your Friend."

The success of that song was unexpected by both Gernhard and LaVoie.

"Phil had to have everything his way or he threw a tirade. That's one of the reasons that I succeeded and a lot of other guys didn't with him, because I could put up with Phil," said LaVoie. "Phil kind of let me put 'Don't Expect Me to Be Your Friend' on the album."

LaVoie did everything on that song — all the guitar parts, vocals, and background vocals.

"Phil said, 'OK, that's your toy; you can play with it,'" said LaVoie. "The song is about basically being in a relationship and breaking up and then saying, let's just be friends. I've been quoted before as saying, 'Don't Expect Me to Be Your Friend' is my favorite song. And I think it's because I liked what it said. It's very easy and it was a very unlikely hit on the radio. There wasn't anything in it, just a few strings and my guitar. But everybody can get into the idea of, if we're going to break up, just get out of my face. I don't want to be friends. But it was a real personal song because I'd done most of the stuff on it. I guess that's why I liked it."

There is a photo of LaVoie on the *Of a Simple Man* album cover, sitting on the front of a boat, with his head tilted slightly forward, looking downward. Barry Harwood, a guitarist who also played on the album, took the photo. Harwood would go on to play with Lynyrd Skynyrd, the Rossington Collins Band, and the Allen Collins Band.

"I'm one of those who doesn't take a very good picture, so I think it was just used because we had it," said LaVoie. "I liked the picture myself because it's really what I look like."

The *Of a Simple Man* album, on the strength of the two big hit singles, reached No. 37 on the U.S. Billboard 200 Albums chart. It would be the highest charting album of Lobo's career.

But LaVoie is quick to point out that he wasn't an "album" artist; he was more of a singles hit-maker. That's how Gernhard saw him.

"Because of Phil, I was an AM singles artist. He never thought in terms of albums; he thought in terms of how many hit singles can we get," said LaVoie. "He'd say, 'We've got a couple of hits; we'll just fill up the rest of the album and go.' There were never album concepts and that's probably why I didn't sell a lot of albums relative to other artists."

But being under contract to Gernhard and following his direction, while successful in some aspects, didn't allow LaVoie the opportunity to grow as an artist.

"I was never given the freedom — because I was under contract to Gernhard — of trying to be anything other than a hit-maker. That was my job. Between 1971 and 1975, you couldn't get away from the Lobo sound anywhere in the world. It was everywhere," said LaVoie. "I fully appreciated after the fact what I didn't do, but I also know what I was capable of doing as far as being famous. I took that as far as I could do it. It just didn't work for me."

That's why he decided to take the stage name "Lobo" at the beginning of his career.

"It was so I could hide. I didn't want my name known. Phil said if it's a gimmick, then stick with it. Once again I just did what he said. He said think of some names. And on the first list of names I had — I don't remember any of the others — 'Lobo' was on there. Phil asked what does it mean? And I said it's a wolf. He said, 'That's cool; let's go with that.' When 'Me and You and a Dog Named Boo' had some of its first big reviews, 'Lobo' was mentioned as being a cool group name. There was really no meaning to it. It was just a name to hide behind."

LaVoie said that Lobo didn't really fit into any one place during the 1970s, and he believes that hasn't changed over the years.

"I don't think past the end of the week. My goal in the music business was to write a hit and have $50,000 in the bank. I was very realistic because back in the early 1970s as a radio musician playing clubs, I made $10,000 a year," said LaVoie. "You have to remember, I was completely unhyped. My records just showed up. I didn't care. I didn't have a manager, didn't have an agent and didn't want one. Just Phil. Everybody thought 'Lobo' was a group and that was fine with me. I couldn't have cared less."

Discography

"Of A Simple Man"
Lobo
1972

"Intro" 0:23
"There Ain't No Way" 3:14
"A Big Red Kite" 4:06
"Recycle Sally" 3:10
"Don't Expect Me To Be Your Friend" 3:38
"A Simple Man" 3:05
"I'd Love You To Want Me" 4:04
"Let Me Down Easy" 2:45
"Pee-Ro Juan Valdez Sam Quixote" 4:04
"Running Deer" 3:25
"Gypsy And The Midnight Ghost" 3:08
"Am I True To Myself" 3:38

People all over the world get on board
Back Stabbers
The O'Jays

Kenny Gamble had written a song, but it wasn't complete. He was stuck without a second verse, and he couldn't quite get it.

But the O'Jays were in the studio — Sigma Sound Studios at 12th and Race Streets in Philadelphia — and ready to go. They had already laid down nine other tracks for an album, as well as the background vocals to the final song and were anxious to see how the rest of it would sound.

Gamble called for a five-minute break, left the recording booth and retired to a small back room at Sigma Sound to work on writing the second verse of the song.

The O'Jays — Walter Williams, Eddie Levert and William Powell — thought that a couple of songs for the album had the potential to be something special. They had a technique they used with background vocals: they would double and sometimes triple the background vocals so that they would sound more powerful, and had recorded those first for the song.

When it came to lead vocals, Williams and Levert — who shared lead vocals and sometimes double-lead vocals on some songs — each had a microphone and baffle so that their voices wouldn't bleed into each other. During the recording of the album, the O'Jays had introduced the idea of double-lead vocals to Gamble and Leon Huff, co-founders of Philadelphia International Records, and the producers liked it because they could better control the sound.

Philadelphia International Records co-founder Kenny Gamble was still writing some of the lyrics to "Love Train" while The O'Jays were waiting in the studio to record the song. (Photo by Mike Morsch)

So everything in the studio was set up and ready to go. Now, the O'Jays were just waiting on Kenny Gamble to finish writing the lyrics.

A few minutes later, Gamble came out and said he had it. He gave the second verse to the O'Jays and they went back into the recording studio to learn it.

"You know, you've got to try it a couple times so you can get it right. And it fit like a glove," said Walter Williams.

"We were able to use those words and make them fit into the feeling and the spirit of it."

By 1972, Williams had already learned a valuable lesson about singing from his friend Stevie Wonder, a lesson that he was eager to employ now for Gamble and Huff.

"He told me, 'You can sing a song and you can sing it perfect. But if the spirit doesn't live in it, you have nothing.' And he's absolutely right about that," said Williams. "It didn't dawn on me that was the case until I started to experience it. You know you can even sing bad notes, flat notes, but if the spirit lives in it, it's a good song.

"What he meant by that is that songs are accepted from other people and from the singer. If I'm the singer, it's from my heart to yours, from my soul to yours. And I've got to make you feel what I feel. Once I understood that concept, then I was able to go into the studio and record and set up lyrics and put the right kind of touch on things."

That's what the O'Jays did with the song they were recording for Gamble and Huff that day in 1972.

It was from their hearts, their souls, and they recorded it with such spirit that it would become the biggest hit the group would ever have.

The song was "Love Train," and it would go to No. 1 on both the Billboard Hot 100 Singles and the Billboard R&B Singles in early 1973.

It would also be the final song that would complete the O'Jays' first album for Philadelphia International Records, *Back Stabbers*, a breakthrough album for the group that would be released in 1972 and hit No. 10 on the Billboard Pop Albums chart.

"The Bible speaks of love. So how could you not accept the song that speaks about love, especially love all over the world? Global love. We singled out some of the places that were special and that we thought needed more love, and those places were talked about in the song — England and China and Russia," said Williams. "We knew the song was special, but we didn't know it was going to be like that. Once that song came out, I think in two weeks, it was damn-near platinum. That's moving a lot of records. And you know what? You can't really keep up with a record that moves like that."

Signing with Philly International was a new experience for the O'Jays in the late 1960s. At the time, Gamble and Huff were independent producers whose records were being distributed by Chess Records, owned by brothers Leonard and Phil Chess. But Leonard Chess died in 1972, just as Gamble and Huff were getting Philly International up and running.

In the interim, the O'Jays found themselves working, but not at the kind of gigs that were going to advance their careers. It wasn't until Gamble and Huff regrouped, with the help of a distribution deal from CBS Records in 1972, that things started moving in the right direction for Philadelphia International Records, and subsequently, the O'Jays.

In addition to the O'Jays, Philly International was building a high-quality stable of artists. The company had also signed Harold Melvin & the Blue Notes, Lou Rawls, the girl group The Three Degrees, and Billy Paul.

"We were aware that there was some really strong talent at Philadelphia International at the time," said Williams. "But we didn't know Harold Melvin & the Blue Notes, hadn't worked with them a lot. But we knew they had something special as well. It was a five-man group with good harmonies. But they didn't really impact the industry until they discovered that the drummer could sing and had a dynamic voice."

The drummer was Teddy Pendergrass. He would leave the Blue Notes in 1975 and have a successful solo career throughout the rest of the 1970s and into the 1980s before being in a car accident in March 1982 that left him a paraplegic.

Stacks of Wax

By the time the O'Jays got to Philly International, they had honed their craft on the theater circuit. In New York it was the Apollo; in Washington D.C. it was the Howard; in Chicago it was the Regal; in Baltimore it was the Royal; and in Philadelphia, it was the Uptown.

"And those theaters were incredible. What they would do for an artist that cared about his appearance and his performance really helped a lot," said Williams. "I mean, we were workhorses during the week. We would do three shows during the day. The 'half' would be posted at 9:30 or 10 in the morning, and they would post it on the blackboard at the Apollo. The 'half' meant a half-hour before the show. You had better be there.

"Three shows a day during the week, Monday through Friday. And then on Friday, sometimes even Thursday, four shows, and then five shows Friday, Saturday and sometimes Sunday. That's a lot of shows," said Williams. "You should be able to, as a group, as entertainers, hone your craft. You should be able to become excellent doing that many shows a day."

With that groundwork already in place, Williams devoted himself to learning more about the craft and the business. And he did that by watching Gamble and Huff and how they operated in every facet of the industry.

"These guys were professionals' professionals. I used to just go in to sit and see how they put tracks together. They would work a track at least 10 different ways until they really felt they had it. That sometimes would happen in an hour, sometimes it would happen in two or three hours. They were that focused on making that track work with the song. It was no joke," said Williams.

The "house band" for Philly International was an integral part of helping Gamble and Huff develop the "Philly Sound," sometimes called "Philly Soul." The group consisted of about 30 studio musicians based at Sigma Sound Studios. Working with Gamble, Huff, and producer/arranger/songwriter Thom Bell, the musicians became known as Mother Father Sister Brother (MFSB). They not only backed many in Philly International's stable of talent, but the group also recorded as a name act, releasing the single "TSOP" — The Sound of Philadelphia — that hit No. 1 in 1974 on the both the Billboard pop and R&B charts. It sold more than a million copies and eventually became the theme song for the *Soul Train* television show.

"Huff was the most fantastic piano man I'd seen ever in those days," said Williams. "The crew that they worked with — Earl Young on drums, Ronnie Baker on bass, Norman Harris on guitar — those guys were incredible. They knew what Gamble and Huff wanted, they were very creative, and when they found the right groove, they would finish it off. Sitting there I learned how to do that, I learned how to write good songs, concentrate on great lyrics and stay focused and come up the best that I could come up with. ... just by sitting and being with them and watching them put things together."

When it was time to go into the studio, Williams was hyped up and ready to sing because he had witnessed the process firsthand.

"I was right there. When it came time to put my part into it, I wanted to be as great as they were. We were all able to do that and be the professionals that we turned out to be. We were inspired by the people we were working with," he said.

The other aspect that helped make those early years at Philadelphia International a success were the songwriters hanging around Philadelphia at the time.

Williams said the O'Jays would work with six or seven different teams of writers and hundreds of songs. It was a long and tedious process to sift through all the material and whittle the list down to the 10 songs that would eventually get onto the *Back Stabbers* album.

The O'Jays were already aware of who they thought were the best songwriters in Philly. In addition to Gamble, Huff, and Bell, there was the team of Gene McFadden and

John Whitehead, who would go on to write, produce, and perform the O'Jays' hit single, "Ain't No Stoppin' Us Now" in 1979; and Walter "Bunny" Sigler, a performer in the 1960s who had the hit record *Let the Good Times Roll/Feel So Good* in 1967.

But the process of going through all the songs and trying to pick the right ones was challenging for Williams.

"You already knew who the big guys were, who the great writers were, and that was Bunny Sigler, McFadden and Whitehead, Gamble and Huff," said Williams. "But we would have to go through all of those other people and hear their songs. Not only would they sing them to us, they would perform them. That's what I didn't like. Going through all of that. Actually, they never would have anything that would be strong enough to compete with Gamble and Huff, McFadden and Whitehead, and Walter Sigler."

Bunny Sigler was thrilled to be considered among the best songwriters at Philly International in the early days of the company, but he still wanted to be a performer.

"I wasn't thinking about writing. I wanted to be a singing star," said Sigler. "So while I was waiting to get another record contract, I started writing. And that's the best thing that could have happened to me. But I didn't enjoy it at first. Me and McFadden and Whitehead, we wanted to sing." Sigler was working with Billy Paul at Sigma Sound Studios while Gamble and Huff were making the *Back Stabbers* album for the O'Jays. Gamble asked Sigler to also work with the O'Jays on the album.

"Writing for Eddie and Walt was the easiest thing in the world because they sing their hearts out and it's wonderful," said Sigler. "If you saw the O'Jays recording, it was like they were onstage. I remember that when they finished recording 'Love Train,' Walt came dancing out of the studio. He was still singing as if he was on stage. I can see it now, him dancing out of there singing 'People All Over the World.' He was doing a dance step."

Walter "Bunny" Sigler was thrilled to be considered among the best songwriters at Philly International in the early days of the company, but he still wanted to be a performer when he was asked to work on the "Back Stabbers" album for The O'Jays. (Photo by Mike Morsch)

Sigler would end up sharing producing credit with Gamble and Huff on the *Back Stabbers* album. Of the 10 songs on the album, Sigler would also have songwriting credit on the first track, "When the World's at Peace," the third track "Who Am I," and the ninth track "Sunshine."

Huff, McFadden, and Whitehead would write the single "Back Stabbers," which would reach No. 1 on the Billboard Hot 100 Singles chart and No. 3 on the Billboard Hot Soul Singles chart.

"That's one thing Kenny said to us back then, that the songs had to stand the test of time. Those songs — they're still played and they sound great now," said Sigler. "What makes it cool is when you leave Philly, and other people recognize you for it. One guy told me, man, I made ten babies on your songs. You should help me pay the child support."

Williams believes the combination of the quality songwriting, the expertise of Gamble and Huff, and the addition of Charles "Cholly" Atkins, a choreographer who taught the O'Jays the dance steps to go along with the songs, were the perfect elements that were added to the the O'Jays' innate talent. And that was the recipe for the group's success in the 1970s.

"Cholly Atkins was an old hoofer and he actually really knew what he was doing. So he staged our shows, he taught us what to do and how to do it. It was just like the other ingredients that we needed," said Williams. "Eddie and Walter could perform, Gamble and Huff could write and produce, and Cholly Atkins could stage it. That seemed to be the other part of the puzzle that came together that shot us out into orbit, where we needed to be.

"But the fuel was the songs and the production of the songs. And that was Gamble and Huff."

As for the *Back Stabbers* album, Williams said it's the one that put the O'Jays on the map, both in the United States and internationally.

Mike Morsch

"It's very special. 'Love Train' was on that album and that's our biggest hit today. There's nothing bigger than 'Love Train.' There's no greater message than 'Love Train.' I think that's the one that told everybody — especially after they'd seen it and experienced it — that this is a good, wholesome group. They're not doing any of the sexual, vulgar type things onstage. It's the one I think that told people that they're doing good music and I want to hear it and I want to see them perform it. That's the one that started everything."

Discography

"Back Stabbers"
The O'Jays
August 1972

Side One

"When the World's at Peace" (Kenneth Gamble, Bunny Sigler, Phil Hurtt) 5:21

"Back Stabbers" (Leon Huff, Gene McFadden, John Whitehead) 3:07

"Who Am I" (Sigler, Hurtt) 5:14

"(They Call Me) Mr. Lucky" (Gamble, Huff) 3:20

"Time to Get Down" (Gamble, Huff) 2:53

Side Two

"992 Arguments" (Gamble, Huff)... 6:09

"Listen to the Clock on the Wall" (Gamble, Huff, Whitehead, McFadden)... 3:48

"Shiftless, Shady, Jealous Kind of People" (Gamble, Huff, Whitehead, McFadden)...3:36

"Sunshine" (Sigler, Hurtt) 3:42

"Love Train" (Gamble, Huff) 2:59

A new Cadillac for the guy who couldn't even drive
Spinners
The Spinners

Atlantic Records had added Thom Bell, a rising star, to its stable of producers, arrangers, and songwriters, in 1972. And the first thing record company officials did was hand Bell a list of the artists recording for Atlantic at the time and tell him to pick out an act to produce.

Without hesitation, he chose the Spinners.

Bell had been in on the ground floor of establishing the Philadelphia style of soul music in the early 1970s. As a teenager, he had met Kenny Gamble and Leon Huff, and Bell would join them as an arranger for some of the early hits produced at Gamble and Huff's Philadelphia International Records.

Bell arranged the O'Jays' 1972 breakout album *Back Stabbers*, and would be a songwriter and producer for the Stylistics. He and his songwriting partner Linda Creed would go on to write the classic hits "Betcha By Golly, Wow," "Break Up to Make Up," "You Are Everything" and "You Make Me Feel Brand New" for the Stylistics.

By 1972, Atlantic officials were more than happy to give Bell the pick of the company's roster of talent.

"Thom Bell is a genius," said Henry Fambrough, an original member of the Spinners. "Thom used to be the keyboards man at the Uptown Theater in Philadelphia when all the acts went through there [in the 1960s]. And he said he remembered the Spinners coming through there. He said we were the only group who came through that sang the harmony that he liked."

It was fortuitous timing for the Spinners. They had formed in 1954 with members Fambrough, Billy Henderson, Pervis Jackson, C.P. Spencer and James Edwards, calling themselves The Domingoes.

The group had a couple of personnel changes, most notably adding lead singer Bobby Smith, and was renamed the Spinners in 1961. They became the first artists to sign with Harvey Fuqua's Tri-Phi Records, and Fuqua not only became the group's manager, he taught its members how to sing harmony.

Fuqua's girlfriend at the time was Gwen Gordy, sister of Motown founder Berry Gordy, and the two of them penned the first song that did anything for the Spinners, "That's What Girls Are Made For." The song reached No. 27 on the Billboard Hot 100 Singles chart and No. 5 on the Hot R&B Songs chart.

"We thought we had it made," said Fambrough.

They didn't, though. Not yet, anyway.

By 1963, Fuqua and Gwen Gordy had married and Fuqua ended up selling Tri-Phi Records and its entire roster of artists to his brother-in-law, Berry Gordy. The Spinners now were part of the Motown label.

The group, sometimes known as the Detroit Spinners, debuted as Motown artists in 1964 and stayed with the company until 1970, without much success. The group's single "I'll Always Love You" reached No. 35 on the Billboard Hot 100 charts and peaked at No. 8 on the Billboard R&B Singles chart.

There was a time in the mid- to late-1960s, when there were no hit records for the Spinners, and the members of the group had to find other ways to make a living. Motown used them as road managers, chaperones and chauffeurs for other artists on the label.

Henry Fambrough, an original member of the Spinners - seen here during a 2015 performance of one of the group's signature songs, "The Rubberband Man" - said that producer Thom Bell was convinced that "Spinners" was going to be a breakout album and that the group would soar to heights that it had not previously experienced. (Photo by Mike Morsch)

"When we weren't on the road, we worked as drivers," said Fambrough. "I was Berry Gordy's mother's chauffeur. The others would drive different groups to different shows."

The Spinners didn't make another significant appearance on the Top 40 charts until 1970 with the Stevie Wonder song "It's a Shame," — with G.C. Cameron on lead — which got to No. 14 on the Billboard Hot 100 Singles chart and No. 3 on the Billboard R&B chart. By that time, though, the group's contract with Motown was coming to an end.

"We were locked into Motown until 1970," said Fambrough. "Berry had the Temptations, the Supremes, Marvin Gaye, the Four Tops, the Miracles, and on and on. And the radio stations could only play so many hits and so many artists an hour. We got lost in the shuffle."

It was Aretha Franklin who suggested that the Spinners move to Atlantic Records, her label at the time, when their contract was up.

"She knew that we had left Motown. And she said, 'Listen guys, I'm with Atlantic Records; go there and talk to them. I think it would be a good company for you,'" said Fambrough.

It turned out to be the right advice from The Queen of Soul. Atlantic signed the Spinners. Then the company signed Thom Bell.

And it was time to make a new record.

In mid-1972, Bell went to Detroit to meet the Spinners on their home turf. He brought along his tape recorder. By this time, Philippe Wynne had replaced Cameron in the group.

"He got everybody's voice individually on his tape recorder. It was the first time we had someone concentrate on our sound," said Fambrough. "He said, 'I'm going back to Philadelphia and I'm going to have my team start writing some songs for your voices.'"

Bell returned to Detroit several months later. With him, he brought back the songs "I'll Be Around," "One of a Kind (Love Affair)," "How Could I Let You Get Away," and "Could It Be I'm Falling in Love."

"When Thom brought the songs back to us, he said, 'Bobby, you be the lead, and Philippe, I want you to do this part.' He cleared all that up and he said, 'Within a couple of months, I'm going to bring you into Philadelphia and we're going to record,'" said Fambrough.

Those songs would all be on the album *Spinners*, released in April 1973, which would be recorded in Philadelphia.

Although the Spinners and Bell were under contract to Atlantic at the time, Bell would record the album in the same studio that was being used to develop the "Philly Soul" sound in the early 1970s.

Sigma Sound Studios, at 212 North 12th Street in Philadelphia, was closely associated with Gamble and Huff's Philadelphia International Records.

By the time the Spinners got to Sigma Sound, some of the early Philly International albums were also being recorded there, including *Back Stabbers* in 1972 by the O'Jays, *360 Degrees of Billy Paul* in 1972 by Billy Paul, *Love Is the Message* in 1973 by MFSB (Mother Father Sister Brother), and *Black & Blue* in 1973 by Harold Melvin & the Blue Notes.

It is for that reason that the *Spinners* album is among those credited with being part of the birth of the Philadelphia Sound.

Bell was confident that *Spinners* was going to be a breakout album and that the group would soar to heights that it had not previously experienced.

In fact, he predicted it. The Spinners themselves were still unsure when they arrived in Philadelphia to begin recording.

"As we were getting ready to record, Thom said, 'By the way, man, I want to tell you, y'all are gonna be the number one group within the next year,'" said Fambrough. "And we all went, 'Right.' Bobby said, 'We've heard that before.' And Thom said, 'OK, remember I said that.'

"So Purvis said, 'Thom, if that's true, we're going to buy you a Cadillac.' Thom said, 'OK now, remember you said that,'" said Fambrough.

"How Could I Let You Get Away" was the first single released from the album and it took off up the charts. On the B-side was "I'll Be Around." As was sometimes the case with radio stations and records in that era, a disc jockey flipped the record over to the B-side and "I'll Be Around" took off as well.

"How Could I Let You Get Away," with Wynne on lead vocals and Fambrough on close harmony, reached No. 14 on the Billboard R&B chart. But "I'll Be Around," with Smith on lead vocals, moved even faster and higher and would become the group's breakthrough hit, reaching No. 1 on the R&B chart and No. 3 on the Billboard Pop Singles chart.

"Could It Be I'm Falling in Love" was released as the follow-up single to "I'll Be Around," and it, too, would be a hit. Smith handled the lead on that one, with vocal backing by MFSB. The song would also reach No. 1 on the R&B chart and No. 4 on the Pop Singles chart.

"One of a Kind (Love Affair)," with Wynne on lead and once again with the backing vocals of MFSB, became the third consecutive hit off the *Spinners* album, reaching No. 1 on the R&B chart and No. 11 on Pop Singles chart.

Bell was right. Atlantic got behind the album and the Spinners did indeed become one of the top-selling groups in the country.

Fortunately, though, the Spinners avoided having to spend some of their newfound wealth on Bell.

"Thom was sitting at the controls one day and he said to us, 'Where's my car?' But we never bought him a car because Thom didn't drive. He said, 'Man, I can't drive. I don't even have a driver's license. You don't have to buy me a car,'" said Fambrough.

The *Spinners* album started a huge run through the mid-1970s for the group. The album itself reached No. 14 on the Billboard 200 Albums chart and No. 1 on the Billboard R&B Albums chart.

That success was followed in 1974 by two albums, *Mighty Love*, which was No. 1 on the R&B Albums chart; and *New and Improved*, which was also No. 1 on the R&B charts.

Pick of the Litter in 1975 reached No. 2 on the R&B Albums charts and *Happiness Is Being with the Spinners* checked in at No. 5 on the R&B Albums chart.

The *New and Improved* album in 1974 also featured the group's only No. 1 single on the Billboard Hot 100 Singles chart, "Then Came You," a collaboration with Dionne Warwick.

"At the time, Dionne was in between hits. She contacted Thom, she wanted him to produce an album for her," said Fambrough. "He said, 'I won't record you by yourself, but I'll do you and the Spinners together. And she said OK, because we were hot then."

Warwick and the Spinners had toured together in 1974. Bell had two songs for Warwick to record. The first was a slow song, "Just as Long as We Have Love," which she would sing with Fambrough; the other was the more up-tempo "Then Came You."

Once again, Bell was predicting success. But not for the song that the group thought would be the hit.

"The slow song, that was the first one. 'Then Came You' was the second song," said Fambrough. "Everybody was making a bet that the slow song was going to be the hit. But Thom kept telling everybody, 'I don't know about that.'"

Dionne Warwick collaborated with the Spinners on the song "Then Came You," and it became the only No. 1 hit of her career. (Photo by Mike Morsch)

Bell apparently again sensed something the others didn't, despite the fact that Warwick didn't appear to like the song either.

"Thom said, 'I have a piece of music I want to do with you and the guys.' We had just finished our tour," said Warwick. "I said, 'I don't know about this song, Thom.' It wasn't so much that I didn't like it, I just didn't think I could do it."

Bell remained confident. He ripped a dollar bill in half, and he and Warwick each signed a half. They then exchanged halves. "He said, 'I'll tell you what, I'll make a bet with you. You keep one half of this dollar and I'll keep the other half. This is going to be a monster hit," said Warwick.

The idea was that whoever was right on whether the record would be a hit or not, the other would mail back the missing half of the dollar bill to the winner.

"And by the way, it was my first number one recording. Ever," said Warwick. "I loved working with the Spinners. We had such a wonderful time and a wonderful tour."

"Then Came You" would be featured on the *New and Improved* Spinners album of 1974, while "Just as Long as We Have Love" would be on the group's next album, *Pick of the Litter*, released in 1975.

The music wasn't the only thing that made the Spinners hugely popular in the 1970s. In addition to the good songs that were finally being written for them, they added in an experienced stage presence and some great dancing.

According to Fambrough, Harvey Fuqua played a major role in the 1960s with the first part, the stage experience, and choreographer Charles "Cholly" Atkins was responsible for the smooth moves, well-honed by the 1970s.

"Harvey brought in Cholly Atkins from New York. We did all the dance steps. We did a show at the Twenty Grand in Detroit, the Spinners and Marvin Gaye. And we had a seven-day stand there. And for seven days, man, two shows each night that were sellouts," said Fambrough. "Berry [Gordy] was in the audience almost every night watching the Spinners. I'm not sure, but I think that's what made Berry form the artist development [portion of Motown] and he put Cholly in charge of it. It was a good thing for him."

Atkins had been hired by Gordy in 1964 and was the choreographer for Motown's biggest acts during the decade, including the Supremes, the Temptations, the Four Tops, the Marvelettes, and Gladys Knight and the Pips. In the 1970s, Atkins also developed the dance steps for the O'Jays at Philly International.

The Spinners would continue making more memorable songs throughout the 1970s, including "The Rubberband Man," another No. 1 hit for the group on the R&B chart that also made it to No. 2 on the Hot 100 Singles chart; and "Working My Way Back to You" in 1979, which was a Top 10 hit on both the R&B and Hot 100 charts. Fambrough said that he didn't particularly like "The Rubberband Man" the first time he heard it.

"It's so different. Thom had that song in the back of his mind for five or six years. It's about his son. The other kids called him Fat Man. Thom wrote it about his son, but he changed it to Rubberband Man," said Fambrough. "When I first heard the track, I didn't like it. What the hell is this? Thom said, 'Don't worry about it.' We put that song out and it took off so fast. Everybody was singing it."

The Spinners even incorporated oversized rubber bands into the dance routine when they performed the song live.

Fambrough is the only surviving member of the group from its heyday in the 1970s. Wynne died in 1984; Henderson in 2007; Jackson in 2008; and Smith in 2013.

"All my guys are gone now. I don't think a day goes by when I don't think about them. It was a great ride. I look back on them and I miss them. But that's something you can't do anything about. That's a road everybody has to walk down," said Fambrough.

He said the music of the Spinners has survived for decades because it is about love.

"If you listen to all the songs that we produced in the '50s, '60s and the '70s, you will hear love and good things. Even now, when we go on stage, we sing about love. Bringing people together, puppy love. Love your girlfriend and kiss her, all that stuff. Young love, old love, everything on the positive side of the human condition," said Fambrough.

As of 2015, Fambrough was still performing with the Spinners, known now as The Mighty Spinners.

"As the guys passed away, I replaced them. And I was fortunate enough to find four great guys. They've got good voices and their minds are right. No dopers, no alcoholics.

Four great guys. We're still doing sellout rooms," said Fambrough.

"And I'm still doing all the dance steps. The younger guys are having to keep up with me."

Discography

"Spinners"
The Spinners
April 1973

Side one

"Just Can't Get You Out of My Mind" (Vinnie Barrett) 3:42

"Just You and Me Baby" (Yvette Davis) 2:56

"Don't Let the Green Grass Fool You" (Jerry Akines, Johnny Bellman, Victor Drayton, Reginald Turner) 4:01

"I Could Never (Repay Your Love)" (Bruce Hawes) 6:56

"I'll Be Around" (Thom Bell, Phil Hurtt) 3:10

Side two

"One of a Kind (Love Affair)" (Joseph B. Jefferson) 3:31

"We Belong Together" (Yvette Davis) 4:12

"Ghetto Child" (Linda Creed, Thom Bell) 3:47

"How Could I Let You Get Away" (Yvette Davis) 3:46

"Could It Be I'm Falling in Love" (Mystro & Lyric (Melvin and Mervin Steals) 4:13

It was a movement, not a rock band
Wovoka
Redbone

Pat Vegas was exhausted. The bass player and his band Redbone had just played a gig in mid-1973 that included the Steve Miller Band and Nils Lofgren on the bill at the Spectrum in Philadelphia.

Immediately after the show, Vegas and the other Redbone members boarded a late flight back to Los Angeles, finally arriving home around 3 a.m.

Vegas was just getting ready to climb into bed when the phone rang. It was his brother, Candido "Lolly" Vegas, lead guitarist and vocalist for the band.

"Lolly called me and said, 'Hey, Pat, I've got an idea for a song that's really, really good, man. You wanna come over and we'll write it together?' I said 'Lolly I'm tired and I want to go to bed.' But he said it was a great song and that we could do it together," said Vegas. "He was up and ready to go, so I said, 'If I come down there Lolly, we're going to write this together.' And he said, 'OK, what do you think I'm talking about? We'll write it together.'"

So Vegas got dressed and drove over to his brother's house. When he arrived, Lolly played the chords of the song for Pat. Lolly had titled the song "I Want to Give You My Love."

"It was a different song with a different kind of feeling. But it was kind of milky and went on forever," said Vegas. "So I said no, no, no Lolly. Leave me alone with it for about an hour by myself and let me work on it with my bass."

Pat went into another room and started to work on the song. He broke down the chord changes and started to rebuild the song around the bass, to give the song more of a structure.

"I broke it down with that bass beginning. That's the first opening I put to it. Lolly came in and he heard it and he said, 'Damn, I like that man, I like it.' He had been drinking some vodka before I got there, so he was a little bit out of it. But when he came in and heard it, he loved what I did with it."

After about three hours of working on the song, Pat Vegas went home and finally went to bed. Later in the day, after the brothers had both gotten some sleep, Lolly again called Pat.

"He calls me up and says, 'You gotta come and hear this song I wrote.' And I said, 'What do you mean *you* wrote?' He didn't remember anything because he had been drinking heavily that night," said Vegas. "I said 'Wait a minute Lolly, I was at the house for three hours. What do you mean *you* wrote it?' And he says, 'Yeah, you were?' And I said, 'Yes, I was. Ask your wife.' And he asked her and she confirmed it. He didn't remember a damn thing."

The name of the song would eventually be changed to "Come and Get Your Love" — at the suggestion of Pat Vegas — and would go on to be the band's biggest hit. It appeared on the album *Wovoka*, released in November 1973. By April of 1974, the song had reached No. 5 on the Billboard Hot 100 Singles chart and would spend 18 weeks in the Top 40. It became the fourth most popular song on the Hot 100 chart for all of 1974.

But the song would cause a rift between the brothers that would never heal.

When the band went into the studio to record "Come and Get Your Love" for the *Wovoka* album, its drummer was Pete "Last Walking Bear" DePoe, who had joined the band in 1969. But right in the middle of the recording session, DePoe was served with divorce papers.

"Pete was all distraught and crazy. So then we got Butch Rillera in to play it. Butch came in and recorded it with me and Lolly and that's the one we used, the one with Butch Rillera," said Vegas.

The following week, CBS Records pressed the record and prepared to release it as a single ahead of the album. When the single came out, it had only one name listed as the songwriter: Lolly Vegas.

Pat Vegas was upset and he made his feelings known to his brother.

"I said, 'What the hell is this? What's going on?' Lolly just flat out wrote me off. And I've been stewing over that ever since," said Vegas. "I did all the work putting it together and changing some of the words. Lolly's version was seven minutes long. He insisted he wanted it just the way it was. And I said, 'Lolly, you're crazy, man. It's not gonna happen. It's too long.'

"When you hear the song, it's all bass. But he told me, 'My wife told me not to give you writer's credit or she'd kill me.' I said, 'That's no fuckin' excuse, you asshole.' He got all the royalties," said Vegas.

But there was still an album to complete. And the disagreements between the brothers were kept between the two of them. However, there was another song on *Wovoka* that would cause more of a public dust-up.

It was called "We Were All Wounded at Wounded Knee."

Redbone, which originally included the Vegas brothers, DePoe, and guitarist and pianist Tony Bellamy, was a group of musicians of Native American and Mexican descent. The band's name, Redbone, is a term for a mixed-race or "half-breed" person.

According to Pat Vegas, it was Jimi Hendrix — himself part Cherokee — who encouraged the formation of an all-

Native-American rock band. Bellamy, Pat, and Lolly had jammed together with Hendrix on a few occasions at a club called Thee Experience, a psychedelic nightclub on Sunset Boulevard in Hollywood that was popular from 1967 to 1969. Pat Vegas said that it was during those jam sessions that Hendrix recognized the potential of the band, and encouraged the members to continue to work to get their music in front of the public.

For historical context, the Battle of Wounded Knee happened on December 29, 1890, on the Lakota Pine Ridge Indian Reservation in South Dakota. The U.S. 7th Cavalry Regiment had tried to disarm the Lakota, but hostilities broke out between the troops and the Indians. When it was over, more than 200 Lakota men, women, and children had been killed, although some reports have the number of dead closer to 300.

But the original idea for the song "We Were All Wounded at Wounded Knee" came from a chance meeting Pat Vegas had on an airplane with a comedian.

Once again, Vegas was on his way back to Los Angeles after a gig at the Spectrum in Philadelphia, when Sandy Baron sat down in the seat next to him.

In addition to being a standup comic, Baron went on to establish himself as a Broadway stage, film, and television actor. He played himself in the opening scene of the 1984 Woody Allen film *Broadway Danny Rose*, as well as narrated the film. And in the 1990s, Baron would have a recurring role in the television sitcom *Seinfeld* as Jack Klompus, who consistently held some kind of a grudge against Jerry Seinfeld's television dad, Morty Seinfeld.

Baron also wrote music, and that's what he wanted to discuss with Pat Vegas on that flight from Philadelphia to Los Angeles in the early 1970s.

"So he introduces himself and he says, 'Pat, I've got this lyric for a song and I think I'd like you and me to put a treatment to it, some music to it. Put it together for me.' But he just had a long poem," said Vegas. "I said, 'Yeah, we can maybe get together and do something with it.' He said, 'I think the combination of you and me could make it a hit song.' He said it was something important that needed to be said.

A couple of days later Baron called Vegas and invited him over to the house. There, Vegas met Baron's wife, Mary Jo Webster Baron, and the three of them had a bite to eat and a glass of wine before Vegas and Baron got to work on the song.

They finished it in five days and called it "We Were All Wounded at Wounded Knee."

But record company officials decided it would not be included on the U.S. release of the *Wovoka* album. Not only that, but CBS wanted nothing to do with it as a single in the United States. Even 80-plus years after the Battle of Wounded Knee, record company officials considered the song and its lyrics too controversial and would not allow it to be distributed for radio play in the U.S.

That was disappointing to Vegas, but it did not stop him from trying to get the song in front of the public. Redbone had an upcoming European tour scheduled in mid-1974 and the European release of *Wovoka* would include "We Were All Wounded at Wounded Knee."

So according to Vegas, he snuck into the CBS San Maria record pressing plant and had the crew there press him 500 single copies of "We Were All Wounded at Wounded Knee."

"I paid for it out of my pocket. Then I hand-carried that box of 500 records to Europe with me," said Vegas. "And everywhere we went to do an interview, I started passing the record out to all the radio stations in Europe. I even gave a copy to CBS Europe as well. And they loved it and they put it out.

"It hit the airwaves in Europe and everybody was screaming for it, they wanted to hear it. And sure enough it became our biggest-selling album of the year in Europe. We got a double platinum from it. It became the biggest record there, but CBS refused to play it here. CBS didn't spend a dime on that record. But they reaped the rewards anyway," said Vegas.

Still, the record company's refusal to release the song in the U.S. cut deeply for Vegas. He had for years, to that point, been determined to have a Native American band that was more than just a club act, a band that could be successful recording artists on a national level. He had visited Native American reservations and had seen how poverty stricken they were.

"They had nothing. And that really upset me," said Vegas. "So I was really disappointed, especially for the Native American people" when "We Were All Wounded at Wounded Knee" didn't get released in the U.S.

Wovoka would be the fifth studio album released by Redbone, but Vegas didn't think it was the best album the band ever recorded. That distinction, in his opinion, goes to *Message from a Drum*, released in 1971. And Vegas thinks it's the best album because of the title song.

Written by Pat Vegas, its opening verses include the lines "When the ones you thought you knew, turn their backs on you, another side of life to face, some haven't used a thing; 'Cos it hurts to find some people unkind, yes it hurts to find some people unkind," and suggest an already established rift between the Vegas brothers that would come to a head a few years later over the band's biggest hit, "Come and Get Your Love."

"That song, 'Message from a Drum,' is really saying something about my brother and his wife, people that you know and you love that turn their backs on you and fuck you over. I truly got fucked over on 'Come and Get Your Love' because they refused to give me any credit for it. I worked hard on that one. On top of that, I edited it down and still got no credit," said Vegas.

Redbone would record only two more albums in the 1970s after *Wovoka—Beaded Dreams Through Turquoise Eyes* in 1974 and *Cycles* in 1977—but would never again achieve the commercial success of *Wovoka*.

Original Redbone member Tony Bellamy died of liver failure in 2009 and just a few months later, Lolly Vegas died of lung cancer.

These days, Pat Vegas hosts a radio program called *Chance to Have It All*, a nonprofit 501(c)3 organization that showcases Native American musicians, and helps mentor those artists as they navigate today's music industry.

And although he still carries the weight of those disputes with his late brother, Vegas does recognize that *Wovoka* and the hit single "Come and Get Your Love" helped establish Redbone as "the royalty of that era" for Native Americans.

"We had accomplished something that no one ever expected, that no one even thought about. Redbone wasn't a rock group per se; Redbone was a movement for a people that were being unjustly treated and being ignored, like they were non-existent. I didn't want that to be. So it was a movement, not a rock band," said Vegas.

"That's my satisfaction. That, I can live with. I did what I had to do to uplift an entire race of people, to make America a little more aware of what was going on [with Native Americans]. A lot of people didn't have a clue about what was going on. It didn't help just Native Americans; it helped a lot of people. The awareness was there, and I'm proud of it," he said.

Discography

"Wovoka"
Redbone
November 1973

Side one

"Wovoka" (P. Vegas/L. Vegas) 3:00

"Sweet Lady of Love" (L. Vegas) 3:08

"Someday (A Good Song)" (P. Vegas/T. Bellamy) 4:12

"Liquid Truth" (L. Vegas) 5:03

"We Were All Wounded at Wounded Knee" (P. Vegas/L. Vegas)....
[European release only] 3:34

Side two

"Come and Get Your Love" (LP version) (L. Vegas) 4:59

"Day to Day Life" (P. Vegas/T. Bellamy) 2:42

"Chant Wovoka / "Clouds In My Sunshine" (P. Vegas) 4:42

"23rd and Mad" (L. Vegas/P. DePoe) 6:46

A worn-out, ragtag bunch of musicians
Bloodshot
J. Geils Band

When the J. Geils Band started recording its third studio album in early 1973 at the Hit Factory, the only studio time they could get was around 7 p.m.

Band members would show up and then just play through the night.

"There was a lot of red wine and a lot of other stuff going around. We would just literally play all night until about six or seven in the morning, go back to the hotel, which was kind of like a flophouse, and start the next day," said Peter Wolf, lead singer for the band.

That made the J. Geils Band — Wolf, guitarist John "J." Geils, keyboardist Seth Justman, bassist Danny "Dr. Funk" Klein, harmonica player Richard "Magic Dick" Salwitz, and drummer Stephen Jo Bladd — a worn-out, ragtag bunch of musicians during the recording sessions.

Famed photographer David Gahr would notice that. During a photo shoot for the new album cover, Gahr — who had established himself by taking some iconic images of Bob Dylan, Janis Joplin, and Bruce Springsteen by that point — could see through his lens that the J. Geils Band members were a tired group of musicians.

"We would talk amongst ourselves and we would say, 'Man, did you get any rest?'" said Wolf of the late hours the band was keeping during the recording sessions. "Everybody would say, 'No.' And then one day we were taking pictures with David Gahr and he said, 'You guys are all beat up. You look like a bunch of bloodshot gang members from the street.'"

It was the word "bloodshot" that stuck with Wolf when he went into Atlantic Records to update company officials on the album project.

"I said, 'Listen, we're going to call the album *Bloodshot*. To coincide with it, could we make it a red vinyl? And that's how all that came about," said Wolf. "They [record label officials] were OK with that. But unbeknownst to us, they charged us for the extra cost of making a red vinyl record. That's how the record industry worked in those days."

The J. Geils Band had first signed with Atlantic Records in 1970. Wolf, an ex-disc jockey on radio station WBCN in Boston, had managed the band for a short time during the early days.

It recorded its self-titled, debut album in 1970 and followed that up in 1971 with *The Morning After*, neither of which made huge splashes. *The J. Geils Band* album charted at No. 195 on the Billboard Pop Albums chart. *The Morning After* charted substantially better, getting to No. 64 on the Billboard Pop Albums chart. And it featured the single "Looking for Love," which got to No. 39 on the Billboard Pop Singles chart.

But there was very little help from Atlantic Records in promoting either of the first two albums.

"Atlantic didn't quite know what to do with us. I was managing the band, but we decided to hook up with a manager who was pretty well known at the time," said Wolf. "He came to a couple of shows and he said, 'You know, the energy of your shows is just so different than your first two records. Why don't you do a live record?'"

Wolf said the band's first reaction was that it did not want to do a live album, but eventually relented. *Live Full House* — the band's third album and first non-studio album — was recorded April 21-22, 1972, at the Cinderella Ballroom in Detroit.

Stacks of Wax

"It's basically the same songs from the first and second records, but they're done at ninety mph and the arrangements are so different," said Wolf. "And with the crowd, it created an excitement. That became the record that radio DJs first started playing. FM radio started playing it quite a lot."

When they went back into the studio to make *Bloodshot* — the band's third studio album but fourth album overall — they once again took producer Bill Szymczyk with them. Szymczyk had co-produced *The Morning After* album with J. Geils' keyboardist Seth Justman, which was recorded at the Record Plant in Los Angeles.

In the mid-1960s, Szymczyk had worked his way up at the Hit Factory, which was located at 421 W. 54th Street in New York City. The Hit Factory was then owned by Jerry Ragovoy, a songwriter and record producer who had, in 1963, under the pseudonym Norman Meade, written the song "Time Is on My Side" for the Rolling Stones.

By 1973, Szymczyk had produced successful albums for B.B. King, the James Gang, Joe Walsh, the Edgar Winter Group, and Michael Stanley. In 1974, Szymczyk would start producing a string of albums for the Eagles, including *On the Border* in 1974, *One of These Nights* in 1975, and *Hotel California* in 1976.

Both Walsh and the Eagles had shared the concert bill with the J. Geils Band and that's how Szymczyk eventually ended up producing for the Eagles, according to Wolf.

Another aspect of the recording sessions for *Bloodshot* had to do with Wolf's personal life at the time: He was dating actress Faye Dunaway.

One of Dunaway's early screen roles was as bank robber Bonnie Parker in the 1967 film *Bonnie and Clyde*, which starred Warren Beatty as Clyde Barrow. It is now considered a landmark film and it catapulted Dunaway into stardom.

But while she was dating Wolf, Dunaway was shooting *The Three Musketeers* and was able to hang around the Hit Factory on occasion during the *Bloodshot* recording sessions.

Wolf and Dunaway would eventually marry in 1974, and divorce in 1979.

Bloodshot, released on April 12, 1973, was a breakthrough record for the band. It reached No. 10 on the Billboard Pop Albums chart and had two singles, both written by Justman and Wolf, that broke onto the Billboard Pop Singles chart: "Make Up Your Mind" made it to No. 98, and "Give It to Me" got to No. 30.

"There was a sort of New York energy on *Bloodshot* that we didn't have on the other two [studio] records," said Wolf.

The issue of a red vinyl record instead of the customary black vinyl would also resonate with fans, despite the fact that the band members paid extra to have the records pressed in red vinyl. In fact, there are both red and black vinyl versions of the album, with the red vinyl a little more difficult for collectors to find today.

The album also featured another trademark that producer Szymczyk would continue when he later began producing the Eagles — that of placing a message in the run-out groove of the record.

The run-out groove is the gap on an album between the end of the last song and the label in the middle of the record. The space is about three-eighths of an inch wide, and when the needle on the record player reaches this gap, the arm of the turntable automatically picks up and returns to the start position.

On the master copy of a completed album, Szymczyk would sometimes take a steel pen and write something into the run-out groove so that when pressed, all the albums would contain the message.

There is no message from Szymczyk on the A-side of the J. Geils *Bloodshot* album. But on the B-side, Szymczyk wrote "Nice to see your face in the place."

"I think it means exactly what it says. I think it's a message to our audience, meaning it would be nice to see you out at the shows," said Wolf.

Although there was a hitch in the band's ascent after the *Bloodshot* album, the group's commercial fortunes improved in the late 1970s with the release of two albums, *Monkey Island* in 1977 and *Sanctuary* in 1978. But the band would take it to the next level in 1981 with the release of the album *Freeze Frame,* which became its only No. 1 album and biggest seller. It featured the Billboard Hot 100 Singles chart No. 1 hit "Centerfold," written by Justman.

Wolf said the band didn't really worry about its place in the 1970s music scene, because it was just busy working hard and making music.

"When you're out there working constantly, you don't have the advantage of looking back in a historical scope. You just kind of do what feels natural," said Wolf. "We were just making music. There was James Taylor, there were so many artists. The Stones were coming into different things. Van Morrison . . . there were so many great soul records . . . Aretha Franklin, John Lee Hooker was still with us, Muddy Waters was still with us."

Wolf believes the game changer for many bands from the 1970s and the beginning of the 1980s was the launch of MTV in 1981.

"I think that sort of changed the landscape dramatically. At one time, most rock and roll was played on AM radio. And when FM started, it changed the landscape. Listeners moved from singles to albums," said Wolf. "And then I think the landscape again dramatically changed when MTV came along. It became so powerful. People were more interested in your video than your record."

The late 1970s also featured a changing of the guard, as it were, according to Wolf. Or at least the appearance of a changing of the guard.

"A lot of newer bands started coming along and the Rolling Stones and Cream and even J. Geils — they were part of the old order," said Wolf. "It was basically that newer audiences were coming along and the bands were saying, 'Hey man, we're making music for you; we're not going to fall into the same traps that these bands did. We're dedicated to a different kind of music.'

"At the end of the day, it really was all the same. Elvis Costello was part of the new wave. But it really was just a term, like San Francisco rock. The Grateful Dead was San Francisco rock, Jefferson Airplane was San Francisco rock," he said. "But there really wasn't anything similar about these bands. Janis Joplin had nothing similar to Jefferson Airplane other than that she and Grace Slick were female singers. The Grateful Dead had nothing in common with Sly Stone, who was also from San Francisco. These are just terms that were placed on different styles; it wasn't necessarily a unifying kind of music.

"But as far as the term 'new wave,' it was just basically a term used by the media to define the newer bands that were coming out at the time," he said.

Although he doesn't consider himself a vinyl collector, Wolf admits to having "walls and walls and walls" of vinyl records in his home.

"But it's not quantity, it's quality. I still have the first Little Richard record that I bought and the first Chuck Berry record I bought and the first Elvis record I bought," he said. "I still have my first Rolling Stones record and my first Springsteen record and my first Aretha record. These are, to me, treasures. It's sort of like if you were a painter and had Matisse paintings or Picasso paintings. You don't give them away, you treasure them. So I treasure the recordings."

As for the J. Geils Band records, he's got those, too. And he has a red vinyl copy of *Bloodshot*.

"I even have the first test pressings. I have all the Geils records. Some of my solo records, unfortunately I don't have because I was negligent in holding onto them. I was always passing them out. But I'll get them," said Wolf.

Although the band's namesake, J. Geils, no longer performs with the band and has sued his band mates over use of the band name, original members Justman, Klein, Magic Dick, and Wolf still tour on occasion as the J. Geils Band.

"A good part of my life was spent working on songs, writing songs, being part of that band. A great deal of my life and energies went into the band," said Wolf. "So to have the opportunity to go back and revisit a lot of material I helped create, helped make popular, it's always interesting. We don't do it very often, so it's always special when we get together."

Wolf points out that many bands, like the Rolling Stones and the Eagles, have had personnel changes over the years. But when the core group of the J. Geils band gets back together, it's like they've never been apart.

"You get back and you hit a song, something like 'Lookin' for a Love,' or a song like 'Give It to Me,' when you have the players that can really play it, it all just snaps back. Especially when you get out to an audience and there's a crowd that is so into it. You can close your eyes and feel like you're back in 1972. It's really all the same," he said.

"Many of the people are coming to hear the body of work you made popular. It's sort of like if I go to a Stones show, if they add some new songs, that's fine, but I'm also wanting to hear 'Tumbling Dice,' 'Start Me Up,' 'Jumpin' Jack Flash.' I think it's the same for people who go see Springsteen; there are songs people want to hear. They're open for everything, but they primarily want to hear a lot of the body of work that the artist is known for. People come out and they want to hear the songs that made the artist famous or popular."

Whether he's pursuing a solo project or reconnecting with the J. Geils Band members for a tour, Wolf admits the bottom line is that he himself is just a music fan.

Mike Morsch

"When the J. Geils Band gets together and we start kicking in those songs, I'm still awed by it. And when I get out there with my solo band, I'm still awed by that because they're amazing musicians. And when I go see a show, I don't go as someone who plays music, I go as a fan, because that's what really got me into it in the first place," he said.

Discography

"Bloodshot"
J.Geils Band
April 12, 1973
(All songs written by Seth Justman and Peter Wolf, except where noted.)

"(Ain't Nothin' But a) House Party" (Del Sharh, Joseph Thomas) 4:43
"Make up Your Mind" 3:31
"Back to Get Ya" 5:22
"Struttin' With My Baby" 3:16
"Don't Try to Hide It" 2:45
"Southside Shuffle" 3:43
"Hold Your Loving" (Bernice Snelson, Titus Turner) 2:30
"Start All Over Again" 4:15
"Give It to Me" 6:32

They don't know you, but they know these people
Friends and Legends
Michael Stanley

Michael Stanley's band had only one night to rehearse. It was late 1973 and Stanley had just released his second solo album, *Friends and Legends*. The next evening, the band was scheduled to appear — along with Ike and Tina Turner and Redbone — on *Don Kirshner's Rock Concert*.

Kirshner's syndicated television show featured live performances by its artists, which made it different from most other shows of the time that had artists lip-sync to prerecorded music.

Stanley and his producer, Bill Szymczyk, had flown to Los Angeles, as had almost all the musicians who played on the album, and had congregated at one of the Studio Instrument Rentals (SIR) studios to tune up for the Kirshner gig the next night.

The band members were all milling around the studio, waiting for the rehearsal to begin. There was Joe Walsh, who had finished a successful run with the James Gang, but was now with a band called Barnstorm. Along with Walsh was Barnstorm band mate Joe Vitale and three guys from Stephen Stills' band Manassas: Al Perkins, Paul Harris, and Joe Lala. In addition, solo artist Dan Fogelberg was there, as was saxophonist David Sanborn. All had been involved in the recording sessions for *Friends and Legends*.

And now they were all standing around in a studio in Los Angeles looking at Stanley.

Mike Morsch

Joe Walsh had left the James Gang and formed his own band Barnstorm when he contributed to Michael Stanley's "Friends and Legends" album.
(Photo by Kevin Hughes)

"And Joe came over to me in his great Joe Walsh fashion and said, 'Michael, you've got to take charge.' In probably the most honest moment of my entire life, I looked at him and said, 'Joe, I don't know how to take charge,'" said Stanley. "And he goes, 'OK, I'll take charge.' All of a sudden, Joe started telling everybody what to do."

That's where Michael Stanley found himself in late 1973. With the help of an all-star band, he had a new album, an appearance on a popular live music television show, and a potential tour in support of that album.

The only thing he didn't have was the desire to tour. It freaked him out. Stanley hadn't been able to make a living in the music business to that point. In fact, in between making albums, he paid the bills as the regional manager of a chain of record stores covering seven-states.

How, he thought to himself, did he end up here, with all these fabulous musicians, some of whom were well on their way to making big names for themselves?

That road was full of a wonderfully timed series of events and, as it turned out, a bit of luck that would make *Friends and Legends* one of the most enjoyable experiences of Stanley's musical life.

He had done an album as a member of the band Silk in 1968, and that's where he first met Bill Szymczyk. The producer had come to Cleveland, Stanley's hometown, and signed Silk and the James Gang to record deals.

"Ours was a really horrible record and the James Gang's was a really good record," said Stanley. "So I went back to college and decided at that point, I guess it had been five years of being in rock bands, that I didn't want to be in a band anymore, I wanted to be James Taylor. I set out to do that."

Stanley concentrated on his songwriting. He no longer cared about being in a band; he just wanted to write songs. But he and Szymczyk stayed in touch.

About a year after the failed Silk album, Szymczyk called Stanley.

"He said, 'Are you still writing songs?' I said, 'Yeah, I'm writing a whole bunch of songs.' And he said, 'You want to make an album?'" said Stanley.

Szymczyk had been with ABC Records in the late 1960s and had produced B.B. King's 1969 live album *Live & Well*, which became King's first-ever Top 100 album.

By the early 1970s, Szymczyk had left ABC Records and formed his own label, Tumbleweed Records, where he produced the J. Geils Band as well as the James Gang's first three albums. When Joe Walsh left the James Gang and formed Barnstorm, Szymczyk produced that band's albums.

At the time, Tumbleweed Records, based in Denver, Colorado, had six artists signed to the label. One of those was a Canadian named Arthur Gee.

Stanley's real last name is Gee.

"What are the odds of having two people on this little label in Colorado with the same last name that nobody else has?" asked Stanley.

Tumbleweed had orchestrated a sort of signing ceremony to announce that Stanley had joined its stable of artists. A photographer from Billboard magazine was there to record the event.

Just minutes before the unveiling of Stanley's signing, Szymczyk approached him.

"Bill said, 'You have to change your name.' I had never thought about that. It's kind of a big decision. He said, 'Well, it's a big decision that has to be made in the next fifteen minutes,'" said Stanley. "It was one of those things. In those days, they sent a photographer from Billboard to report that Tumbleweed Records was signing an artist to his record contract. Bill said, 'What's your middle name?' 'Well, my middle name is Stanley.' He said, 'Michael Stanley. That won't offend anyone; let's do that.' In the span of ten minutes, my whole persona changed."

When it was time to make an album, Stanley had songs, but he didn't have a band.

"I told Bill, it's just me sitting at home with my wife in the apartment and I'm writing songs," said Stanley. "He said, 'I'll take care of it,' as he always did in most cases."

As it turned out, the Cleveland connection was instrumental in Stanley's early development as an artist. Walsh and the James Gang, Eric Carmen and the Raspberries and Rick Derringer were all playing in bands in and around Cleveland at the same time Stanley was trying to make a career in music. But the artists rarely crossed paths because they were all playing gigs on the same nights in different parts of town.

Walsh actually played on Stanley's first album for Tumbleweed, the self-titled *Michael Stanley* in early 1973. When it came time for Stanley's second solo album, *Friends and Legends*, Walsh had gravitated to Colorado, where Tumbleweed was based.

The timing couldn't have been more perfect. Barnstorm was off the road. Stills and Manassas were off the road. And everybody was in Colorado.

From Manassas, Szymczyk got Paul Harris on keyboards, Joe Lala on percussion and Al Perkins on steel guitar. From Barnstorm, Szymczyk added Walsh, Joe Vitale on drums and Kenny Passarelli on bass.

And that was the nucleus of Stanley's band for *Friends and Legends*.

Everyone met at a small recording studio called Applewood, which was in a strip mall in the shadow of the Coors Brewing Company factory. Next to the studio was a liquor store, which was convenient at times.

"We rolled in and nobody had heard any of the songs," said Stanley. "The way it went down was, I'd pull up a chair in the middle of the studio and I'd sit down with my acoustic guitar and play. Everybody would gather around. I'd play the song three or four times and they'd all take notes and ask questions. Then we'd all go to our respective corners and Bill would push play and we'd record."

Stanley doesn't recall any song taking more than four or five takes to record.

"It was very casual. These guys were all great. But I didn't know what I was doing at that time. I had no idea about being a band leader or anything of that nature," said Stanley.

"They'd say, 'Well, what do you want me to play here?' And I'd say, 'Play whatever you want. You're in Manassas, you're in Barnstorm, play whatever you want. I'm just happy to be here.'"

"That's the way it all went down. I think we did nine tracks; we did them all in like five days. And that includes those guys leaving and me doing the lead vocals. It was just a lot of fun. It's the way you envision making music."

After the sessions, Stanley took a month or two off, then went back into the studio — this time at Caribou Ranch, Joe Guercio's place in Nederland, Colorado — to do overdubs, and record some of Walsh's vocals as well as some background vocals.

"We were in the studio and we were up in the mountains and once again I was just happy to be there," said Stanley.

"We were trying for some high things and we weren't getting it. I was like, 'Man, I wish we had some high voices.'"

Walsh chimed in with a suggestion.

"Joe said, 'Well, I know a guy who sings really high.' I said, 'Who?' And he said, 'Dan Fogelberg,'" recounted Stanley.

Stanley happened to be a fan of Fogelberg's debut solo album, *Home Free*, which was released in 1972.

"I said, 'How are we going to get him?' And Joe said, 'Well, he lives about 300 yards from here. He'll come over and sing.' And then Joe said, 'You know, it would be nice to have somebody else, too. We should call Richie,'" recalled Stanley.

"I said, 'Richie who?' And Joe said, 'Richie Furay.' 'You mean Richie Furay from freakin' Buffalo Springfield?' And Joe said, 'Yeah, he lives like a mile from here.'"

Stanley was star-struck by the way it was unfolding.

"In like an hour and a half, there is Danny and Richie in the studio learning the songs. They ended up singing on two or three things," said Stanley. "Nobody knew Fogelberg at that time, but I was impressed because I was a fan of his first album. And Richie, obviously, was amazing.

"It was neat for me. Once you dissect it, when you're sitting in the studio with these guys, you realize that it's really just a bunch of Midwestern guys out there in Colorado. It wasn't like a bunch of L.A. guys getting together. Everybody was really nice and really normal.

Stacks of Wax

Richie Furay is one of the most wonderful people to walk the face of the earth. And everybody was great," said Stanley.

After the Caribou Ranch sessions, in the early spring of 1973, the final recording sessions for *Friends and Legends* moved to New York.

Stanley had a song on the album called "Let's Get the Show on the Road" and he was hearing a saxophone solo in it. He asked Szymczyk if he knew any sax players, and of course, Szymczyk did.

David Sanborn was living in Woodstock, New York at the time. Back then, Sanborn was the stereotypical hippie — beard and hair down to the middle of his back, and often sporting a fringed jacket and moccasins. All he carried was his saxophone case.

Szymczyk was producing the *Bloodshot* album for the J. Geils Band at the Record Plant at the same time. To finish the *Friends and Legends* album, Szymczyk bought an hour of studio time from J. Geils, which would get Sanborn into the studio and get his sax on "Let's Get the Show on the Road."

"So J. Geils gave us an hour. They were all sitting around while we were doing this. Faye Dunaway was sitting there back in a corner, reading a book," said Stanley.

Peter Wolf, lead singer for the J. Geils Band, was dating actress Faye Dunaway at the time [they would later be married from 1974 to 1979]. Dunaway was a huge star and had just completed filming *The Three Musketeers* around that time in 1973.

"Once again, I'm like the Midwestern guy in New York looking up at all the buildings," said Stanley.

Two other songs on *Friends and Legends* stand out for Stanley, one of which he planned to put on the album, and the other that unfolded organically during the recording sessions.

"Help" by John Lennon and Paul McCartney had always been one of Stanley's favorite Beatles songs. And the prevailing attitude at the time among new artists was that they should cover a song that was familiar to music fans because that had a better chance to get radio play.

"It was like, 'Oh, he did "Help," let's see what he did with that,'" said Stanley. "I didn't realize it at the time, but if you were doing a Beatles song then, you're basically messing with the Holy Grail. But I had this idea of doing it slow. I had no intention of recreating the Beatles' version of the song. That's what it is, and it's perfect."

A few years later, Stanley became friends with somebody who was friends with Lennon. And the guy played Stanley's version of "Help" for Lennon.

"This is unsubstantiated, but Lennon said that of all the covers he heard, this was his favorite version of the song because it was pretty much the way he wrote it," said Stanley. "He wrote it slow like that. So that was very cool."

The other song that was never intended to go on the album is called "Funky Is the Drummer," and it evolved during the recording sessions.

"It was probably done after one too many beers and one too many joints. We were all just sort of goofing around in the studio and we got into this thing. As sort of a joke at the time, I just decided I was going to introduce the band," said Stanley.

"And that's what it is, an introduction of the band. It's just everybody just jamming. Then Joey Vitale started singing the words, 'Funky is the drummer, who plays the funky beat.' Where that came from, I have no idea. That's how the whole title of the song came about. I don't think we even intended it to be on the record. But every time we played it, everybody laughed. So we said, well let's just put it on," said Stanley.

Once *Friends and Legends* was completed, it was time for Stanley to figure out how to promote it. He had hooked up with a local disc jockey named David Spero, whom he asked to serve as his manager. And Stanley made it clear to Spero that he didn't want to tour in support of the album.

"We talked about it. What's the best way to cover the most things with the least amount of effort? And the obvious answer was television," said Stanley.

Somehow — and to this day Stanley doesn't know how — Spero secured Stanley a spot on Don Kirshner's *Rock Concert*. But there was one contingency: Kirshner's people wanted the band that played on the album backing Stanley on the show.

"The unstated thing was, they don't know who the hell you are. But they know who these people are," said Stanley.

Once again, though, good timing was on Stanley's side.

"When they wanted to tape the show, it just so happened that both Barnstorm and Manassas were off the road. If you tried to plan these things, you couldn't. So everybody got contacted and everybody said yes," said Stanley.

The only one not available was bassist Kenny Passarelli. He was replaced by Bryan Garafalo, who would go on to play on Fogelberg's 1974 *Souvenirs* album —coincidently produced by Walsh — and on Walsh's 1975 *So What* album.

Also added for the performance was Teddie Neeley, who starred as Jesus Christ in the 1973 film *Jesus Christ, Superstar*.

Stanley and the band would do six songs on the Kirshner show. Oddly enough, Stanley didn't see a tape of that performance until 35 years later.

"After all those years, I was like, man, I don't know if I even want to see this. I didn't know what I was doing. And then I watched it and I was like, boy, I know I was scared to death but I didn't look scared to death. And obviously, the band was great. It was just very cool," said Stanley.

Since the release of *Friends and Legends* in 1973, there hasn't been a show that Stanley has performed that hasn't included the song "Let's Get the Show on the Road." He also still regularly performs his version of the Beatles song "Help."

"There are things over a career that you do get tired of, but I don't get tired of doing those songs. I still look forward to that every night," said Stanley.

Primarily because Stanley and the all-star band didn't tour in support of *Friends and Legends*, it made little impact on the music charts in 1973.

Stanley would go on to form the Michael Stanley Band and record five more albums throughout the 1970s, including *Stagepass* in 1977, which was recorded live during four shows over three days in Cleveland. It has become a favorite album for the Cleveland crowd.

But *Friends and Legends* still stands right at the top of Stanley's list of career accomplishments.

"I think it's the first time I felt that it was a pretty unified thing, songwriting-wise. The quality was pretty good across the board," said Stanley. "I had a great time making this music. When you look at the people involved, they're all so accomplished and they're all such great players and such nice people. There were no egos, nobody was overdosing, nobody was saying I need a better hotel room or to fly first class. It was just a bunch of guys who wanted to make music and they lent their talents to my tunes and brought their creative things to it as well. And that's priceless."

Discography

"Friends and Legends"
Michael Stanley
(All tracks composed by Michael Stanley except where indicated)

"Among My Friends Again".. 2:40
"Help!" (John Lennon, Paul McCartney)................................... 4:17
"Yours for a Song"... 3:28
"Let's Get the Show on the Road"... 7:29
"Just Keep Playing Your Radio".. 2:41
"Roll On"... 3:59
"Bad Habits"... 3:40
"Funky Is the Drummer" (Stanley, Joe Walsh, Paul Harris, Joe Vitale, Kenny Passarelli).. 2:53
"Poets' Day"... 6:41

A vintage look with a different sound
Self-titled
The Pointer Sisters

From the beginning of their careers, the Pointer Sisters wanted to be different. Their manager at the time, David Rubinson, stressed to them in the early 1970s that not only should they try to be different from every other musical group out there at the time, but that they should aspire to having long careers in what certainly was a tough business.

The sisters - Anita, Ruth, Bonnie, and June - along with Rubinson, decided they wanted to create a sound that combined jazz music, jazz singing, and be-bop music. And they also wanted to develop a unique visual style for their act.

"David was a big jazz fan. And coming out of the Bay Area at the time, there was a lot of jazz music there. But there was also a pop, rock, and R and B mixture of music with Tower of Power, and Sly and the Family Stone, that whole thing going on there," said Ruth Pointer.

Rubinson was so intent on making the Pointer Sisters something more than a flash-in-the-pan act in the early 1970s that he went to great extremes to develop the group. And that included having the sisters take tap dancing lessons and experimenting onstage with what was called "pop-up changes" — costume changes right on stage in front of the audience.

"We had a big drum case that has a lot of different hats in it and props and things," said Pointer. "And we just had a lot of fun because we wanted to be different. We wanted to stand out. And our music was so different because we were just a different type of group. It was really hard to pinpoint a genre of music that we were going after, because we liked singing everything."

However, the sisters learned early on that their approach, while different, did create an unexpected challenge for their audiences.

"I remember people saying to us, 'We really love your live shows but it's hard for us to make a decision dance-wise on what to do when we listen to your music," said Pointer. "So we were learning right along with our audience, I think."

The sisters also loved vintage clothing, which fit right in with their desire to create a unique visual image as well. It was right around the time in 1972 that Diana Ross was starring in the film *Lady Sings the Blues*, a biographical drama about the life of Billie Holiday that featured a lot of the vintage clothing that Holiday wore during her career.

"We were in love with that film. We had been listening to a lot of Billie Holiday songs and some of the other old jazz singers. There was just a lot going on at the time and we loved all of it," said Pointer. "I remember just enjoying the experience of singing all these types of songs we were singing at the time and making our harmonies tight. I don't know that we were even aware of what was happening to us, other than we were just enjoying singing together."

At the end of 1972, the Pointer Sisters had signed a record deal with Blue Thumb Records and began working on their self-titled debut album.

"Like so many artists' experiences, you get with a record company and they set a date for when they want the album out and they set a certain amount of money that they're going to spend for the album," said Pointer. "As an artist, that is something that just sort of stops you cold because you've got these limits, that's it's got to be out at a certain time, it's got to go into this certain category, we only have this much money. It's like, oh, God, really?"

The album would be recorded at Wally Heider Studios in San Francisco and would be produced by Rubinson. The backing band would be the Hoodoo Rhythm Devils, a local blues-funk band, which had already cut a couple of albums itself for Blue Thumb Records.

The first single planned for release from the album was "Yes We Can Can," a song written by Allen Toussaint. The song had been a minor R&B hit for Lee Dorsey in 1970. Rubinson loved just about everything that Toussaint wrote and he especially loved "Yes We Can Can," and urged the Pointer Sisters to record it.

"The first time I ever heard the song I was at my mom's house and we were playing Lee Dorsey's version of it. And I thought it was really a cool song. So we had been listening to it for a while," said Pointer. "And it came up as a suggestion to go on our album when we first started getting ready to record. I don't think there was any big deal about us singing the song other than we just liked it. We liked the little bluesy sound of it and we just wanted to make it our own. We loved the lyrics."

But when Ruth first heard the Pointer Sisters' version of the song on playback, she initially had a different opinion about it.

"I have to admit I wasn't that crazy about it. I really wasn't. As a matter of fact, as we continued to perform it live, we made some changes in the way we sang it. It's not exactly the same way as we sing it on the record," said Pointer. "It was just the timing, I guess. We were so naive at the time the first album came out. I guess I felt that sometimes we weren't allowed — or didn't have the opportunity — to really take the time to hone in on the certain specialties about the direction we were going."

"The Pointer Sisters" was released in May 1973. The album reached No. 13 on the Billboard 200 albums chart and No. 3 on the Billboard Hot R&B/Hip-Hop Albums chart. (Photo by Phil McAuliffe)

The other planned single from the album was a cover of "Wang Dang Doodle," a blues song written by Willie Dixon, first released in 1961.

The Pointer Sisters was released in May 1973. The album reached No. 13 on the Billboard 200 Albums chart and No. 3 on the Billboard Hot R&B/Hip-Hop Albums chart.

The two released singles also did well: "Yes We Can Can" made it to No. 11 on the Billboard Hot 100 Singles chart and No. 12 on the Billboard Hot R&B/Hip-Hop songs chart. The follow-up single "Wang Dang Doodle" peaked at No. 24 on the R&B Singles chart and No. 61 on the Hot 100 Singles chart.

The album cover features the four sisters sitting around a table in front of a big curtain, wearing their own vintage clothes.

Stacks of Wax

"I love the cover. We got the call that we were going to do the photo shoot and were told to just bring our own things with us. Those are our clothes. That hat is my mother's hat that I'm wearing," said Pointer. "We dressed like that all the time, even when we weren't doing anything. We just loved vintage clothing. Plus it was cheap back then. The record label people said we should wear what we did all the time when we just showed up to hang out at the studio. So that's what we did."

Pointer considers that first album the one that got the Pointer Sisters in the door of the music industry.

"It was what we hoped it would become, and more," she said.

But the evolution of the Pointer Sisters had only just begun. Fans loved seeing the group live, but were still having trouble dancing to those jazz tunes. And the Pointer Sisters themselves were still trying to decide where they fit into the music scene of the mid-1970s.

As an example of that, the group's second album, *That's a Plenty*, released in February 1974, contained the single "Fairytale," a country-flavored tune written by Anita and Bonnie. It became the second hit for the group, reaching No. 13 on the Billboard Hot 100 Singles chart. But it also crossed over and became a Top 40 country hit, reaching No. 37 on the Billboard Hot Country Singles. The success of the crossover hit enabled the Pointer Sisters to perform "Fairytale" at the Grand Ole Opry in Nashville, Tennessee, marking the first time an African-American vocal group appeared on the Opry stage.

So the Pointer Sisters were still trying to decide what type of group to be when the 1970s entered the disco era in the mid-1970s.

"We started thinking that we wanted to be more mainstream so that people would enjoy dancing to our music. But we weren't sure how to make that kind of a transition," said Pointer. "And we were only like two or three years into our careers. My sister Bonnie wanted to embark on a solo career and leave the group. So that took us for another turn. It was life things that happened that make you sort of make different decisions than you would have made, had things stayed the way they were at the beginning."

And they were keeping a high profile as well, despite having not settled entirely on a direction for the group. They were regulars on television variety shows at the time, including those starring Helen Reddy, Flip Wilson and Carol Burnett.

"We were right in the thick of it. We were never at home. I had children, Anita had a child. People don't consider that we had other things going on, too. We had relationships coming and going — mostly going. It's like juggling all these balls, trying to hang on and stay relevant as artists," said Pointer. "It was something that we were just moving right along with on this train, and not being able to get off. We were going through a lot of different emotional things as far as raising our children, taking care of our parents, who were aging. And we were trying to make sure that our careers were continuing to flourish. It was a lot."

Despite the challenges of trying to build their careers in the 1970s, Pointer said that in hindsight, it wasn't as difficult for the Pointer Sisters to fit into the music scene at the time as it may have appeared while they were going through it. They were versatile and could sing many different styles of music.

"There was so much variety and people were interested in everything. There were different types of shows on TV; there were different types of music everywhere. You had hard rock, heavy metal, R and B, pop, jazz," she said.

The rest of the 1970s saw the Pointer Sisters continue to change and evolve. By 1977, June and Bonnie had left the group, with Bonnie starting a solo career. Ruth and Anita signed a deal with Planet Records, convinced June to rejoin the group, and released the album *Energy* in 1978. The first single from that album was a cover of Bruce Springsteen's "Fire," which got to No. 2 on the Billboard Hot 100 Singles chart.

But the best was yet to come for the Pointer Sisters. The 1980s brought a string of Top 10 songs on the Hot 100 Singles charts, including "He's So Shy" at No. 3 in 1980, "Slow Hand" at No. 2 in 1981, and four Top 10 songs off the group's biggest commercial album *Break Out* in 1984: "Automatic" at No. 5, "Jump (For My Love)" at No. 3, "I'm So Excited" at No. 9, and "Neutron Dance" at No. 6.

Since the mid-1980s, the Pointer Sisters have kept a lower profile, but still continue to perform. Ruth and Anita have been joined in the group by Ruth's daughter, Issa, and Ruth's granddaughter, Sadako. Bonnie no longer performs with her sisters and has battled drug addiction in her later years. June died of lung cancer in April 2006.

But the Pointer Sisters did achieve what manager/producer Rubinson urged them to do, which was to have a long career in the music business.

"I think we had an unusual career. It was definitely not anything that I expected. It's hard to really predict where we probably thought we would go with it. David Rubinson stressed to us that he wanted us to aspire to have a career that was long, and we have managed to do that," said Ruth Pointer.

"I think it probably has a lot to do with the types of songs that we put out that are just timeless. We've always been women who paid a lot of attention to the lyrics. And so if a song wasn't saying something that we connected with, we really didn't have any use for it."

Pointer added that the group's songs were, for the most part, songs that made people feel happy.

"The other thing was that we liked to sing uplifting tunes. There are a few things that we sing that are kind of sort of heartbreak songs, like 'Slow Hand' and stuff like that. Other than that, most of our songs are songs that hopefully make people feel good, and can kind of pull them out of a place where they might not particularly want to be at that moment," she said. "From what I've heard from fans, that's what they enjoy about seeing us now. That our songs take them back to a place where they were enjoying life, where they were experiencing growing as young adults. And I'm happy about that."

As far as being able to perform for more than 40 years, Pointer said it's still fun.

"I'm enjoying it more now than I ever did, I think because I have an appreciation for what we've accomplished. I didn't expect that. And nothing beats a great surprise. Even if you don't like a surprise, if it turns out real good, it's like, wow, I'll remember that forever. And this is one of those great surprises that I wasn't expecting. I wasn't expecting to still be performing at sixty-nine years old," she said.

"I remember when Mick Jagger turned forty. And my sisters and I were going, 'Whoa. I hope I'm not still singing at forty. What the heck am I going to look like at that age?' And then forty came and went and it wasn't as bad as I thought it would be," said Pointer. "I'm still in awe when I walk out on that stage and see a room full of people that are waiting to hear me open my mouth and sing. I am so appreciative and so grateful."

Stacks of Wax

The two released singles also did well: "Yes We Can Can" made it to No. 11 on the Billboard Hot 100 singles chart and No. 12 on the Billboard Hot R&B/Hip-Hot songs chart. The follow-up single "Wang Dang Doodle" peaked at No. 24 on the R&B Singles chart and No. 61 on the Hot 100 singles chart. (Photo by Phil McAuliffe)

Discography

"The Pointer Sisters"
The Pointer Sisters
May 1973

Side one
"Yes We Can Can" (Allen Toussaint) 6:02
"Cloudburst" (Leroy Kirkland, Jimmy Harris) 3:12
"Jada" (Pointer Sisters, Bruce Good, Jeff Cohen) 4:40
"River Boulevard" (Barbara Mauritz) 5:52
"Old Songs" (John Shine, Bruce Good) 4:01

Side two
"That's How I Feel" (Wilton Felder) 7:07
"Sugar" (Pointer Sisters) 2:19
"Pains and Tears" (Norman Landsberg) 2:36
"Naked Foot" (Neal Tate) 3:46
"Wang Dang Doodle" (Willie Dixon) 7:34

Failing at something long enough to be a legend
Sold American
Kinky Friedman

On a trip to South Africa in 1996, Kinky Friedman, a self-proclaimed "Texas Jewboy," met Tokyo Sexwale, a businessman and politician who had been imprisoned with fellow revolutionary Nelson Mandela at Robben Island by the South African government in the mid-1970s for their anti-apartheid beliefs.

Friedman had recorded and released his first album, titled *Sold American* in 1973, and he purposely tried to be controversial with some of the songs on the album in an effort to make his mark on the music scene of the early 1970s. There were songs that were intended to be provocative, with titles like "Get Your Biscuits in the Oven and Your Buns in the Bed," "We Reserve the Right to Refuse Service to You," "The Ballad of Charles Whitman," and "Ride 'Em, Jewboy," which was an extended tribute to victims of the Holocaust. And they had the lyrics to match, oftentimes mixing in social commentary.

"Chuck Glazer produced it and did a great job. But we were not performing to a silent witness. We were calculating. Would the disc jockeys play any of this stuff?"

Another thing Friedman and Glazer didn't know in 1973 was something that Sexwale shared with Friedman more than 20 years later, during Friedman's trip to South Africa: That Mandela liked the song "Ride 'Em Jewboy" and would listen to it on a smuggled cassette tape in his prison cell at Robben Island.

"When I met Tokyo, he told me that Mandela would play the record late at night. It was the last thing he would play. Sometimes he would play it twice," said Friedman. "Then Tokyo said, 'Now, Kinky, don't get a swelled head about this, because although he loved the song and he listened to your stuff on a smuggled cassette tape, you were not his favorite singer. His favorite singer was always Dolly Parton.' When he said that, I knew this guy spoke the truth. That's so human. So when you record something, you never know who it is going to reach."

Friedman had tried to break into the music scene in the early part of the 1970s after a wave of country rock that elevated artists like the Band, Gram Parsons and the Flying Burrito Brothers, and the Eagles in the public eye. Friedman's *Sold American* album, while not gaining mainstream traction at the time, did gain him a cult following in the Country and Western genre.

Part of that was due to the outrageousness of the band and its songs. Friedman had formed the satirical "Kinky Friedman and the Texas Jewboys" in 1971. Part of the act included the colorful names of the band's members: Little Jewford, Big Nig, Panama Red, Wichita Culpepper, Sky Cap Adams, Rainbow Colours, and Snakebite Jacobs.

Sold American was recorded on the Vanguard label. In addition to the provocative songs on the album, Friedman and Glazer also included songs that they hoped would be more attractive to mainstream Nashville fans.

"Somehow Chuck found a way to bring together these songs that were not like anything written in Nashville at the time," said Friedman. "There were a bunch of them that could have been country hits if we didn't have the outrageous stuff happening."

In addition to the title track "Sold American," Friedman and Glazer calculated that another song, titled "Western

Union Wire," might have a chance to break through on the Country and Western charts.

But it was the other calculation, the outrageous songs, that overshadowed the songs Friedman and Glazer thought had a legitimate shot at succeeding with the mainstream audience.

"That shit was coming from all sides. In the East, they understood the lyrics to 'Ride 'Em Jewboy,' but they didn't really relate to the music. In the South, they got the music but they really didn't relate to the lyrics," said Friedman. "There were bomb threats from the Jews and the Jewish Defense League when we first got to New York. And there were radio stations that refused to play the album and record stores that refused to stock it. It was expected. You just deal with that.

"But when you listen to it, that record allows your imagination to come into play."

"The Ballad of Charles Whitman" is an example of a song on the *Sold American* album that people didn't quite get in the 1970s.

The song was written based on personal proximity. Friedman graduated in 1966 with a bachelor of arts degree in psychology from the University of Texas at Austin. Just a few months later, in August 1966, Charles Whitman, a former Marine and a student at the university, brought a big arsenal of guns onto campus and stationed himself in the tower of the school's main building. Shooting from the observation deck of the tower over the course of about 90 minutes, Whitman killed 14 people and wounded 32 others in a mass shooting before being shot and killed by a police officer.

"I wrote the 'Ballad of Charles Whitman' and I realized it really is a brilliant song. It's about a mass murderer, but it tells us a lot about ourselves. There is a little bit of Charlie in all of us," said Friedman. "That's kind of the thing. The more I learned about him afterwards, he apparently was a

Kinky Friedman purposely tried to be controversial with some of the songs on the 1973 "Sold American" album in an effort to make his mark on the music scene of the early 1970s. (Photo by Phil McAuliffe)

really nice guy. A lot of people liked him. I met people who had been in class with him who liked Charles and nobody could understand it."

The single "Sold American," which Friedman believes should have been a hit, was also recorded by Glen Campbell for Campbell's 1973 album *I Knew Jesus (Before He Was a*

Star) and although the album got to No. 13 on the U.S. Billboard Country Album chart, the single itself wasn't a hit for Campbell, either.

Friedman changed labels in 1974 and recorded his second album, *Kinky Friedman*, for ABC Records. It would be the only album of his career to crack the U.S. Billboard 200 Albums chart, getting to No. 132.

In 1975, Friedman got a big break opening for Bob Dylan, which exposed his music to both Dylan's audience and Dylan himself. The two became friends. By then, Friedman had added songs like "How Can I Tell You I Love You (When You're Sitting on My Face)" and "They Ain't Makin' Jews Like Jesus Anymore," a song in which Friedman wrote about beating up a drunken White racist who is berating Blacks, Jews, and Greeks in a bar.

Friedman said that both Dylan and Paul Simon really liked "Ride 'Em Jewboy," but that Willie Nelson was the only artist who recorded it. Nelson performed the song for Friedman's 1998 album *Pearls in the Snow — The Songs of Kinky Friedman*.

Friedman and Dylan have remained friends over the years.

"A member of Bob's band, who I will not mention for his own protection, was interviewed one time and said that the only time he could see what the real Bob was like was when Kinky Friedman came around to the show. 'When he's hanging out with Kinky, he's a different guy.' That's a real compliment," said Friedman.

Friedman added that the Band's late drummer, Levon Helm, used to tell stories about when the Band played with Dylan and how dreadful it was at times when they were booed by audiences, because Dylan had transitioned from his acoustic folk roots and started playing electric guitar.

"But they [the Band] followed Bob's lead, which was, 'Fuck them, fuck this, we're going to stick with it.' Most people who had success playing one style of music, like

'Blowin' in the Wind,' which is a great song, but most people would resort back to that. They would cave and they would go back to playing acoustic folk," said Friedman. "You don't need people shouting 'Traitor! Fuck you!' And then to hear Bob's old friends come backstage afterwards and right in front of Levon and the other guys say, 'Look at these clowns you're playing with. They're killing your career.' And Levon had to listen to that shit every night, and it really rankled him. I think, though, that if Bob had not done that, he too would be a footnote in music."

Despite the flak he caught in the early part of his career for not being politically correct, Friedman said it's easier being Kinky Friedman now than it was back in the day.

"It's a helluva lot easier. If you fail at something long enough, you become a legend. That's all there is to it," said Friedman.

He does, however, miss the "country outlaw" days and what he calls the great songwriting that used to come out of Nashville.

"I was asking myself the other day that, why is it that we haven't had a great song come out of Nashville in thirty years, ever since Shel Silverstein died and Roger Miller died, and Willie and Kris Kristofferson left Nashville. Why is that?" said Friedman. "I think the gene pool may have dried up. Everything is derivative. There are great musicians, but the stuff they play, people will say, 'Oh, it sounds like Steve Earle met Alan Jackson.' It's really strange; it just seems to have dried up.

"And some of it is that real success distances you from your heart. That's true. That's why Bob Dylan and Willie Nelson aren't writing the way they used to," he said. "But being a struggling songwriter, I find that, now in retrospect, to be about the highest possible calling you can have. I would love to see what Willie and Bob and Kris could produce if they were convinced that they were struggling songwriters again. It would be impossible to recreate that ambiance, but it would be really interesting."

Friedman said that, over the years, he did notice one similarity between Dylan and Nelson that he thought was significant but that may have escaped non-musicians.

"Both of them seem to have their guitars a little out of tune. And they like to keep it that way. And if anybody fucks with them, if a producer came in with Willie and tuned his guitar, Willie would be furious and just about bail out of the project. I think they're both great and they know that. And they kind of challenge themselves like that," said Friedman. "And I don't know any other artists I can think of that do that. I've got a little device that now tells me when my guitar is in tune. But any musician can tell me I'm out of rhythm, out of sync, out of tune, whatever. Those are the same kind of people who have never really understood Willie Nelson's success."

Nelson once told Friedman that Nelson's vocal style had been patterned after Frank Sinatra.

"And when Frank Sinatra was interviewed, he said his vocal style came from Billie Holliday. And Billie Holiday said her vocal style was inspired by Louis Armstrong's horn. That's an amazing family tree of American music," said Friedman. "Not that I'm a part of that, but we all are. We're all a part of that."

As for the *Sold American* album, Friedman said it's still relevant today in the context of his career.

"The album *Sold American* has a lot of songs that took a while to catch on, but *Sold American* has kept selling," he said. "Back then, people listened to a whole record."

Discography

"Sold American"
Kinky Friedman
1973

Side One

"We Reserve The Right To Refuse Service To You" (J. Maizel, K. Friedman, R. Goldberg) 4:02

"Highway Cafe" 3:36

"Sold American" 3:15

"Flyin' Down The Freeway" 2:11

"Ride 'Em Jewboy" 5:35

Side Two

"Get Your Biscuits In The Oven And Your Buns In The Bed" . 2:23

"High On Jesus" 3:51

"The Ballad Of Charles Whitman" 3:04

"Top Ten Commandments" 3:22

"Western Union Wire" 3:13

" Silver Eagle Express" - (Kinky Friedman, Roger Friedman) . 3:47

Re-launching a career with help from the Rocket Man
Sedaka's Back
Neil Sedaka

When Neil Sedaka first heard Carole King's 1971 album *Tapestry*, like a lot of people, he was impressed.

Tapestry was King's second studio album and featured the hit singles "It's Too Late," "I Feel the Earth Move," and "You've Got a Friend," a song that would also be a hit for James Taylor, who recorded it for his *Mud Slide Slim* album that same year.

But there was something about *Tapestry,* which would go on to be one of the best-selling albums of all time, that did something besides impress Sedaka.

It inspired him.

"When I heard it, I said to myself, 'Gee, I can do that,'" said Sedaka. "Carole and I were from the same ilk, the same generation, and we were both from the Brill Building. I said to myself, 'I can do that.'"

The Brill Building, at 1619 Broadway in Manhattan, New York, housed music industry offices and recording studios where some of the most popular songs in American history were written. The music that came out of there became known as the "Brill Building Sound."

Many songwriters and songwriting teams worked in the Brill Building from the late 1950s through the 1960s. Among them was a veritable *Who's Who* of the music industry at that time, including Burt Bacharach and Hal David, Tommy Boyce and Bobby Hart, Jerry Leiber and Mike Stoller, Barry

Mann and Cynthia Weil, Sonny Bono, Neil Diamond, Marvin Hamlisch, Paul Simon, and Phil Spector.

Also among those songwriters were two other teams: Gerry Goffin and Carole King, and Neil Sedaka and Howard Greenfield.

Goffin and King, who were married then, had written several No. 1 hits in the 1960s, including "Will You Love Me Tomorrow," "Take Good Care of My Baby," "The Loco-Motion," and "Go Away Little Girl."

Sedaka and Greenfield also had written their share of No. 1 hits, including "Everybody's Somebody's Fool" and "Breakin' in a Brand New Broken Heart," both for Connie Francis; and "Breaking up Is Hard to Do" and "Love Will Keep Us Together," both of which were recorded by Sedaka himself.

The shared pedigree and environment of the Brill Building years went a long way toward giving Sedaka the confidence that he could create an album as good as King's *Tapestry*.

The only thing that seemed to be standing in his way was that by 1974, Sedaka hadn't been on the U.S. record charts in 13 years.

"Everybody thought I was a ghost from the 1950s," said Sedaka. "In America, I couldn't get arrested. People would come up to me and say, 'Didn't you used to be Neil Sedaka?'"

He indeed had a pretty good start to his career in the late 1950s and early 1960s. Sedaka had his first Top 10 hit in the U.S. with "Oh! Carol," which reached No. 9 on the charts in 1959 and followed that up in 1960 with another No. 9 single, "Stairway to Heaven." In 1961, he had two more hits, "Calendar Girl," which rose to No. 4 and "Happy Birthday Sweet 16," which got to No. 6.

Sedaka's streak stretched into 1962 with the original version of "Breaking up Is Hard to Do," which became his first No. 1 hit, and then "Next Door To an Angel," which reached No. 5.

Then the Beatles came to America in 1964. And Sedaka's career for the remainder of the decade and into the early 1970s waned. Fortunately, he remained a popular concert attraction in both the United Kingdom and Australia. In 1972, Sedaka did a tour of England, and that's when he met the members of the English rock band 10cc, whose members included Graham Gouldman, Eric Stewart, Kevin Godley, and Lol Creme.

Sedaka would record an album called *Solitaire* in 1972 with the members of 10cc. It had two songs that made the Top 40 in the United Kingdom including the title track, which would become a hit for the Carpenters in the U.S. three years later in 1975.

But for the most part, Sedaka was still having trouble gaining any traction back in the United States.

Enter Elton John.

John and Sedaka met at a Bee Gees concert in England in 1973. And it turned out that John was a big fan of Sedaka's music.

"Elton read everything and knew every record. I had a few hits in England, even though I was not having anything in America," said Sedaka. "He said, 'May I come over and listen to the record that you've been recording with 10cc?' He was very impressed. And he asked me to join his record label, which I did."

John had just founded Rocket Record Company, which was named after his hit single "Rocket Man," written with songwriting partner Bernie Taupin, and featured on John's 1972 album *Honky Chateau*.

Among the artists joining Sedaka on the new label at that time were Cliff Richard, the Hudson Brothers and Kiki Dee.

Sedaka's first album for Rocket Records would be called *Sedaka's Back* and included a compilation of songs from his previous three albums, all of which were released only in the United Kingdom.

Three singles would be released from the album: "Laughter In the Rain," which Sedaka co-wrote with Phil Cody; "The Immigrant," also co-written with Cody and dedicated to John Lennon, who was experiencing some immigration issues at the time; and "That's When the Music Takes Me," on which Sedaka had a solo songwriting credit. A fourth song, "Love Will Keep Us Together," co-written by Sedaka and his old partner Greenfield, would not be released as a single by Sedaka, but would be covered by — and become a hit a year later as well as help launch the careers of — the Captain & Tennille.

"'Laughter In the Rain' took three or four hours to write with Phil Cody. And 'Love Will Keep Us Together' took about two hours with Howard Greenfield," said Sedaka. "First, I wrote them on the piano, but you really have to get it on the record. I said, after writing them on the piano, that if the record comes out as good, these would be number one hits. I could tell in those days."

Sedaka was in a songwriting groove.

"I think it was just one of those magic moments, that I've had several times, where I was touched by something spiritual and I just sat there very calmly and wrote them," he said.

"Laughter In the Rain" would be released as the first single off of *Sedaka's Back*. It would reach No. 1 on the U.S. Billboard Hot 100 Singles chart, the U.S. Billboard Hot Adult Contemporary Tracks chart and the U.S. Cash Box Top 100 Singles chart.

"The Immigrant" reached No. 22 on the U.S. Billboard Hot 100 Singles chart and got all the way to No. 1 on the Billboard Adult Contemporary chart in May 1975.

The album itself would reach No. 23 on the U.S. Billboard 200 Albums chart.

Sedaka was indeed back in the U.S. music scene.

"I'm very, very proud of 'The Immigrant' and it's very relevant today with the immigration situations that are happening," said Sedaka. "I loved the song so much that I put it out as a single, and I'm glad I did."

As *Sedaka's Back* re-established Sedaka in the U.S. market, there were some questions at the time why he decided "That's When the Music Takes Me" would be the third single released off the album, rather than "Love Will Keep Us Together."

The song actually first appeared on Sedaka's 1973 album *The Tra-La Days Are Over*, but it did not have a U.S. release until it appeared on *Sedaka's Back*.

The Captain & Tennille cover of "Love Will Keep Us Together" became the title track of the duo's debut album in 1975. It was a monster smash for them, reaching No. 1 on the U.S. Billboard Hot 100 Singles chart and the U.S. Billboard Easy Listening chart, and also won a Grammy for Record of the Year in 1976.

Listeners of the song on the Captain & Tennille album can hear the duo acknowledge Sedaka, by working in the words "Sedaka is back" into the fade-out of "Love Will Keep Us Together."

But the reason that Sedaka didn't release the song as a single off the *Sedaka's Back* album was that he thought that the Captain & Tennille's version was something special.

"I thought the Captain and Tennille's record was better than mine. It won a Grammy and was the most-played song of the year," said Sedaka. "And I'm very happy that I helped launch their success. My record was very pleasurable, very lilting, but theirs was better and more to the times."

The cover photo for *Sedaka's Back* shows Sedaka dressed in a pinstripe suit, holding a cigar and wearing a pink fedora.

"Elton had a photographer at the time that he used many times. The hat was just lying around during the photo shoot and Elton's manager at the time just picked it up and said,

'Try it on, Neil.' And it worked," said Sedaka. "I remember seeing these thrilling billboards on Sunset Strip with my face and that hat. I'm glad it worked because it was an eye-catcher."

The photographer was Terry O'Neill, who had established himself in the 1960s photographing the Beatles and the Rolling Stones as well as some of Hollywood's big names, among them Judy Garland. O'Neill would go on to take some of the most iconic photos of Elton John, a selection of which appeared in the 2008 book *Eltonography*. And O'Neill continued his links to Hollywood in the 1980s by taking famous photos of his then-girlfriend and later wife, Faye Dunaway, lounging next to the Beverly Hills Hotel swimming pool in 1977 the morning after she won the Oscar for her role in the film *Network*.

The back cover features another O'Neill photo of Sedaka in a more classic pose, sitting backward on a chair in front of a jukebox with his arms folded. There is also a note to fans from John, which reads: "Neil is proud of his past but he's even prouder of what he's doing now. And so he should be — this album contains some of his best work ever. Listen to songs like 'Solitaire' and 'Laughter in the Rain,' then you'll see what I mean. We at Rocket Records have been given the privilege of releasing these tracks, which are a compilation of Neil's hit albums in Great Britain. If you watch the charts in the next few months, you'll see that even though he's never been away — Sedaka's back — Elton John."

As for the title of the album, it reflected what Sedaka was going through in his career at the time, and what he hoped to achieve as the music moved through the decade of the 1970s.

"I hadn't been on the charts for 13 years. I was only working in England and Australia because they have a great love for the original American rock and rollers. I started with Elvis and Buddy Holly and Ritchie Valens. Dick Clark launched me as an unknown at nineteen years old," said Sedaka. "I didn't have any work, so people didn't see me for quite a few years. That's why I called the album *Sedaka's Back*."

And he had a sense that this was the album that was going to put him in front of U.S. audiences again after so many years of trying to re-establish his relevance.

"I woke my wife up in the middle of the night when I got the first pressing and I said, 'Holy shit, this is going to be a number one record.' And it was," said Sedaka.

"I was determined to come back on the charts," he said. "I take music very, very seriously. It was never the gimmicks; it was never the funny clothes. It was all about the music. And I did everything from the writing to the arranging to the mixing. I had help, but I was always at the helm. To me, it was the most important thing to have something sincere, emotional, and that would hit home."

These days, Sedaka still performs to sellout crowds, although he believes 2016, his 60th year as a performer, will be his final year onstage.

"They can lose themselves in the music. It's very emotional, but very happy. I have a big body of work that goes from up-tempo songs to ballads. And they bring a lot of nostalgia. People remember exactly where they were when they hear each song," said Sedaka. "I've been writing for sixty-three years. It's about seven hundred songs — not all great, but a lot of them are. But the people do come because I'm one of the few who still writes at this age and one of the few from the original Brill Building days who still performs and still loves it.

"But you have to go out when you're in good shape. I don't want to mention any names, but some artists have gone on too long, cannot sing, cannot perform. So I'm going out while I'm on the top."

After a long career, Sedaka still recalls something his father once told him.

Mike Morsch

"My father always said, 'Neil, these songs will outlive you.' And he was right. I still hear 'Happy Birthday Sweet Sixteen,' I still hear 'Calendar Girl,' 'Breaking Up is Hard to Do' and 'Laughter in the Rain.' It's an amazing thing," he said. "It's been very rewarding. I've had an interesting life because it's really about the music. And I'm really proud of that."

Discography

"Sedaka's Back"
Neil Sedaka
November 1974

Side One

"Standing On The Inside" (Neil Sedaka)..3:55

"That's When The Music Takes Me" 3:35

"Laughter In The Rain" (Phil Cody, Neil Sedaka)..................... 2:50

"Sad Eyes" (Phil Cody, Neil Sedaka)... 3:38

"Solitaire" (Phil Cody, Neil Sedaka).. 5:02

"Little Brother" (Phil Cody, Neil Sedaka) 3:27

Side Two

"Love Will Keep Us Together" (Howard Greenfield, Neil Sedaka.... 3:35

"The Immigrant" (Phil Cody, Neil Sedaka)................................ 4:23

"The Way I Am" (Phil Cody, Neil Sedaka)................................. 3:50

"The Other Side Of Me" (Howard Greenfield, Neil Sedaka)..... 3:34

"A Little Lovin'" (Phil Cody, Neil Sedaka)................................. 2:52

"Our Last Song Together" (Howard Greenfield, Neil Sedaka) . 4:00

Wacky cover photo, cool music inside
Daryl Hall and John Oates (The Silver Album)
Hall & Oates

Daryl Hall was sitting in Tommy Mottola's office one day in late 1975 when the telephone rang.

"This guy is on the phone and he says he knows you," said Hall, recalling the story and what Mottola, who was then managing Hall and his band mate John Oates, said.

"Who is it?" Hall asked.

"His name is Sylvester Stallone," said Mottola.

Hall did indeed know the name. Sylvester Stallone's brother, Frank, was a fellow Philadelphian and had — during the pre-Hall & Oates days — once been in a Philly band called Valentine, whose lead guitarist was John Oates.

"Let me talk to him," Hall said as Mottola handed him the phone.

Hall & Oates had just released their fourth studio album in August 1975. Titled *Daryl Hall and John Oates,* the album would go on to become known as *The Silver Album* and include the duo's first Top 10 hit single.

Sylvester Stallone had heard the album. And there was a song titled "Grounds for Separation" written by Hall, that he really liked.

"So I get on the phone and Sly is on there and he goes, 'Hey, man, this is Sly,'" said Hall. "I said, 'What's going on, man? What have you been doing?'"

Stallone told Hall he was working on a film project and he wanted to ask the musician a question.

"And he said, 'I've got this new idea and I'm really hot on it. It's called "Rocky." It's all about this boxer who never gives up. It's all about Philly and about the Philly mentality,'" recalled Hall. "He said he had heard 'Grounds for Separation,' he thought it was unbelievable, and he wanted to use it as the theme for the movie."

Hall thought it was a good idea.

"I had no idea Sly was into anything important. It was like he was just throwing this idea out there. So I said, 'Sure, if you want to use it, go ahead,'" said Hall.

Filming for *Rocky* would begin shortly thereafter, in January 1976, throughout Philadelphia. The musical score for the film was to be composed by Bill Conti, an unknown in the film industry at the time.

According to a 2014 interview with *Rocky* director John Avildsen in *Philadelphia Magazine*, nobody involved with the film cared much about who was going to do the score. In fact, according to Avildsen, the budget for the score was only $25,000, which included everything — the composer's fee, the pay for the musicians, the rental of the studio and the cost to buy the tape on which the music was to be recorded.

"So we had one three-hour session with a thirty-two piece orchestra," said Avildsen in the magazine article. "When the producers came into the recording studio and they saw all these guys, they looked at Bill and said, 'Bill, how are you going to make any money?' Bill put it all into the music. When we were recording the montage music, I said, 'Bill, you ought to put some words to this thing, because this sounds like a song.' He said, 'No, it's just for the montage.' I said, 'Well, you got some people there and they're recording. Why don't you get them to come up with a song? We've got an hour." He said, "Oh, OK." And that's where 'Gonna Fly Now' came from."

That apparently eliminated the Hall & Oates song "Grounds for Separation" from being further considered as a possible theme song for *Rocky*.

There have been reports in subsequent years that Hall & Oates pulled the song from consideration prior to "Gonna Fly Now" being chosen for the film's theme.

"Something happened, but I don't know what it was," said Hall. "In the Mottola camp, anything could happen. It just sort of went away."

But Stallone himself may have believed that somebody in the Hall & Oates camp did indeed pull "Grounds for Separation" from being considered, a theory that may have been confirmed years later when Stallone crossed paths with Hall at a nightclub in the mid-1990s.

"I hadn't seen Sly in a long time," said Hall. "We were at a club and he walked up to me and said, 'You remember that phone call? You fucked up.' I said, 'Sly, I definitely fucked up, brother.'"

"Grounds for Separation" may not have found immortality in what would become a classic American film, but there was another song on *The Silver Album* that would make an impact on the music world and the careers of Hall and Oates.

The two had recorded their third studio album in 1974, *War Babies*, produced by Todd Rundgren, who had relied heavily on his progressive rock band Utopia to perform on the record. With Rundgren's heavy influence, *War Babies* was a departure from the Hall & Oates interpretation of Philly Soul that they had produced in their second album, *Abandoned Luncheonette*, in 1973.

So when it was time to make their fourth album, Hall & Oates decided to go back to their soul roots. The duo had changed labels, from Atlantic Records to RCA Records, for *Daryl Hall & John Oates*, which ended up being known as *The Silver Album* because of its glam-rock-style cover.

Hall was living on the Upper East Side of New York when he and Oates began producing material for *The Silver Album*. Living with Hall, was his girlfriend Sara Allen.

Mike Morsch

When it was time for Daryl Hall and John Oates to make their fourth album, they had changed labels and decided to go back to their soul and R&B roots for what would be called "The Silver Album." (Photo by Mike Morsch)

Oates had introduced Allen to Hall a few years earlier. According to Oates, he had met a flight attendant — called "stewardesses" in those days — and a girlfriend of hers on the streets of New York and had struck up a conversation with them. Oates eventually took that meeting and turned it into a song titled "Las Vegas Turnaround" that appeared on *Abandoned Luncheonette*. He also introduced Hall to Allen.

By 1975, Allen and Hall were a few years into a personal relationship that would end up lasting more than 30 years. And Hall was inspired enough by his feelings for Allen that he wrote a highly personal song, one that would end up on *The Silver Album*.

That song was "Sara Smile," which became the first Top 10 hit for Hall & Oates, reaching No. 4 on the U.S. Billboard Hot 100 singles chart in early 1976.

"It was a song that came completely out of my heart. I've said this many times — it was a postcard. It's short and sweet and to the point," said Hall.

But there was no big first-time reveal of the song to Allen.

"She was there, in the house. I was just writing the song. I don't think there was a first time that I played it for her. She listened to the evolution of the song," said Hall.

Hall & Oates was touring England when "Sara Smile" broke in the R&B world, becoming a hit on African-American radio. The song then crossed over into mainstream radio and became a pop hit as well.

"I will never forget the first time I heard it on the radio," said Hall. "I was in California. I heard it on the radio amidst all the other songs, and I thought to myself, 'This doesn't sound like anything else that's being played around it.' It was totally unique and stuck out like a sore thumb — well, maybe not a sore thumb — but it stuck out. I have a distinct memory of that. I'm sort of proud of that idea."

It wasn't the only song about a woman, though, that would end up on *The Silver Album*. Oates would write a song titled "Camellia," also about a woman, which would be sequenced as the first song on the A-side.

The difference was that while "Sara Smile" was written about a real woman, "Camellia" was about a real woman in a fictional story inspired by a drunk guy in a club.

Oates has told the "Camellia" story for years at his solo shows. The idea first came to him in the early 1970s. It was at a time when Hall & Oates had started to regularly tour.

"Going on the road for the first time was really exciting, especially in the seventies," said Oates. "We were playing this little club in Atlanta called *Richard's*. Those were the days when you had to do two sets a night. We pretty much repeated the same songs because we didn't have that many.

"The club had these little tables and I remember during the first set there was a guy right in front of me; he was drinking pretty heavily and I happened to notice him. When I came out for the second set, he had pretty much passed out. And he had his head in his hands leaning down on the table. So the whole night, I had to play looking at the guy and it was not the most inspiring thing to do. I figured to pass the time I would just invent a story about him. I didn't know this guy from Adam, but I figured I'd just make something up. So I made something up."

That fictional story did, though, have some aspects of reality. Oates had met a woman named Pamellia — with a "P" — in Atlanta and they became friends. She had some good friends who owned a hotel in Ocho Rios, Jamaica, and she invited Hall and Oates to travel there and hang out at the hotel with some reggae artists.

"That's where the whole lyrical idea — 'Oh Camellia, won't you take me away, to paradise tropical moon, don't you leave me sitting here in Atlanta' [came from]. It was a combination of the drunk at the table in the club, and using her name, and the trip to Jamaica. It was a combination of all those things," said Oates.

The eventual name change on the song was actually Hall's idea.

"I had written the song and Daryl and I were getting together in New York going over material, putting our songs together and getting prepared to record," said Oates. "I played it for him and he really dug it. But he said, 'Man, that name, that's too weird. Nobody is going to be able to relate to that name.' And he actually said, 'What about Camellia? It's the same thing.' And I said, 'Yeah, close enough.'"

Recording for *The Silver Album* would be done on the West Coast, at Larrabee Sound Studios in Los Angeles, in the summer of 1975. The co-producer for the album, along with Hall and Oates, was Christopher Bond, a former Philadelphian and member of the Hall & Oates band who had been a guitarist on *Abandoned Luncheonette* and who had assisted producer Arif Mardin in the production of the album.

After that album was finished, Bond moved to Los Angeles and spent time recording his own music and being a session musician, often working at Larrabee Sound Studios. Bond had made a solo album called *Good Love*, which Hall and Oates heard and liked.

"I got a phone call — it must have been like two or three in the morning New York time because I remember Johnny Carson was on in Los Angeles — from John Oates, saying that they had a new record deal with RCA," said Bond. "John said they had one record, one shot with RCA. He said, 'We keep going through lists of producers and yours is the only name that's left. Do you want to do it?'"

Hall and Oates had put a band together in New York in anticipation of using it to record *The Silver Album*, but Bond had heard the band and didn't like it.

"For *The Silver Album*, I didn't really want to be a producer," said Bond. "And then I got that phone call from John. He and I had always been great friends and Daryl and I had had some collisions, but nothing major. It was creative tension. But it was good because something good always came out of it. And producing the album sounded like a fun thing to do. I thought I'd get it done in a couple of months and then go back to doing my sessions."

Bond flew to New York to meet with Hall and Oates as well as with Mike Berniker, president of RCA. Berniker was convinced that "Camellia" was a hit and made his feelings known to Bond at the time.

In his meetings with Hall and Oates, Bond discussed going back to the R&B vibe that they had achieved on *Abandoned Luncheonette*. But this time around, they'd give it what Bond called "a rock and roll edge."

While in New York, Bond listened to the material that Hall and Oates had planned for *The Silver Album* and even went to a couple of rehearsals with the Hall & Oates New York band.

"But it just wasn't happening," said Bond. "I said I've got some fabulous players in L.A. and I'd really like to do this album in L.A. By now, I had it in my head that I had to make 'Camellia' a hit. I had never produced a record for anybody else all by myself at that point. So I took their word that 'Camellia' was a hit."

Hall and Oates agreed to record the album in Los Angeles.

"They came to a little apartment I had in Studio City and we went through the entire record," said Bond. "All the songs and a couple that weren't finished, including one that was really unfinished but had a great opening and first verse and chorus called 'Rich Girl.' But Daryl just didn't want to finish it at the time for *The Silver Album*."

Along with Hall on keyboards and Oates on guitar, the L.A. studio musicians, those who would essentially be the next wave of the 1960s studio musicians known as The Wrecking Crew, would play on the record. Among those were three drummers — Jim Gordon, Michael Baird and Ed Greene; Gary Coleman on percussion; Leland Sklar and Scotty Edwards on bass; and Clarence McDonald on keyboards.

While doing session work at Larrabee Studios, Bond met engineer Barry Rudolph. The two hit it off, and with Hall & Oates deciding to record *The Silver Album* in Los Angeles instead of New York, Bond asked Rudolph to be the engineer on the record.

"On the first day at Larrabee, in they [Daryl and John] walked and John announced, 'We're cutting the first single today.' And I'm going, whoa. Not one note has been played yet, not one song, I've heard nothing," said Rudolph. "But they were just so together. To come in and announce that what they were going to do that day was the first single, I just thought, 'Wow. Of all the pros I had worked with, nobody had ever said that.'"

The song that Hall and Oates recorded that first day was "Camellia."

"I was familiar with *Abandoned Luncheonette* and I'd heard some of the *War Babies* record," said Rudolph. "Daryl and John were incredibly together. They knew exactly what they wanted to do. They had very clear ideas about how it should sound and the arrangements. They worked with Chris on that stuff quite a bit."

With "Camellia" being the first-planned single, Hall and Oates had decided that another Oates-penned song "Alone Too Long" was slated to be the second single. At that point in the process, "Sara Smile" wasn't being considered for release as a single.

"When 'Sara Smile' was recorded, it was probably tracked in a half hour at the most. Daryl did all the vocals. In fact, the lead vocal is a live vocal tape. We punched in one word, the first 'Sara' before the first chorus because it was flat," said Rudolph. "Daryl is very much a live and immediate artist; he's not much for punching in lead vocals. Backing vocals are different. But he really was a real-by-feel kind of singer."

But Bond and Rudolph didn't think "Sara Smile" was destined to be a single from the album.

"The first time I heard 'Sara Smile,' I thought it was a really neat song. And that's all I thought about it. But it did definitely belong on this record," said Bond.

"To be honest, everyone kind of thought that 'Sara' was a really cool kind of album cut. It was a really nice song and everyone loved working on it," said Rudolph. "It was a very simple production, a very simple song. Daryl said to me, 'When we do the backing vocals, I want it to sound like the Dells.' I said OK. I sort of knew who they were."

The Dells were a doo-wop group popular in the 1950s and 1960s, who had an R&B hit with the single "Oh What a Night."

"When I heard the playback the first time of the first take that we'd done of 'Sara,' I thought oh, something was happening," said Bond. "I'm sitting in the control room thinking to myself, oh my God, to me this sounds like a hit record. But everybody kept insisting the hit single was 'Camellia.' This was the 1970s. Albums all had concepts — that's what it was all about. And the concept with 'Sara' was that it was like an Al Green song. I wanted it to sound like an old Al Green song from Memphis.

"I cut 'Camellia' three different times, with three different sections. I did two different string dates on it. I tried it with two different drummers. I even tried cutting it in different studios to see if I could make it sound like a hit to me and it never did," said Bond.

Once *The Silver Album* was released, the two singles, "Camellia" and "Alone Too Long," did OK on the charts, but nothing spectacular. At that time in the music business, according to Oates, artists had to give a single six to eight weeks to see if it would make the charts and get regular radio play.

"By the time those two singles had been released — the album had been released prior to that — you're talking about being into this album for more than six months. At that point in our careers, six months was an eternity. We were already getting ready to make a new record," said Oates.

Hall and Oates accepted that the album was what it was, had done what it was going to do, and that it was time to move on.

"Don't get me wrong; we very happy with the record artistically. We thought it was a really good record. We really liked it and we were touring a lot," said Oates. "Our focus was not only on promoting the record itself but promoting ourselves in terms of becoming a real, solid touring band. We had developed a new band at the time that we were very high on, and we really felt that this band was a great support system for where we were at. We were very focused on touring."

After touring the United States for six months in support of *The Silver Album*, Hall & Oates toured England for the first time in their careers.

"It was a very exciting time to be there. We were perceived by the British music press as the cool, hip, new Americans," said Oates. "We were wined and dined and treated like the Second Coming. We thought that was pretty amazing because it wasn't really happening in America like that."

Still, RCA had no intention of releasing a third single from *The Silver Album*.

"In their minds, we were going to make another record, and in our minds, we were going to make another record," said Oates.

But while the duo was still in England, a disc jockey on a small R&B radio station in Toledo, Ohio, decided to start playing "Sara Smile" as an album cut — just because he liked the song.

"Simple as that. And as soon as he began to play it, the phones lit up, people kept calling and asking, 'Who are these guys, what is this song that you're playing, and where do we get it?'" said Oates.

Bond and Rudolph remember the "Sara" story differently. It may or may not be rock and roll urban legend, but it does support Hall's theory that "in the Mottola camp, anything could happen."

"The story goes that Tommy took a second loan out on his house and borrowed a bunch of money and basically got the top ten stations in the country to play 'Sara' in regular rotation for a week. And that put it over the edge," said Rudolph.

Nevertheless, word of the song's popularity in Ohio quickly got back to RCA offices in New York and the record company officials decided to release "Sara Smile" as the third single off *The Silver Album*.

The song went to No. 4 on the U.S. Billboard Hot 100 Singles, No. 6 on the U.S. Cash Box Top 100 Singles, No. 18 on the U.S. Billboard Hot Adult Contemporary Tracks and No. 23 on the U.S. Billboard Hot Soul Singles chart.

Tommy Mottola was also the inspiration for another song on the album called "Gino (The Manager)," co-written by Hall and Oates. On the back cover of the album, there is a credit that reads "And introducing Tommy Mottola as 'Little Gino.'"

"It's more or less about him. But it wasn't nasty enough, though," said Hall.

"We loved that lyric. We thought that was right on the money," said Oates. "It was totally inspired and directed at Tommy Mottola. If you read the lyrics closely, it was basically just kind of describing who he was in a song. Not necessarily in a negative way. But he had a very strong personality. He was a very unique person and we just wrote a song about it."

Years later, in 1990, Mottola would go on to become president of Sony Music Entertainment and help develop the careers of Celine Dion and Mariah Carey, the latter whom he married in 1993.

When *The Silver Album* was done, Rudolph said the consensus among those in his circle was "wacky cover photo, cool music inside."

The cover for *The Silver Album* has become one of the most memorable in their careers. It shows a black and white photo of Hall and Oates, heavily made up in the glam rock style of the era.

"Oh, Christ — that's called naiveté," said Hall.

Pierre LaRoche, a makeup artist, was responsible for the cover. LaRoche had been a makeup artist for Mick Jagger and David Bowie. He was responsible for Bowie's *Aladdin Sane* lightning bolt, his *Ziggy Stardust* rhinestone-gold forehead circle, and he had created the look for the characters in *The Rocky Horror Picture Show*.

"We were sort of hanging out with the Stones at the time. And Pierre said, 'Can I do your album cover?' We said, 'Sure,'" said Hall. "The next thing we knew, we were in the studio and he was painting our faces and doing all this stuff. We went along with it.

"You have to put it into the context of the time. It was the height of glam rock, KISS was just starting, Todd Rundgren and even Edgar Winter were doing highly made-up album covers. So we were just another two of those fools who did that. It certainly was . . . striking. That's the best word I can use," said Hall.

"Glam rock was fashionable in New York City. We were living in New York City and we were very much a part of the downtown hip New York scene," said Oates. "If you look at our previous albums up to that point, we had never been on the cover of an album. So we decided we wanted to be on the cover. We figured if we were going to be on the cover, let's go big."

Oates still recalls the exact words that LaRoche said to the duo about doing the album cover.

"I will quote him directly. He said, 'I will immortalize you.' And he was right. To this day, it's probably the only album cover that anyone ever talks about," said Oates.

"To me, the whole idea of the artwork on an album cover is that it should somehow impart — if not literally, at least emotionally — that it represents what you're about to experience when you listen to that music," said Oates. "I will say, though, that I don't think *The Silver Album* cover necessarily did represent the music inside. It was more about making a statement that was shocking and in a way, very bold. That's what it was all about."

The Silver Album reached No. 17 on the U.S. Billboard 200 Albums charts and was the first Hall & Oates album to crack the U.K. Albums chart, getting to No. 56.

Hall looks at *The Silver Album* now as "a time and a place" record.

"It was two Philly guys who had recently moved to New York City and then were transplanted out to Los Angeles to make a record. And that's what *The Silver Album* was," said Hall. "It was a combination of all of those realities. We were trying to figure out how to interact with the Los Angeles musicians. They were great musicians, but they were California musicians, and I was trying to get a certain kind of sound that was in my head.

"The fact that such good results came out of that record was a surprise to me. It was kind of like pulling teeth, though. 'Sara Smile' happened very naturally, but a lot of these songs were really hard," he said.

Oates calls *The Silver Album* "one of the four or five most important albums" that Hall & Oates recorded in their careers.

"For the first time, we were able to coalesce a sound. If you look at our first three albums — *Whole Oats*, *Abandoned Luncheonette* and *War Babies* — if you take those three albums and combine them together stylistically, you'll find elements of all three of those records finally finding some sort of homogenous form in *The Silver Album*," said Oates.

"Not to say that was the final expression of it, because it wasn't. But at that moment, it was the most coherent musical record we had made," he said. "And it had a lot to do with a lot of things — the songs we were writing, the fact that we were touring all the time, and that we were experiencing life on the road, and we were expressing that energy. It had to do with going to L.A. for the first time and working in L.A. in a different studio environment, and it had a lot to do with different but incredibly great studio musicians. And also working with Chris Bond, who was really kind of coming into his own at that moment."

Bond said that with their work on *The Silver Album*, Hall and Oates were also coming into their own as songwriters.

"I gotta say, 'Sara' was a brilliant piece of work, and as a writer, I give Daryl credit for that. I think, at the time, the two of them were on a road to becoming important songwriters in the history of pop and rock music," said Bond. "'Sara' was a flat-out kind of brave song to do. And it was pure. It was real. When you heard it, it just said this is a real emotion. This was a feeling. This is what it's all about.

"And it continued on," said Bond. "They were writing some really wonderful stuff, creating that new sound that we'd all talked about two years prior during the *Abandoned Luncheonette* album. And it wasn't blue-eyed soul, because blue-eyed soul was the Righteous Brothers. That's who created blue-eyed soul. This was something new. And it was good and I was proud to be part of it."

Oates said that *The Silver Album* was kind of a perfect storm of creative collaborations.

"I think *Abandoned Luncheonette* certainly was one of those moments, with Arif Mardin and Atlantic Records and the studio musicians of New York, and the songs we had written. That was a moment. And *The Silver Album* was another moment," said Oates.

Discography

"Daryl Hall and John Oates" (The Silver Album)
Hall & Oates
August 18, 1975
(All songs written by Daryl Hall and John Oates except where noted)

Side One

"Camellia" (Oates) 2:48

"Sara Smile" 3:07

"Alone Too Long" (Oates) 3:21

"Out of Me, Out of You" 3:28

"Nothing at All" 4:24

Side Two

"Gino (The Manager)" 4:10

"(You Know) It Doesn't Matter Anymore" 3:07

"Ennui on the Mountain" 3:15

"Grounds for Separation" (Hall) 4:12

"Soldering" (Ewart Beckford, Alvin Ranglin) 3:24

A 'reunion song' for two different solo albums
Breakaway
Art Garfunkel

Art Garfunkel had a real spring in his step that morning. It was a beautiful day in the summer of 1975, so he left his hotel in London and decided to walk to AIR Studios, where he was cutting his second solo album, *Breakaway*, for Columbia Records.

Garfunkel was feeling good, enjoying what he said was "the London experience of 1975" during his walk. He and his co-producer, Richard Perry, had the tapes of the instrumentation for the songs that would appear on the album — which Garfunkel always did first — and he had spent endless hours stroking and tweaking the instrumentation and overdubs, trying to make the songs sound interesting and fresh.

"You keep putting layers of sound on a song, and then you subtract. Then you sculpt," said Garfunkel of the process.

The songs also had what he called "dummy Art Garfunkel vocals" on them, but now it was time to put the "real" Garfunkel vocals on the tracks.

"I had walked through the streets of London in a wonderful mood," said Garfunkel. "And I was realizing that I was in good voice. I had gotten a good night's sleep."

When Garfunkel got to the studio, Perry had the microphone ready for him, with the echo adjusted just the way Garfunkel liked it.

"And I went out, put on the cans [headphones] and within an hour, I was in the zone," said Garfunkel. "And the very first take was the one. It takes years before you realize you don't have to do it again and again and again. You don't always get better when you repeat; you sometimes make things stale.

"But it's very rare to have it happen right at the top. We're talking about the immediacy of your good results. The take on the very first try, for me, it's very rare. "It was a case of 'Richard, I think the very thing I just gave you is worth listening to. Let's listen to it. We can try again, a few more takes, but I have a funny feeling you're not going to top it."

The first take was indeed the best one of "I Only Have Eyes for You," a song written by composer Harry Warren and lyricist Al Dubin in 1934 and recorded by several artists. A doo-wop version of the song got to No. 11 on the U.S. Billboard Hot 100 Singles charts and to No. 3 on the R&B chart in 1959 for the Flamingoes.

Garfunkel's version would be his first No. 1 single in the United Kingdom.

The *Breakaway* album featured some of the biggest names of the 1970s music scene, including David Crosby and Graham Nash of Crosby, Stills, and Nash; Toni Tennille of the Captain and Tennille; Bruce Johnston of the Beach Boys; and a young Stephen Bishop, who just a year later would release his debut album *Careless* — on which Garfunkel would return the favor with vocals and background vocals — and would feature two hit singles for Bishop, "On and On" and "Save It for a Rainy Day."

The second single from the *Breakaway* album, the title track, which featured Crosby and Nash on backing vocals, cracked the Top 40 on the Billboard Hot 100 Singles chart, coming in at No. 39, but did substantially better on the Easy Listening chart, holding the No. 1 spot for a week in February 1976.

The 1975 "Breakaway" album would feature the song "My Little Town," written for Art Garfunkel by his former partner, Paul Simon, who liked it so much that he put it on his solo album, "Still Crazy After All These Years, also released in 1975. (Photo by Mike Morsch)

The *Breakaway* album would also feature one more hit and a little of the old magic for Garfunkel — "My Little Town," written for Garfunkel by his former musical partner, Paul Simon.

Simon and Garfunkel had split up after their final studio album, *Bridge Over Troubled Waters*, had taken six awards at the 13th annual Grammy Awards in 1971.

At the time, Simon was quoted as saying he didn't think the duo would record together again. But they were getting along, at least well enough for "My Little Town" to change that four years later in 1975.

"That's true — Paul wrote that song for me," said Garfunkel. "Sweet, melodic, pretty — those are flavors I go to time and again. I love to be a man who can be pretty. But maybe I overdo that."

Simon happened to agree with Garfunkel's self-assessment in that regard.

"Paul said, 'Artie, you do overdo it. You need an up-tempo stomping song on this album,'" Garfunkel recalled Simon saying to him. "The song is not pretty and not melodic. It has anger, a bite.

"I'm very much in tune with Mister Simon, his musical sense, his thinking. As soon as he said that and showed the song to me, I was right with him. I knew just what he meant. I thanked him and said, 'Let's go to work on it,'" said Garfunkel.

Simon was working on his own solo album at the same time, *Still Crazy After All These Years*, which would also be released in October 1975, the same month that *Breakaway* was released.

Simon and Garfunkel, who shared lead vocals on the song, both liked it so much that they agreed that "My Little Town" would appear on both their solo albums.

Stephen Bishop would write two songs for Art Garfunkel's 1975 "Breakaway" album. Just a year later, Bishop would release his album "Careless," on which Garfunkel would return the favor contributing background vocals on the record. (Photo by Mike Morsch)

"We both had albums coming out at the same time. When we saw the marketing coincidence, we said we should relate to it," said Garfunkel.

And the "reunion" song helped generate interest for both solo albums. It would become the duo's eighth Top 10 hit on the Billboard Hot 100 chart, peaking at No. 9 in late 1975. It was the only song on the *Breakaway* album that wasn't produced by Perry; production credit instead went to Simon, Garfunkel, and Phil Ramone.

In addition to the contribution from Simon and two songs written by Bishop, Perry also suggested that Garfunkel cover "I Believe (When I Fall in Love It Will Be Forever)" written by Stevie Wonder and Yvonne Wright; and Bruce Johnston's "Disney Girls" on the *Breakaway* album.

"Disney Girls," with Johnston on lead vocals, had first appeared on the 1971 album *Surf's Up* by the Beach Boys.

"The one thing that was great for Art's album was Richard Perry is a guy that musically is kind of like Clive Davis [then president of Columbia Records] as far as finding songs," said Johnston. "Clive is smart. He just found songs. And that's exactly what Richard Perry did for the *Breakaway* album.

Johnston's involvement in the album was minimal, but memorable.

"Richard called me and he said, 'You know, we've decided we'd like to record 'Disney Girls' and if you're interested, maybe you'd like to work on it," said Johnston. "So I came down to the session. Richard had great musicians — Joe Osborn on bass and Russ Kunkel on drums, Andrew Gold on guitar. And then there was Toni Tennille and David Crosby — voices who I liked to sing with on Beach Boys background vocals — and of course, Art Garfunkel."

Johnston did contribute one other small part on "Disney Girls": the whistling at the end of the song. Johnston had done the whistling on his own version of the song and he was the best whistler in the studio that day.

Stacks of Wax

Bruce Johnston of the Beach Boys wrote the song "Disney Girls" that Art Garfunkel covered on "Breakaway." After he heard Garfunkel's version, Johnston said: "My first impression was that I wished I could sing it as good as he did." (Photo by Mike Morsch)

"They couldn't believe it because there was no air on the microphone. That probably was the most astonishing thing to [Garfunkel and Perry] on the recording of the song, that during the whistling there was no air on the mic," said Johnston.

When he first heard the playback on "Disney Girls," Johnston said it was evident to him that Garfunkel had more than done justice to the song.

"My first impression was that I wished I could sing it as good as he did," said Johnston. "When somebody like Art Garfunkel covers one of your songs, you say thank you, but I'm not worthy. You're so humbled by the fact that an artist is going to share his career with you for three or four minutes and place some faith in your abilities.

"Art was definitely the voice on my song," said Johnston. "And that's all I had to do with it. It's like going to Baskin-Robbins and getting an ice cream cone with sprinkles on top of it. That's my contribution to this album — sprinkles with background vocal parts on one song."

The cover for the *Breakaway* album, featuring Garfunkel sitting at a table with a woman on each side of him, still means a lot to him, even more than 40 years later.

The woman to Garfunkel's right having her cigarette lighted is actress Helena Kallianiotes, who had appeared in the 1970 film *Five Easy Pieces*, starring Jack Nicholson. In 1973, Kallianiotes was nominated for a Golden Globe for best supporting actress for her role in the film *Kansas City Bomber*, starring Raquel Welch.

"I met Helena through Jack Nicholson. She was his friend and she's fascinating. I love this woman; she's an actress and very talented. I wanted her in the photo because I have a sweeter look on my face and she has a contrasting, darker look."

But it's not Kallianiotes who makes the album cover special to Garfunkel. It's the woman to his left, the one nuzzling up to his cheek, as she was his girlfriend at the time, Laurie Bird.

The photo shoot for the album was going to be done by photographer Norman Seeff, who in the early 1970s had established himself as a "rock" photographer.

But in 1971, Seeff left New York to take a job as a professor of photography at Bennington College in Vermont. After only a year, Seeff was still unsatisfied with his career and relocated to Los Angeles to take a job as a creative director for United Artists Records.

Seeff had scheduled the photo shoot for the *Breakaway* cover late one evening at Dan Tana's Restaurant, right next to the famous Troubadour nightclub on Santa Monica

Boulevard in Hollywood, and he was ready to go. But there was no Garfunkel.

Garfunkel and Bird were staying at the Chateau Marmont Hotel, also on nearby Sunset Boulevard, and weren't much interested in leaving their room.

"I had just gotten to know Laurie. We were new to each other and excitedly in love," said Garfunkel. "We were asleep; it was 10:30 at night. I got a call from someone saying, 'Artie, you're supposed to be down here for the photo session.' See, I was really in love. I'm a perfectionist who takes his work so seriously, but not that time. It was trumped by Laurie Bird.

"So I scrambled and put on some clothes and Laurie and I came down to do the picture. I hadn't really woken up that much yet, so I have this blasé look in the photo. And I kept thinking, I like it, that's fine. I don't want to be a choirboy now. Let me look a little wasted. And put more things on the table, make it look messier."

Bird and Garfunkel would be together until 1979, when she committed suicide by taking an overdose of Valium in the New York apartment she shared with Garfunkel, who was in France making the movie *Bad Timing* when she died. She was just 26 years old.

According to Garfunkel on his website, after Bird's death, when he sang the line "Remember me to one who lives there, she was once a true love of mine," in the Simon and Garfunkel hit "Scarborough Fair," it was sung with Laurie Bird in mind.

Breakaway would be a success for Garfunkel. It was a Top 10 album in the U.S. reaching No. 9 on the Billboard 200 Albums chart and No. 7 on the U.K. Albums chart.

Garfunkel calls the record "a make-out album."

"There's always a place for sex in the arts. And I tried to make this album so that you'd want to dance with her in the living room and then want to take her into the bedroom," said Garfunkel. "And it's creamy. That's what we were looking for. When Richard and I got to the fadeout ending of a song, we extended it and extended it. It was saying, 'No, he's not finished holding her yet. Keep the fadeout going.'"

And he calls the album "a proud piece of work."

"We were all chasing after the Beatles and *Sgt. Pepper* in those days. John, Paul, George, and Ringo, and George Martin, taught us all how to make an album into an artistic endeavor. And make the album as an art form a bigger deal, make it into a fleeting movie. Let it flow from song to song and have a connection. And we were all under the sway of album-making in that more artistic sense."

Discography

"Breakaway"
Art Garfunkel

Side one

1 "I Believe (When I Fall in Love It Will Be Forever)" (Stevie Wonder, Yvonne Wright) 3:47

2 "Rag Doll" (Steve Eaton) 3:03

3 "Break Away" (Benny Gallagher, Graham Lyle) 3:31

4 "Disney Girls" (Bruce Johnston) 4:32

5 "Waters of March" (Antônio Carlos Jobim) 3:34

Side two

1 "My Little Town" (Paul Simon) 3:51

2 "I Only Have Eyes for You" (Al Dubin, Harry Warren) 3:36

3 "Looking for the Right One" (Stephen Bishop) .... :20

4 "99 Miles from L.A." (Albert Hammond, Hal David) 3:29

5 "The Same Old Tears on a New Background" (Stephen Bishop) 3:42

Blown away by her own voice on a boom box
Inseparable
Natalie Cole

Producers and songwriters Chuck Jackson and Marvin Yancy thought Natalie Cole sounded like Aretha Franklin. That's one of the reasons that they decided to record some demo songs with Cole that they hoped to shop to all the record studios.

But none were interested. Except one: Capitol Records. Coincidentally, it was the same label that had recorded Cole's father, the legendary Nat "King" Cole.

And her first album for Capitol, *Inseparable*, made her an instant star.

"When we went into the studio, I had no idea what I was doing. I just went in there and sang. I was really young and very naive. Everyone thought that I had come from a gospel background, but I had no gospel experience. I wasn't a gospel singer," said Cole.

Recorded in 1975, the album shot to the top of the R&B album charts based on the strength of the hit single, "This Will Be (An Everlasting Love)," which also reached No. 1 on the U.S. Hot Soul Singles chart and No. 6 on the Billboard Hot 100 charts.

While making the album, Cole said "something just kind of came out of me, and it just clicked." Even after the release of *Inseparable* and its single "This Will Be," Cole admitted she had no clue where it was all going.

Natalie Cole's first album "Inseparable" made her an instant star. "But I never really thought I was that great of a singer, truthfully," she said. (Photo by Patti Myers)

"I was around these wonderful musicians that I had never been around before. They thought I was the next I-don't-know-what. I never really thought I was that great of a singer, truthfully," said Cole.

And then in early summer of 1975, while walking down the street in New York, she heard "This Will Be" for the first time on the radio.

"I heard it on this lady's big boom box and I was blown away," said Cole. "I still didn't know. It was such a new thing for me because I'd never planned on being a singer. It was like 'This is probably a one-time wonder.' When it started to actually hit and take hold, it turned into a whole different thing and my life totally changed."

It had all started with Jackson and Yancy. In 1974, Cole was living in New York and playing small clubs in the Northeast. Her manager at the time, Kevin Hunter — who also thought she sounded a lot like Aretha Franklin but wanted Cole to develop her own sound and not sing any of Franklin's songs — had arranged for Cole to open for Jerry Butler at a club in Cherry Hill, New Jersey. One of the reasons Hunter was pushing hard for the gig was that he was still working on getting Cole a recording contract, and he had gotten word that Kenny Gamble and Leon Huff — producers, songwriters, and the creative forces at Philadelphia International Records — had plans to attend the performance.

But Gamble and Huff never showed. After the show, Butler suggested to Hunter that he get in contact with two Chicago songwriters, Jackson and Yancy, who would be traveling to New York soon after the Cherry Hill show.

Hunter did just that. He and Cole scheduled a meeting with the songwriters a few weeks later at the Lillian Tang Dance Studio in New York.

Jackson and Yancy were in an R&B group called the Independents, which had a hit single in 1973 called "Leaving Me" that got to No. 21 on the U.S. billboard Hot 100 Singles chart. But the group had recently broken up, and Jackson and

Yancy had struck out on their own as songwriters and producers and they were looking for their big break.

According to her 2000 autobiography *Angel on My Shoulder*, written with Digby Diehl, Cole recalled that after the introductions, Jackson and Yancy got right down to business in that first meeting.

"Marvin [Yancy] asked me to start singing — 'Sing anything' he told me," Cole wrote in her autobiography. "I don't remember what I sang but it felt good. I wasn't more than eight bars into the song when I saw Marvin look at Chuck and Chuck look at Marvin and say 'Yesssss!' Chuck's eyes were lighting up and Marvin was laughing. I had no idea what was going on but something was happening in that room. It didn't seem like anything earth-shattering to me, but the two of them knew right away that they'd found what they'd been looking for."

Jackson and Yancy returned to Chicago and immediately began writing songs for Cole. They also had connections in Chicago with recording studios. The plan was to make a demo tape of four songs that Hunter could shop to the record labels.

Cole was still working gigs in the Northeast, but in between commitments, she would travel to Chicago and work on one song at a time for the demo tape.

Once the tape was finished, the rejections from the record labels came quickly — Columbia, RCA and Motown all said no, despite Cole's musical talent and famous father.

But Capitol said yes, thanks to Larkin Arnold, who had just been named head of the new R&B division at the label. According to Cole's autobiography, Arnold knew Jackson and Yancy from their work with the Independents, and Arnold liked what he heard from Cole, particularly two songs on the demo, "I Love Him So Much" and "You," both of which would eventually be on the *Inseparable* album at the suggestion of Arnold.

Larkin signed Cole to Capitol Records and asked Jackson and Yancy to write more songs to fill out what would become Cole's debut album.

Before recording could begin on the album, though, Cole had to fulfill the rest of her scheduled shows that had already been arranged for her by Hunter. One of those shows was in Toronto, Canada.

"We had just arrived in Toronto and I was settling into my room at the Lake Shore Boulevard Motel when there was a knock at the door," Cole wrote in her autobiography. "I opened it and what seemed like a platoon of Toronto police rushed in — both two-legged and four-legged. Between the uniformed officers, the detectives, and the German shepherds, it got real crowded in there real fast. The cops started tearing the room up until they found what they were looking for. And from the moment they arrived, it was obvious they knew what they were looking for. Eventually they unearthed a little $25 bag of heroin along with my hypodermic needles and various paraphernalia from my suitcase, and I knew I was in deep shit. To make it all a little worse, the bust came right on my birthday, February 6, 1975."

Hunter knew that Cole had struggled with a drug problem from an early age, but had tried to keep a tight rein on it. In the book, Cole called the heroin addiction "manageable" at the time.

The arrest on drug charges threatened to derail Cole's shot at the big time before it even got started. A Canadian judge eventually sentenced Cole to probation in Ontario province, which was good in one sense, in that she wasn't jailed on felony drug charges. But it created the issue of Cole not being able to leave Canada in the short term because she had to check in with Toronto police every Wednesday for a couple of months.

This delayed her getting to Chicago to begin recording for the *Inseparable* album and her commitment to Capitol

Records. That, in turn, created the issue of trying to keep the drug issues away from Capitol officials.

According to *Angel on My Shoulder*, Hunter had to scramble to arrange a series of shows for Cole throughout Canada, to give the impression that work commitments — and not probation restrictions as the result of a drug bust — were preventing Cole from getting to Chicago to record the album.

After serving out her probation in Canada, Cole was finally able to return to Chicago, but she kept her arrest and drug issues from Jackson and Yancy. The three started work on the album in early spring, 1975.

Recording was done mostly in the studio at Curtom Records, a label started by Curtis Mayfield, lead singer of the Impressions, which was a former RCA studio at 1 North Wacker Drive in Chicago. Additional recording for *Inseparable* was done at Universal Recording Studios and Paragon Studios, also in Chicago.

"After they [Jackson and Yancy] had a song roughed out, they'd bring it to me. I'd sing a little of it and if it felt like it was going somewhere, I'd keep singing right there in the studio around the piano," Cole wrote in her autobiography. "It was just ridiculous how much fun we had.

"Everything was done in Chicago, because that's where we came up with this kind of Chicago sound. It was a combination of Chuck and Marvin's songs, the way the musicians played, the attitude they had. It was distinctive, just like the Motown sound or the Philly Sound. It was unmistakable, and they created this sound for Natalie Cole. Whenever a Natalie Cole record came on, everybody knew right away what it was, and I was very proud of that," Cole wrote.

Although Jackson and Yancy had what they thought were seven or eight good songs for the album, Arnold still wasn't hearing what he thought would be a breakout single among them.

According to *Angel on My Shoulder*, Cole recalls the moment that changed everything — while they were all at Jackson's home one evening, Arnold suggested the album needed an up-tempo song with more energy.

"Chuck rose from his chair and said, 'I've just been working on this song.' He pulled this little raggedy piece of yellow paper out of his pocket and handed it to Marvin at the piano," wrote Cole. "Marvin played a few chords of what became 'This Will Be' and Larkin said excitedly, 'That's it! That's exactly what we need!'"

Cole was less convinced.

"My first reaction was, 'I can't sing that! All the hugging-and-squeezing-and-kissing-and-pleasing — forget it!' I said, 'I'm never gonna get that right,'" wrote Cole.

But she would get it right and the first single released from the *Inseparable* album would indeed be "This Will Be (An Everlasting Love)." And it would indeed become a No. 1 hit.

The title track from the album would also be a hit, reaching No. 1 on the U.S. Billboard R&B chart and No. 32 on the Billboard Hot 100 Singles chart.

Inseparable, released in May 1975, would be the first of four Top 10 R&B Natalie Cole albums released between 1975 and 1977.

A little more than a year later, in July 1976, Cole and Yancy would marry. They divorced in 1980 and Yancy died of a heart attack in 1985 at the age of 34.

Cole went on to win nine Grammy Awards and have a successful career for more than three decades, although drug addiction and health issues plagued her throughout the years.

She detailed her decades-long battle with drug addiction in *Angel on My Shoulder*. In addition, she was also diagnosed with hepatitis C in 2007, a result of those years of drug abuse. The treatments for hepatitis C led to kidney failure, and Cole had a kidney transplant in 2009.

In March 2015, Cole was still performing sold-out shows and seemed to have her health issues under control.

"I'm feeling pretty good. I've had some really crazy, crazy health issues for a while, but I feel so much better now," she said.

It would not last, though. She ended up having to cancel several shows in December 2015 due to health issues. On December 31, 2015, Natalie Cole died at the age of 65 at Cedars-Sinai Medical Center in Los Angeles of congestive heart failure.

Discography

"Inseparable"
Natalie Cole
1975

1. Needing You (Chuck Jackson / Marvin Yancy).........................2:45
2. Joey (Chuck Jackson / Marvin Yancy).....................................2:57
3. Inseparable (Chuck Jackson / Marvin Yancy) 2:26
4. I Can't Say No (Chuck Jackson / Marvin Yancy) 3:30
5. This Will Be (Chuck Jackson / Marvin Yancy) 2:50
6. Something For Nothing (Chuck Jackson & Maxine Brown / Marvin Yancy) 2:57
7. I Love Him So Much (Chuck Jackson & Maxine Brown / Marvin Yancy) 3:24
8. How Come You Won't Stay Here (Chuck Jackson & Maxine Brown / Marvin Yancy)...3:03
9. Your Face Stays In My Mind (Chuck Jackson / Marvin Yancy) 2:45
10. You (Kay Butler / Chuck Jackson / Marvin Yancy) 3:30

Surviving the stranglehold of a big psychological mess
Self-titled
Ted Nugent

It was around 3 a.m. on a Saturday in 1971, and Derek St. Holmes had just arrived home. The high school senior was in a band called Scott, and it had a Friday night gig that had kept him out late, something that his parents usually weren't too happy about.

The St. Holmes family lived in Riverview, Michigan, known as "downriver" from Detroit. St. Holmes' sister, two years his senior, was off to college, which was a break for St. Holmes. Her bedroom was bigger than his, and when she left, St. Holmes got to move into her room and claim it as his own.

On this night, though, his parents were asleep by the time St. Holmes got home. He got to his bedroom without waking them up, but he was still hyped up from the band's performance.

So with his guitar in hand, he sat on the edge of his bed and started to write a song. He got out a piece of paper and a pen and started playing the guitar and writing the lyrics, trying hard not to wake his parents.

"The next day I ran it by the band to see how we could put it together and play it. And it sounded great," said St. Holmes.

A few years later, in 1974, Scott had progressed to the point where the band opened for The Amboy Dukes.

The Dukes had formed in Detroit in 1964 and for the next decade, had numerous lineup changes . . . except one.

The only constant through that entire period was lead guitarist, songwriter, and Detroit native Ted Nugent, the "Motor City Madman."

Because Scott had opened for him, Nugent was aware of St. Holmes' talent, as was bassist Rob Grange, who had joined The Amboy Dukes lineup in 1971.

"We were opening up shows for him. I looked over many times and I saw Ted standing and watching me," said St. Holmes.

By late 1974, though, Nugent had tired of The Amboy Dukes. He decided to leave the band and start a new one, simply calling it the Ted Nugent Band. He would bring bassist Grange with him, and eventually would add drummer Cliff Davies.

But Nugent still needed a vocalist and rhythm guitarist.

At about the same time, St. Holmes had decided that a career in music wasn't in the cards. Young and newly married, he and his wife had decided to move to California because his wife's stepfather ran a construction company and had promised St. Holmes a job.

"That was hard for me, man, because I didn't want a real job," said St. Holmes. "But I was married, obligated to this girl, and at the time, loved her. And I thought that's what I needed to be doing as a man to hold up my end of the marriage."

The 16-foot U-Haul truck was packed and the couple's car was hitched to the back. They were ready to leave Michigan for California when St. Holmes went back inside the apartment one last time to get the final piece to be packed — the telephone.

"I walked into the apartment, it was probably around noon, to unplug the phone. And it rang. So I picked it up and it was Ted's road manager. And he says, 'Hey, I got you an audition with Ted. He wants to know if you can come up to Jackson, Michigan, right now, rehearse, and we'll see how this thing goes,'" said St. Holmes.

St. Holmes hesitated. Because Scott had opened for Nugent, St. Holmes had on occasion hung out with Nugent, having dinner and kicking around Nugent's Michigan farm.

"I said, 'He's not interested in anybody but him being in the forefront.' Not that I wanted to be in the forefront, but Ted didn't want to share anything," said St. Holmes.

Still, the road manager, Phil Nicholson, was insistent that St. Holmes audition for Nugent.

St. Holmes walked outside, cordless phone still in hand, where his wife was sitting in the running U-Haul truck, ready for the journey to the West Coast to start a new life. St. Holmes told her who was on the phone and what the call was about.

"She said, 'Yeah, go ahead, take the car off the back of the truck and drive up to Jackson and see what it's like,'" said St. Holmes.

The audition wasn't at Nugent's farm, but rather at Grange's house, where the band usually rehearsed. St. Holmes played for Nugent and Grange for about 20 minutes.

"Ted stops, looks at me and goes, 'How many Marshall amps do you want?' I'm sitting there thinking, 'Couldn't you just say, "Hey, would you like to join my band? Hey, you sound great; I'd love to have you in my band?" But he couldn't bring himself to do any of that, except be coy and say, 'How many Marshalls do you want?' So I went, 'I'll take two stacks.' And that's how it started," said St. Holmes.

Derek St. Holmes was officially a member of the Ted Nugent Band. And it was time to make an album.

The self-titled *Ted Nugent* album was the new band's first effort. It would be recorded at The Sound Pit in downtown Atlanta, Georgia.

The band members — Nugent, St. Holmes, Grange, and Davies — had decided to co-write the songs for the album. But St. Holmes was about to get his first lesson on working with Nugent.

"Back then, Ted was younger. He's still got an ego, but then he had such an ego that he just didn't want anybody being better than him," said St. Holmes. "I think at that time, he'd been beaten up so badly by other musicians and other managers. He just wasn't going to let it happen again."

As a result, the 22-year-old St. Holmes was overshadowed by the more experienced Nugent.

"For me, that was very lucky and very unlucky, because I couldn't blossom. Every time I came up with what I thought was a really good idea, it was shot down by or controlled by Ted," said St. Holmes. "I really had to fight through all that stuff to make some of my points get across, even though I would get fired, then I'd be rehired, then I'd get fired, then I'd get rehired. Truly, it was just a big psychological mess."

Still, the collective and creative effort — despite the difficulties — became apparent in the songs. The first cut, "Stranglehold," an 8-minute and 22-second song, would set the tone for Nugent's career from that point. Although the songwriting credits for "Stranglehold" are Nugent and Grange, the lead singer on it is St. Holmes.

"I didn't know what co-writing was. And I didn't know that you get royalties for co-writing, that you get paid on that. You actually put together a contract and put percentages on the paper. But we didn't know anything about that. So we didn't get any of that," said St. Holmes.

There was still a collaborative spirit during the making of *Ted Nugent* though, despite the fact the other band members didn't get credit.

"Ted had great, great song ideas. He would bring them in, and — like any good writer — at that point he would go, 'This is what I've got' and we'd go, 'OK, what if we go here, what if I sing this note? I know your melody sounds really good and I can use some of it, but you didn't quite finish," said St. Holmes.

"I know because I sing. Ted was not a singer. So I would melodically change something, but because I'm not a trained musician, I wouldn't know how to write the notes. But I knew how to sing them, so I would sing the melody from what Ted had and it would make the song work. In fact, that means I wrote it. But we didn't get paid for that."

There is one song, however, that was written, arranged, and performed by St. Holmes on the album, and for which he gets all the credit. It's called "Hey Baby," and it is the song that St. Holmes wrote in his bedroom at 3 a.m. that Saturday morning in 1971 when he was a senior in high school and still living in his parents' house in Riverview, Michigan.

The *Ted Nugent* album, released in September 1975, finally reached No. 28 on the Billboard 200 Album charts in 1976. "Hey Baby" was the only single from the album to chart, checking in at No. 72 on the Billboard Hot 100 Singles chart. The album would go on to be a double-platinum album in the United States, and a gold album in Canada.

The album would also start a run of charting albums in the U.S. for Nugent throughout the rest of the 1970s and into the 1980s, including *Free-for-All* in 1976 (No. 24); *Cat Scratch Fever* in 1977 (No. 17); *Weekend Warriors* in 1978 (No. 24); *State of Shock* in 1979 (No. 18); and *Scream Dream* in 1980 (No. 13).

St. Holmes believes the period from the start of the band in 1975 through 1978 was some of the best music the band produced.

"But if you listen to that album [*Ted Nugent*], and you go listen to any other album after *Double Live Gonzo* (a 1978 live album that reached No. 13 on the Billboard chart), they don't sound the same," said St. Holmes. "The reason they don't sound the same is because Cliff Davies and Rob Grange and Derek St. Holmes and Ted Nugent weren't together and they didn't write the songs. But we wrote the songs between 1975 and 1978. We put them all together."

Nugent and St. Holmes had their issues over the years. They first parted ways in 1978 over creative and financial issues. St. Holmes, Grange, and ex-Montrose drummer Denny Carmassi formed a band called St. Paradise and released one self-titled album in 1979.

St. Holmes then hooked up with Aerosmith guitarist Brad Whitford and released a self-titled album called *Whitford-St. Holmes* in 1981. The two have more recently hooked up again and released another album — 35 years later — called *Reunion* in 2016.

Over the years, St. Holmes and Nugent have been able to patch up their differences, and St. Holmes has toured with Nugent the past several years when the latter is on the road.

"It's all water under the bridge now. Ted and I are good buddies," said St. Holmes. "Bottom line — Ted is like my big brother and sometimes we get along and sometimes we don't. But I listen to him because if it wasn't for him, I wouldn't be here. If it wasn't for some of his guidance, I wouldn't be here. But if it wasn't for some of my musical talent, he wouldn't where he is. As you get older, things do become more clear."

St. Holmes said that in the 1970s, Nugent was on a path and St. Holmes understands that now better than he did then.

"Ted is always on a mission. And I get that. The thing is, I'm only on a musical journey. I'm not on a hunting journey, I'm not on a musical/hunting/political journey — I'm on a musical journey. So when you crash into my world, I'm strictly about music, and that's all," said St. Holmes. "I think that was also something that always didn't coincide with Ted."

As for the *Ted Nugent* album, St. Holmes said that was the album that started him on his musical journey.

"I like that album. It formulated my career, so I guess I should say that I love it to death. But there are a lot of things on that album production-wise that I would have done differently," said St. Holmes.

"I'm not trying to be egotistical at all. I just know that I'm sixty-two years old and I don't hear much rock and roll anymore. Especially like in the era of Led Zeppelin, Black Sabbath, Aerosmith, Ted Nugent, all that stuff, that big power rock is just simply gone," he said. "I guess back then we thought we were trying to run with Zeppelin. We were trying to be that kind of band, in that genre with Aerosmith, Led Zeppelin, Black Sabbath. We kind of thought that we were somewhere in there."

Newly married Derek St. Holmes and his wife had decided to move to California because his wife's stepfather ran a construction company and had promised St. Holmes a job. But then he got a phone call to audition for Ted Nugent. (Photo by Mike Morsch)

Discography

"Ted Nugent"
Self-titled
September 1975
(All songs written by Ted Nugent except where noted)

"Stranglehold" 8:22
"Stormtroopin'" 3:07
"Hey Baby" (Derek St. Holmes) 4:00
"Just What the Doctor Ordered" 3:43
"Snakeskin Cowboys" 4:38
"Motor City Madhouse" 4:30
"Where Have You Been All My Life" 4:04
"You Make Me Feel Right at Home" 2:54
"Queen of the Forest" 3:34
"Magic Party" (Studio outtake) 2:55

Encouraging the booty shakers
Part 3
KC and The Sunshine Band

KC and The Sunshine Band was on a roll. Its self-titled second studio album, released in 1975, had shot all the way up to No. 4 on the U.S. Billboard 200 Albums chart on the strength of two No. 1 Billboard Hot 100 hits, "That's the Way (I Like It)" and "Get Down Tonight."

It was in the early stages of the popularity of dance music — commonly referred to as "disco" music — in the 1970s and KC and The Sunshine Band were at the forefront of it.

While touring to support that album, Harry Wayne Casey — a.k.a. "KC" — observed something at the band's shows: People seemed to be what he described as "fighting" the urge to have a good time. They appeared to be having internal struggles and didn't seem to be enjoying themselves as much as Casey thought they should. So he decided to write a song to help people get over that feeling and get up out of their seats. And the result was the single, "(Shake, Shake, Shake) Shake Your Booty."

"While touring and being out there, I'd see people wanting to have a good time, but just not being themselves," said Casey, who wrote the song with his then-writing partner, Peter Finch. "That songs says, 'Don't fight the feeling, give yourself a chance, shake your booty. You're the best in the world, I can tell. You should know too, shake your booty.' Just enjoy it. That's what that song is really about," said Casey.

By the time "Part 3" was ready to be released, Harry Wayne Casey was confident in his songwriting process and even more confident that he had written some more hits. (Photo by Mike Morsch)

"Shake Your Booty" would be one of the anchors of KC and The Sunshine Band's next album, simply titled *Part 3*. Released in October 1976, the album would not only feature another No. 1 hit on the Billboard Hot 100 Singles chart in "Shake Your Booty," but also "I'm Your Boogie Man," which also reached No. 1 on the Billboard Hot 100 Singles chart, and "Keep It Comin' Love," which got to No. 2 on the Hot 100 Singles chart but did reach No. 1 on the Billboard Hot Soul Singles chart.

Despite the success of the singles, the album itself only got to No. 13 on the Billboard 200 Albums chart. But it further solidified KC and The Sunshine Band's position as the hottest dance music group in the mid-1970s.

One reason was that Casey and Finch were always writing and recording songs, but under no pressure from their record label.

"To be honest, the records were recorded almost a year before they came out. So by the time you were hearing 'Get Down Tonight' on the radio, I had already started the *Part 3* album," said Casey. "There was really no pressure. I had finished one album and started right away doing the next one. That's how I operated. We were always just working on the next album, sometimes a year before you were going to hear it."

Casey had begun working at TK Records in Miami, a wholesale record distributor, literally starting at the bottom in the shipping department. It was there that he hooked up with Finch, an engineer at the company, and they started writing songs together.

The duo wrote their first hit, "Rock Your Baby," for George McCrae. The record was released in May 1974 and spent two weeks in July at No. 1 on the Billboard Hot 100 Singles chart.

But KC and The Sunshine Band would quickly become the top stars at TK Records and as such, Casey and Finch would not only write and record the band's albums, they would also produce them.

"TK had a lot of one-hit wonders, so after we had the second album, it was kind of like, 'Holy cow, we're really doing it here.' I think we were the only artists at the label that had more than one or two hits," said Casey. "So I was never under any pressure because I had a great relationship with the record company. I pretty much was the record company in a way. I had the chance to do whatever I wanted to do at whatever pace I wanted to do it at."

So when it came time to release another album, KC and The Sunshine Band was not only well-positioned within the company, Casey and Finch already had songs completed and were ready to record.

The songwriting itself was a process for Casey, but one that he had developed early in his career, and continued to hone through the mid-1970s.

"The original process might have taken a few hours or so, but once lyrics start coming into the play, it flows," said Casey. "Sometimes I start a song and I just keep going until I'm finished with it. Other times, I get through most of it, then come back and re-attack it another day. Or after I've written it, go back over it and start changing a few words here and there to clear up the thoughts that I'm trying to portray in the lyrics."

Casey said that it's important to understand that sometimes in their infancy, songs are just ideas. For example, "I'm Your Boogie Man" was originally called "I'll Be a Son of a Gun."

"It wasn't called 'I'm You're Boogie Man' in the original writing of the words. It became very easy for me to come up with an idea or melody and then I just kind of sing along as we're recording and get the melody down. Some of the lyrics then actually end up on the actual record because I can do that quickly," said Casey. "But sometimes it was like a whole rewrite for me. Not that often, but sometimes. I've been writing since I was a young kid and I would write to deal with life and to deal with situations going on in my life. So that was all kind of natural to me."

He said that the song "Keep It Comin' Love" is exactly what the title says it is.

"Keep love coming, don't stop it. Let the love keep flowing and never let it stop. I mean, sometimes you have all this love and sometimes you let it all go and it disappears and it turns into hate or other things. Keep the love coming; I don't want it to stop. I don't want you to ever stop loving me — just keep coming at me with the same intensity from the very first day we met," said Casey.

By the time *Part 3* was ready to be released, Casey was confident in his songwriting process and even more confident that he and Finch had written some more hits.

"I knew every one of those songs were hits. I definitely knew that. I felt that. There was no doubt in my mind that it was a hit album, too," said Casey. "I was just doing what I loved to do. To me, it was just a process. It was what I did. It was like delivering the mail. It was like working in an office building. What I thought I was doing was no different to me than anybody else who has a talent. Everyone that does something in their lives has a certain talent, and that's why they're doing what they're doing. And so, to me it was just, that's what I do."

But the run didn't continue for KC and The Sunshine Band. And neither did disco music as the decade progressed. The *Part 3* album was followed by two more moderately successful albums, *Who Do Ya (Love)* in 1978 and *Do You Wanna Go Party*, in 1979. The latter featured the band's final No. 1 hit, a ballad called "Please Don't Go."

The band did have one more big success in 1977 with the release of the film *Saturday Night Fever*. The Casey-Finch song "Boogie Shoes," which was on the band's *KC and The Sunshine Band* album from 1975, was included in the film's soundtrack.

Although inclusion in the soundtrack put "Boogie Shoes" back on the Billboard Pop Singles charts at No. 35, it also created some consternation for Casey, which continues to this day.

Bee Gees' songs dominated the *Saturday Night Fever* soundtrack and because of the film's popularity, the Bee Gees themselves have gotten a lot of the credit for popularizing the disco era.

That's rubbed Casey the wrong way since the 1970s.

"I've always felt like the Rodney Dangerfield of music, where I got no respect. My band, I always felt like, got pushed to the side for some reason. We were the main creators and the main engine behind that dance revolution. We were actually the driving force behind what changed music in the 1970s. We've never gotten that kind of credit for whatever reason," said Casey. "People know my songs, but they don't know the names of the songs sometimes. They hear KC and The Sunshine Band and they go, 'Who?' But when they hear the songs, they go, 'Oh, yeah.'"

KC and The Sunshine Band still performs and draws big crowds at its shows. Casey is still writing and producing his own songs. And dance music has become popular again.

"It's bigger than it's ever been. The top songs are dance records," said Casey. "I'm having a blast and there's more to come. I'll stop doing it when I can't do it anymore."

Discography

"Part 3"
KC and The Sunshine Band
October 1976
(All songs written by Harry Wayne Casey and Richard Finch)

Side One

"Baby I Love You (Yes, I Do)"..4:43

"Wrap Your Arms Around Me"...3:47

"I Like to Do It" 2:57

"(Shake, Shake, Shake) Shake Your Booty"................................3:06

Side Two

"Let's Go Party"...2:57

"Come on In"..3:25

"I'm Your Boogie Man" 4:05

"Keep It Comin' Love"..4:23

Avoiding the electric fan in favor of spiders and snakes
Let Your Love Flow
The Bellamy Brothers

It was the late 1960s and brothers Howard and David Bellamy had moved from their home in Darby, Florida, to Atlanta, Georgia, and formed a band called Jericho, hoping to make a living playing music.

The band played gigs all over the Southwest, but the finances just weren't coming in. They couldn't pay their rent, so they dissolved the band and returned home to Florida.

The Bellamy brothers were raised on the gulf side of central Florida, on a cattle ranch that also included orange groves. Many times as a young boy, in that hot, humid Florida weather, the work was so hard that Howard Bellamy thought he would die with a garden hoe in his hand.

Although neither had any formal music training, they came from a household that enjoyed music. The brothers learned how to play guitar and several other instruments, with the hopes that a career in music would some day get them off the ranch and away from working in the orange groves.

But they had given music a shot as young men, and now they were back home, in their early to mid-20s, looking for their next move.

One evening after returning home, the boys went out and tossed down a few beers. Actually, more than a few beers. They had tied one on, but they didn't want their mother to see them in that condition.

Their mother had seen them that way before, and she didn't want to see it again. To discourage them from doing so, she would place an electric fan in the doorway of the home's darkened main entrance.

The boys learned quickly that stumbling home in the dark after a night of drinking and kicking over that electric fan in the doorway made quite a ruckus. So much so that it would wake up their mother, and she would invariably give them seven kinds of hell about their drinking.

On this particular evening, Howard and David decided they didn't want to incur the wrath of their mother by tripping over the electric fan. So they decided to spend the night in a nearby bunkhouse on the grounds of the ranch.

The bunkhouse was in need of a good cleaning, but David and Howard settled into their sleeping bags anyway for the evening.

About an hour into what they thought was going to be a peaceful night to sleep it off, Howard felt something in his sleeping bag. It turned out that a chicken snake, one of the many critters roaming around the wide-open spaces of the ranch, had climbed into the sleeping bag with Howard.

"I literally made a new door running out of that bunkhouse," said Howard Bellamy. "When I woke up the next morning, after all that carrying on, that's when David wrote a song about it. He wrote it, but I guess I inspired it."

That inspiration turned into the song "Spiders and Snakes," which was released by Jim Stafford in November 1973. The single, which by the time of its release featured co-writing credits for David Bellamy and Stafford, was one of the top hits of 1974, reaching No. 3 on both the U.S. Billboard Hot 100 and the Cashbox Top 100 singles charts and No. 1 on the Canadian RPM Top Singles chart.

It also had given the Bellamy Brothers, as they were now going to be known, another chance at the music industry.

Stacks of Wax

    This time they headed to Los Angeles, not knowing anybody but Stafford, with whom they lived upon arrival. When Stafford's road manager, Leo Gallagher, left to pursue other interests — he would end up gaining fame as the comedian Gallagher, who smashed watermelons with a big mallet as part of his act — Howard took over as Stafford's road manager to make ends meet, while the Bellamy Brothers worked local gigs and tried to get noticed enough to get a record contract.

    In the meantime, they were hanging out with the artists in the Los Angeles music scene at the time — Bob Dylan, James Taylor, Van Morrison — as well as West Coast country rock groups like the Byrds and Poco.

    Eventually, the Bellamy Brothers did get noticed and signed a deal with Warner Brothers Records/Curb Records in 1975. They also started sharing the stage with the likes of the Beach Boys, the Doobie Brothers, and Loggins and Messina.

    Among the early friends the brothers made in Los Angeles were a record producer named Phil Gernhard, and members of Neil Diamond's band, most notably Dennis St. John, Diamond's drummer.

    A roadie for Diamond, Larry E. Williams, had written a song for Diamond, but the singer declined to record it. Johnny Rivers, who had a string of hits in the 1960s, including "Secret Agent Man," "Poor Side of Town," and "Baby I Need Your Lovin'," had followed that in 1972 with another hit single, "Rockin' Pneumonia and the Boogie Woogie Flu," also passed on the Williams song.

    St. John, however, thought it was perfect for the Bellamy Brothers.

    "He [St. John] came over to our house one night and said he had a song that really sounded like something we would do. That's just kind of how it happened," said Howard Bellamy.

    The song was "Let Your Love Flow."

"And I thought it was the best song that I had ever heard," said Bellamy.

The Bellamy Brothers did indeed decide to record the song, but they weren't the first. Despite the fact that Diamond and Rivers had passed on "Let Your Love Flow," not everybody did. Singer-songwriter Gene Cotton — who had four Top 40 hits between 1976 and 1978, including "You're a Part of Me," a duet with Kim Carnes — had recorded the song, but had not secured the rights to it.

"We'd written most of our own songs, but this song just felt like our song when we heard it," said Howard Bellamy. "It's so important to have the right marriage between a song and an artist and this one was just the song for us."

But not everybody was as excited about the song, especially record company officials.

"We really had to push to get it out. I'm still surprised that we won out on that. We didn't win many battles in those days. They [record company officials] really didn't want us to record the song. They weren't as hot over it as we were. But we kept on and kept on and finally we talked them into it."

Their persistence paid off. Not only did Curb Records officials relent and let the Bellamy Brothers record "Let Your Love Flow," but the company also decided to release the song as a single.

"I was so pumped about the version that we had," said Bellamy.

And his instinct was right. The song took off like a rocket, first in Europe, and then back around in the United States.

The Bellamy Brothers had a monster pop hit on their hands. And it had created a few more complications for them.

First, the record company wanted an album on which it could place the big single. Second, the record company really didn't know how to market the Bellamy Brothers. "Let

Your Love Flow" had raced up the pop charts to No. 1 on the Billboard Hot 100 Singles, but had also made it as high as No. 21 on the Billboard Hot Country Singles.

Were they a pop group or a country group?

As for an album, the Bellamy Brothers were nowhere ready to make one.

"It was like, oh my, we've got a monster record, what do we do now? The song had made such an impact, we had to scramble to put our career together to go with it," said Bellamy. "In those days, singles were the big thing. You'd get these producers that put more emphasis on singles, and the situation that we were in was kind of that way. We wanted to be more album-oriented, but we were in a big head-butting situation with the label. We didn't really agree with them on anything."

Finally, though, the Bellamy Brothers' debut album, also titled *Let Your Love Flow*, was completed in 1976.

"We got the other songs done, but we scrambled to do them. No one could imagine the battle we were going through with the record company at that time. It was unbelievable," said Bellamy. "We were just two farm boys from Florida saying 'What the hell have we gotten ourselves into?' Thank goodness there were two of us. We just battled through it and somehow survived."

Produced by their friend Gernhard, the album contained 10 songs, including the song "Inside of My Guitar," co-written by David Bellamy and Jim Stafford that had been on the B side of the "Let Your Love Flow" single.

David and Howard Bellamy wrote all the other songs on the album with the exception of "Satin Sheets," the first song on the A side of the album, which was written by Willis Alan Ramsey. In 1972, Ramsey wrote and recorded the song "Muskrat Candlelight," covered in 1973 by the band America, which had a minor hit with it, and again in 1976 by the Captain & Tennille, both with the revised title "Muskrat Love."

Still, the label didn't know what to do with "Let Your Love Flow." In fact, one of the most popular songs of the era that followed "Let Your Love Flow" to the top of the Billboard Hot 100 Singles chart in 1976 was "Disco Duck," a satirical novelty dance song performed by radio personality Rick Dees & His Cast of Idiots.

"We didn't start out as a country act, even though we were country. The people that we were involved with, they didn't know what in the hell we were," said Bellamy. "That was one of big problems. And people still don't know what the devil we are. We've never fit into any particular mold."

While the "Let Your Love Flow" single was a chart-topper, the album itself didn't do nearly as well. It got to No. 21 in the United Kingdom, but only to No. 69 in the U.S. and No. 75 in Canada.

The Bellamy Brothers would make another splash in 1979 with their fourth studio album for Warner Brothers Records/Curb Records, *The Two and Only*, which was solidly country music this time.

Three singles from the album made the country music charts: "Lovin' On," which reached No. 16 in the U.S. and No. 25 in Canada; "You Ain't Just Whistlin' Dixie," which got to No. 5 in the U.S. and No. 11 in Canada; and the big hit, "If I Said You Had a Beautiful Body Would You Hold It Against Me," which reached No. 1 in the U.S., No. 2 in Switzerland, No. 3 in the UK and No. 24 in Canada.

"Thank goodness we could follow up 'Let Your Love Flow.' We didn't do it right away, but we followed it up quickly enough that everybody still remembered who we were. So we took off again," said Bellamy.

The 1980s were even better for the Bellamy Brothers. The band was huge. It had five Top 20 albums during the decade and 22 Top 10 singles, including nine that made it to No. 1 on the U.S. Billboard Hot Country Singles chart.

And it all started with "Let Your Love Flow."

Stacks of Wax

"It makes you believe that anything can truly happen. In our case, it really did. We didn't plan it. It makes you believe in fate a lot. A lot of times when we had tried our hardest to get something going, nothing happened. It was just by fate we fell into an incredible song. It's almost like it was written in the stars," said Bellamy. "But you know, looking back, had we not taken a shot, no one would have ever heard of the Bellamy Brothers. It's strange. People say, 'Why did you do it, why did you move to L.A.?' You have to take a shot and then you figure out how to maneuver after you get into the situation. That's what we did — we took a shot and we really maneuvered."

Over the course of their 40-year career so far, Bellamy estimates that he and his brother have performed "Let Your Love Flow" nearly 8,000 times onstage.

"One great thing about our careers — and there are a lot of great things, even though it's been as crazy as anybody's career how it happened — we have songs that have had long lives," said Bellamy. "And people still get excited. When you go and do one-nighters with new faces, I can honestly say that singing 'Let Your Love Flow' has never gotten old."

And if it ever does, all Bellamy does is remind himself of those hot days working in the orange groves of the Florida ranch where he and his brother grew up.

"Any time we're out there and I think the road is hard, I look back on how we were raised. We don't have bad days now. You think it's great and you appreciate it and think you're very fortunate for what has happened to you," he said.

Discography

"Let Your Love Flow"
The Bellamy Brothers
1976

Side One

"Satin Sheets" (Willis Alan Ramsey) 4:35

"Nothin' Heavy" (David Bellamy)... 3:20

"Rainy, Windy, Sunshine (Roadeo Road)" (David Bellamy, Howard Bellamy) 4:08

"Let Fantasy Live" (David Bellamy)... 4:15

"Highway 2-18 (Hang On To Your Dreams)" (David Bellamy, Howard Bellamy) 3:06

Side Two

"Let Your Love Flow" (Larry E. Williams)................................. 3:16

"Livin' In The West" (David Bellamy) 4:46

"I'm The Only Sane Man Left Alive" (David Bellamy) 3:48

"Inside Of My Guitar" (David Bellamy, Jim Stafford)................ 3:19

"Hell Cat" (David Bellamy) 3:00

Movin' up to the big time with 'Movin' Out'
The Stranger
Billy Joel

Billy Joel was ready to make a change. On his first three albums — *Cold Spring Harbor* in 1971, *Piano Man* in 1973 and *Streetlife Serenade* in 1974 — he had used studio musicians. When he toured in support of those albums, Joel had a different set of musicians in his band.

One of the band members on the *Streetlife Serenade* tour in 1975 was fellow New Yorker, bassist Doug Stegmeyer, who had once been in a band named Topper along with other Long Islanders Russell Javors, Liberty DeVitto, and Howard Emerson.

When it came time for Joel to record his fourth album *Turnstiles*, he wanted to put together a touring band that included other New York musicians, ones who exuded a New York energy that could establish continuity in the music by also being used in the recording studio.

Among the first things Joel was looking for was a drummer — a New York-style drummer — one who was hard-hitting and aggressive. Since Stegmeyer had already established a rapport with Joel on the *Streetlife Serenade* tour, he was comfortable recommending to Joel that he audition Stegmeyer's former Topper band mate, Liberty DeVitto.

Joel agreed to hear DeVitto play. But the audition wouldn't be the first time that Joel's and DeVitto's paths had crossed.

When they were both teenagers in the mid-1960s, there was a Long Island club called My House, which didn't have a liquor license but catered to young people, offering them a place to come and listen to music. Bands like the Soul Survivors and Vanilla Fudge appeared at the club. And opening for those bands in those days were Joel's band the Hassles, and DeVitto's band, the New Rock Workshop.

Joel and DeVitto would see each other in passing at the club, enough to say hello to each other, but nothing more.

Now, 10 years later, DeVitto would try to impress the Piano Man enough to get the gig as a permanent member of Joel's touring and recording band.

"I had to go in to audition for Billy. After I went through the songs on *Piano Man* and *Streetlife Serenade*, Billy said, 'I'm going to record a new album. What would you do on these songs?' And he played me some songs that would eventually be on *Turnstiles*," said DeVitto.

DeVitto laid down his drums on the songs that Joel played for him. And Joel was impressed. DeVitto got the gig.

"Billy was pretty amazed at how fast I picked up the material. What he didn't know until twenty-five years later was that Doug Stegmeyer had slipped me a tape of all those songs ahead of time."

Joel, Stegmeyer, and DeVitto recorded the basic tracks for *Turnstiles* and soon thereafter, Stegmeyer and DeVitto suggested to Joel that he consider adding the other members of Topper: guitarists Howie Emerson and Russell Javors. Joel once again agreed. Saxophonist Richie Cannata was also added to the group and Joel had his band to finish *Turnstiles*.

The *Turnstiles* album marked Joel's musical return to New York from California, where he had gone early in his career. It also was notable because not only was it the first album on which Joel's touring band would appear, but it would also be the first time that Joel would produce one of his own albums.

But according to DeVitto, *Turnstiles*, released in May 1976, only sold about 50,000 copies. It did feature the song "New York State of Mind," but that song wasn't released as a single at the time, only becoming popular years later because it was a fan favorite at Joel concerts.

Joel was now four albums into his career without a real breakthrough. He had moderate success with the *Piano Man* album, which got to No. 27 on the U.S. Billboard 200 Albums chart, and followed that up with getting to No. 35 on the same chart with the *Streetlife Serenade* album.

The song "Piano Man" was Joel's highest-charting single to that point, checking in at No. 25 on the Billboard Hot 100 Singles chart.

By the end of 1976, while still on the *Turnstiles* tour, officials at Columbia Records, Joel's label, were expecting more from him on his next album, which would eventually be called *The Stranger*.

"So Billy is four albums in and that was back when record companies used to have artist development. They would wait if they felt an artist was getting better," said DeVitto. "When *The Stranger* came along, this was the one that Columbia Records was saying, if this doesn't happen, we're dropping Billy Joel from the label. This will be it."

With the pressure on, Joel realized he needed to concentrate on the music. And that he needed a strong producer.

Enter Sir George Martin, the record producer, arranger, and composer for all of the Beatles' original albums. After the Beatles broke up in 1970, Martin had moved on to producing other artists, most notably the band America. By late 1976, Martin had produced America's 1974 album *Holiday,* which reached No. 3 on the U.S. Billboard 200 Albums chart; *Hearts* in 1975, which reached No. 3 on the album chart; and *Hideaway* in 1976, which got to No. 11.

Martin was interested in producing an album for Joel.

"I remember that we heard that George Martin was coming to see us play. We were all excited. This is unbelievable, this is going to be so great, the Beatles' producer, coming to see us," said DeVitto.

The legendary producer caught one of the performances on the *Turnstiles* tour and after the show he approached Joel about a possible collaboration on Joel's next album.

But Martin had one request: He didn't want to use Joel's touring band — the band that Joel had taken such care to put together with the express intent of using it for his studio albums — on the next record. Martin wanted to use studio musicians.

"He tells Billy after the show, 'I want to produce you, but I want to use studio musicians.' Billy says to him, 'Love me, love my band,' and turns him down. Turns down George Martin," said DeVitto. "We were like, 'OK, forget about him. What did he do? Just the Beatles. And maybe America? So what.'"

Joel was still without a strong producer. The next big name to come take a look at the band on the *Turnstiles* tour was Phil Ramone, and by this time, he was as big a deal as George Martin. The list of artists that Ramone had produced was a *Who's Who* of the music industry of that era, including Frank Sinatra, Bob Dylan, the Band, Ray Charles, and Aretha Franklin. Ramone had won his first Grammy as co-producer with Paul Simon on Simon's 1975 album *Still Crazy After All These Years*.

Ramone first heard Joel and his band perform at Carnegie Hall in New York, also during the *Turnstiles* tour.

"When Phil saw us, he saw the raw energy that we had. We had playing live down. We could rock a place. That's how Billy became popular. People liked his records, and the people who didn't like his records would see him live and then they would like him," said DeVitto. "When Phil heard us, he knew how to get what he heard onto a record."

Joel now had a strong producer.

While the *Turnstiles* tour had helped convince Ramone to sign on for the next album, which was a big positive, it also could have provided a negative challenge for Joel in those days. The cycle of making albums and then touring in support of those albums could be an exhausting existence in the 1970s, as record companies demanded that bands deliver albums at a fast pace, which would help capitalize on any momentum that a group had going, and keep the band's music in front of the public.

But Joel continued to write new songs while on the *Turnstiles* tour. DeVitto recalled how one song that would appear on *The Stranger* evolved while he, Cannata, and Joel were sitting around the hotel pool one evening.

"We'd be staying at a Holiday Inn, or something like that," said DeVitto. "We'd pull in, then we'd all go meet outside by the pool. It was kind of a motor inn, rather than a hotel. We'd be out there and Richie would look at Billy and say, 'Man, this is so great. This is wonderful. What you did really paid off.'"

The sarcasm and kidding around would be clearly evident among the road-weary musicians, and Joel would play along.

"Billy would act like he'd moved from the city to Long Island. And he would say, 'Yeah, this has been great; look at the pool I have here.' And then he'd say, 'You've got to come inside and look at the basement, see what I did with the basement. I put a bar in there, it's beautiful.' And then Billy would say, 'When are you people going to move out of the city? Come on out here to the Island — it's beautiful.'"

Joel would use the exchange as the inspiration to write the song "Movin' Out," which would appear as the No. 1 track on the A-side of *The Stranger* album.

Inspiration for songs could come from just about anywhere. DeVitto said that during one stop in Knoxville, Tennessee, the circus was in town. DeVitto and the band's sound guy, Brian Ruggles, decided to take in the circus.

When they got back to the hotel, they encountered Joel, running down the motel hallway, carrying an acoustic guitar, yelling, "I've got a song I want you to hear!"

"Now I'm an Italian Catholic, right?" said DeVitto. "And Billy plays me this song and I say, 'Oh God, you can't say that in a song.'"

The song was "Only the Good Die Young," and Joel put it on *The Stranger* album as well. It was one of four singles released from the album and did confirm DeVitto's worries at the time because of its controversial lyrics about a young man who was determined to take the virginity of a young Catholic girl.

In a 2008 interview with Bill DeMain for *Performing Songwriter* magazine, Joel said that "the point of the song wasn't so much anti-Catholic, as pro-lust."

The girl in the song is Virginia Callahan, whom Joel had a crush on during his high school days on Long Island. According to Joel in the interview, he had originally written it as a reggae song.

Once the *Turnstiles* tour ended and it was time to head back into the studio for the next album, Ramone was indeed in charge. And he made the band members feel comfortable and confident.

"In the studio, Phil made us feel like we were a family. We called him 'Uncle Phil.' We were like his kids. He was developing us into this great recording band. We already played great at our live shows and now he was honing us into this great recording band," said DeVitto.

During the recording sessions, which were done at A&R Recording Studios at 799 Seventh Avenue in New York City in July and August 1977, Ramone had what he called "pre-food takes" and "post-food takes."

"We would order food, usually Chinese food, and Phil would say, 'OK, let's go out and try to get a take.' And we'd run the song down and then we'd be hungry," said DeVitto. "And in the middle of a song, you could see the guys coming in and delivering the food. And you're hungry and you're playing like, 'I got to get this take because I'm starving.'

"We'd finish a take, then we'd go and eat. And then Phil would say, 'OK, go out and do it again.' But now we were satisfied and happy," said DeVitto. "And it was always the pre-food take that made it. Because we were always hungry. And that's the way it should be with a band. A band should always be hungry because if you're hungry, you're going to try harder."

Although the core group of the band — by this time consisting of Joel, Stegmeyer, DeVitto, and Cannata — was responsible for most of the music on *The Stranger*, Ramone and Joel did use a variety of studio musicians and background vocalists on some songs.

And fortunately for Joel, Columbia Records' patience with his development paid off. *The Stranger* was released in late September 1977, and it was the breakthrough album that all involved were hoping it would be, spending six weeks at No. 2 on the U.S. Billboard Albums chart. It was kept out of the No. 1 spot by the *Saturday Night Fever* soundtrack album by the Bee Gees.

Of the nine songs on the album, all credited to Joel as writer and composer, four singles made the Billboard Hot 100 chart: "Just the Way You Are" at No. 3; "Movin' On" and "She's Always a Woman," both of which reached No. 17; and "Only the Good Die Young" at No. 24.

When the album was released, "Only the Good Die Young" wasn't a big deal, according to Joel in the interview with *Performing Songwriter*.

"But then Columbia decided to put it out as a single, and that's when there were problems," said Joel. "There was a radio station at Seton Hall College in New Jersey. They banned it."

The reason the station banned it was because Seton Hall was affiliated with the Catholic archdiocese in Newark, New

Jersey. After that, the song was banned by the St. Louis archdiocese, and then it was banned in Boston.

"The single had been out a short amount of time and wasn't doing well," Joel said in the *Performing Songwriter* interview. "The minute they banned it, it started shooting up the charts, because nothing sells a record like a ban or a boycott."

As is normally the case when a band is recording an album, band members have no way of knowing for sure if they're making a hit record.

"I just knew that it sounded good when we came in and listened. When you record, you play a part and you're concentrating. I'm a drummer that's playing a part. And then I get off the drums and I go into the control room and I'm another person listening to what that guy who just played the drums did. It's kind of an out-of-body experience," said DeVitto.

"The way Phil made it sound, it was like, holy cow, I've never heard anything like that before. It sounded really good. He made it sound very big," he said. "You never think that you're making history. You just think, well, we're just doing what we do. Just a bunch of guys who are doing what they love to do. That's all. Being middle class Long Island guys, I think the music reflected that."

DeVitto does recall, though, the moment after *The Stranger* album hit big that he realized that the band had accomplished something special. It was after a gig at the Daughters of the American Revolution Hall in Washington, D.C.

"When we walked out after the show, Billy got mobbed by the girls. I remember standing off to the side, looking at that and saying to myself, 'I think we did it,'" said DeVitto.

The Stranger eventually overtook Simon and Garfunkel's 1970 *Bridge Over Troubled Water* album to become the best-selling album for Columbia Records at the time.

Stacks of Wax

"On *The Stranger* album, we got paid as musicians, as side guys. It became 'the other album' that everybody bought. If you went into the record store to buy *Saturday Night Fever*, you bought *The Stranger*, too. If you went in to buy any other album, you bought *The Stranger*, too. It was that kind of album," said DeVitto. "It was exciting, but you never really keep that going in your head because you got paid to do it, you were done with that and it was over."

DeVitto still listens to *The Stranger* today, but he listens to it more closely now than he did in the early days.

"Now I think, wow, the tempo on that album is unusually good. And the feel on that song 'The Stranger' itself, it's unbelievable. There is a lot of really good stuff on that record. I listen to Doug Stegmeyer playing the bass and wow, he was really good," said DeVitto.

"When Phil Ramone came to see Billy Joel, he saw Billy and us play live and said, 'I have to take that sound and put it on a record. I'm not going to manipulate that sound. I'm going to take that sound and put it on a record because it's great just the way it is.' And that's what he did," said DeVitto.

Discography

"The Stranger"
Billy Joel
September 29, 1977
(All songs written and composed by Billy Joel)

Side one
"Movin' Out (Anthony's Song)" 3:30
"The Stranger" 5:10
"Just the Way You Are" 4:52
"Scenes from an Italian Restaurant" 7:37
Side two
"Vienna" 3:34
"Only the Good Die Young" 3:55
"She's Always a Woman" 3:21
"Get It Right the First Time" 3:57
"Everybody Has a Dream/The Stranger (Reprise)" 6:38

Building the brick house wasn't so easy
Self-titled
Commodores

By the mid-1970s, the Commodores had developed a routine for recording albums. Band members would get together in the middle of October and spend about two months choosing and arranging songs, take a couple of weeks off for Christmas, fly to Motown Records in Los Angeles and spend January and February recording, release the album in the spring, and tour in support of the album in the summer.

When the band — William A. King, Ronald LaPread, Thomas McClary, Walter Orange, Lionel Richie, and Milan Williams — was getting together songs for its fifth studio album, the self-titled *Commodores* in late 1976, members had chosen and arranged eight songs for the album. They needed one more, though.

But everybody was worn out.

"We had done eight songs and we could not choose the ninth song. Everybody was desperate, everybody was tired, didn't want to see each other anymore, wanted to go home. We had seen each other every day, seven days a week, for two months," said William A. King, the band's trumpet player. "We decided to just do something quick, because we only had two days left to get the songs prepared before we left for L.A."

They all agreed to just throw something together quickly. So Walter Orange sat down at the drum kit and started tapping out a beat. Ronald LaPread added the bass, while William A. King and Lionel Richie tried to figure out the horns part to go with it. Thomas McClary added in guitar and Milan Williams joined in on keyboards.

"We were just jamming," said King. "And we finally got a basic track down."

There were no lyrics to the riff, so it was suggested that King and Orange both head home after the session and try to write some words to go with it. But time was of the essence. The band needed the lyrics the next day if it was going to complete the ninth song for the album before heading to Los Angeles to record.

"At that time we had cassette tapes, so I was playing it over and over and over again. I was just trying to figure out a starting point," said King. "But I knew it was going to be about a woman."

But even after getting home that evening and playing the cassette over and over, King was still stuck. It was getting late, and King's wife, Shirley Hanna-King, was running out of patience.

"She said, 'Look, why don't you turn that tape off? You've played it a thousand times; don't you have that melody in your head yet?'" King recalled his wife saying. "I said, 'No, I don't, which is why I keep playing it over and over again.'"

But Shirley Hanna-King had heard enough and retired to a different part of the house where she didn't have to listen to the tape.

Eventually, King himself ran out of steam.

"I fell asleep, literally with the tape on. It just ran out," said King. "When I woke up, I had a pad of paper and pencil on my chest. I looked at it and it had all these lyrics written on it. I was looking at it thinking, 'God, those are some good lyrics.' And then I looked at the handwriting and it was my wife's handwriting. So I asked her, 'Did you write this?' And she said, 'Yeah, I had to do something to keep you from playing that tape all night long because we couldn't get any sleep.'"

King took the lyrics to the next day's session and presented them to the Commodores.

"Milan Williams said, 'Man, these are the best lyrics you've ever written,'" said King.

Orange had also done some writing the previous evening, and between the two of them, King and Orange combined their lyrics and came up with a song that would be about a woman who was built like "a brick shithouse."

The song was "Brick House." But James Carmichael, who was producing the *Commodores* album, still wasn't sold on it being the ninth and final song for the record.

"Carmichael wasn't convinced," said King. "He listened to it and said, 'Eh, I'm not too sure about this song.'"

But Orange was. So unbeknownst to the other members of the group, he took the assistant engineer into an adjacent studio, had the track put on and then Orange started singing over the track, adding in the lead vocals. He then took the revised track back to Carmichael and the Commodores to hear the results.

"And everybody went, 'Oh my God, this is really nice.' That's actually how the song got on the album, because Walter went in there and did a demo vocal over it, which convinced everybody that the song was worth going on the album," said King. "It probably would not have even made it onto the album. We would have just done one fewer song on the record."

"Brick House" would be released as a single and go to No. 5 on the U.S. Billboard Hot 100 Singles chart and No. 4 on the U.S. R&B chart.

But it wouldn't be the only hit single from the *Commodores* album, which was released on March 30, 1977. There would be another single that was even bigger.

Lionel Richie had a song that, according to King, he must have rewritten a dozen times once the band had gotten to Los Angeles to record. Richie would go into the bathroom at Motown Records, write the lyrics and bring them back out to the band.

"Either Carmichael or one of the guys would go, 'Eh, these suck.' And Lionel would go back into the bathroom," said King. "We had this thing we used to say: 'Has anybody seen Richie? Oh, he's in the bathroom.' The lyrics for that song were written in the bathroom at Motown Studios in Los Angeles."

The song was "Easy," and it would be a smash hit. It got to No. 1 on the U.S. Billboard R&B chart and No. 4 on the U.S. Billboard Hot 100 Singles chart.

"Even though we hated his first lyrics, 'Easy' was easy," said King. "From the first time he played it, I thought it was a hit song. And I wasn't alone. I think everybody in the room thought it was a hit song."

The *Commodores* album itself was also a big hit for the group. It reached No. 1 on the U.S. R&B/Hip-Hop Albums chart and No. 3 on the U.S. Billboard 200 Albums chart.

The album was also notable for a couple of other reasons. It put the group over the top and on a track to bigger stardom. And it was the first album where the group started to transition away from its funk/soul roots and into more ballads, which allowed Lionel Richie to step out front.

When choosing songs for an album, each member of the Commodores wanted his songs to be selected. That meant those songs had to be acceptable to most, if not all, the members of the group.

"We used to say, 'Bring your helmet and your sword' when you bring your songs in because you had to fight to get them on the album," said King. "Everybody wanted to get a song or two or three on the album. But everybody also knew if they got their song on that album and it was nothing, then the album was going to be nothing."

Although King admitted there was some selfishness when it came to getting one's songs on an album, the group

Stacks of Wax

members understood that the goal was to have a hit album. And even though the Commodores themselves would make the initial decisions on which songs would be chosen, producer James Carmichael would make the final decision because they all thought he would provide the most unbiased viewpoint.

"The goal was to have good songs on an album."

It was also around this time, during the emergence of the ballad "Easy," that the group also began to ponder just exactly what kind of sound it wanted to have. Was it going to continue on in the funk/soul genre, or go more toward ballads?

"Most bands start as cover bands, but nobody knows what you sound like. They know what you sound like playing the Temptations, the Four Tops, Three Dog Night, Led Zeppelin, or whatever you're covering. But they don't know what *you* sound like," said King. "I don't know any band that knows what that sound is going to be because you haven't yet developed it. You don't know what it is. Even if you have songs that you've written and you've put your stamp on them, it's amazing how that changes as you see and receive other ideas as you go along in life. It's an evolution."

So the band members started thinking, "Everybody loves a love song. So then we decided, let's all try to write love songs. Let's just head off in that direction, because we know we can do the up-tempo funk stuff. So let's just go and do that. And we all did. That was what the goal was for the *Commodores* album," said King.

As he demonstrated with the single "Easy," it turned out that Richie was the best ballad writer in the Commodores. And the other members of the group recognized that, according to King.

"The other guys were bringing in those types of songs, but in our heart of hearts, everybody knew that 'Easy' and 'Three Times a Lady' and 'Still' and songs like that were better. You have to realize that this guy is writing these hit songs and my songs are getting passed by. But you go back to, do you want a hit album?" said King.

"People would tell us—you know what, you're giving this guy too much power. But here was the deal: Do we want to take a chance and not have a hit? Do we really want to take that chance? And the guys said, no, we don't. So we forged ahead," said King. "That was really how we got into the whole ballad thing. I have to be honest — it kind of took over. We got to be known as balladeers."

Working for Motown in the 1970s also played a part during the transition period. Motown founder Berry Gordy had relocated the company from Detroit to Los Angeles in 1972. By doing so, it had lost some of its stars from the 1960s, most notably Gladys Knight and the Pips, the Four Tops and Martha Reeves, who all either stayed in Detroit or left the company altogether.

The Commodores and the emergence of Lionel Richie, along with Rick James, were among the company's biggest new stars in the 1970s.

But it didn't appear that way sometimes to the Commodores.

"We never felt like we were actually a part of Motown as much as Smokey Robinson or the Temptations or the Supremes or the Jackson Five or Marvin Gaye. That was Motown. We were the newcomers, the guys who came there after Detroit," said King about the company's move to Los Angeles. "Yes, we belonged to Motown and it was incredible. It really was. But it was like we were the second guard. And the first guard always reigned supreme over us. If we were in the studio recording and they needed the studio for one of the other artists, they'd just go ahead and knock us out to get it done."

But that didn't deter the success that was to come for the group following the *Commodores* album. From 1978 through 1981, the group would produce four more Top 10 albums: *Natural High* in 1978, which would soar to No. 1 on the U.S. R&B chart and No. 3 on the U.S. Billboard 200 Albums chart; *Midnight Magic* in 1979, No. 1 on the R&B chart and No. 3 on the album chart; *Heroes* in 1980, No. 3 on the R&B chart and No. 7 on the album chart; and *In the Pocket* in 1981, No. 4 on the R&B chart and No. 13 on the album chart.

Those same albums produced several Top 10 singles as well: "Three Times a Lady," No. 1 on the U.S. Billboard Hot 100 Singles chart off the *Natural High* album; "Sail On" at No. 4, and "Still" at No. 1 off the *Midnight Magic* album; and "Lady (You Bring Me Up)" at No. 8, and "Oh No" at No. 4 off the *In the Pocket* album.

All were written by Lionel Richie with the exception of "Lady (You Bring Me Up)," which was written by William King, Shirley Hanna-King, and Harold Hudson, who was then a member of the Commodores backup band.

"We always thought we had the wherewithal to write hit songs. By then, we were very confident about our position and where we were. We were selling albums left and right. At one point we were ranked number four in the world in album sales. You name it, we had done it," said King.

And then Lionel Richie decided to embark on a solo career.

"It was kind of rough. We did *In the Pocket'* and I had written this song called 'Lady (You Bring Me Up).' Richie was going to do the lead on it," said King. "I called him and said, 'You know we have to get this song done. I want you to do the lead on it. I thought about Walter, but I think your voice is better because it's more pop and Walter is more an R and B-type singer.' He said OK."

The Commodores had set up studio time in Los Angeles to record the song, but Richie didn't show. When King called Richie to find out what happened, Richie said he had forgotten about the recording session.

The session was rescheduled for the next day and Richie assured King he would be there. Although he was late, Richie did show up this time.

"He finally comes in and I said, 'The song is up; you can just walk in and get the lead. You got time, right?' And he said, 'Oh, yeah,'" said King. "He got warmed up and then did the first verse and second verse. And then he said, 'I have to go now.' I said, 'But you haven't finished the song yet.' He said, 'Tomorrow.' And he never came back."

According to King, the final version of "Lady (You Bring Me Up)" includes the first and second verses that Richie did in the studio that day, then the ad-libs that he did during his warm-up to fill out the song.

"We took those and fit them in all over the song where we could fit them in. We piecemealed it together," said King.

Without Lionel Richie, the Commodores would break into the Top 20 with only one other album and single in the 1980s: The album *Nightshift* would get to No. 1 on the R&B chart and No. 12 on the U.S. Billboard 200 Albums charts, and the title cut off that album would get to No. 1 on the R&B/Hip-Hop chart and No. 3 on the U.S. Billboard Hot 100 Singles chart.

As for the 1977 *Commodores* album, King calls it "the album of all of our albums."

"We were on the cusp — right before we cut that album — and that album took us over the top. All of a sudden, not just Black America or R and B America knew the Commodores. The pop world knew about the Commodores. And not only did they know about us, but they loved us," said King.

"'Brick House' and 'Easy' just scampered through the world. I don't care what part of the world we went to, you could hear those two songs. We're still talking about those songs nearly forty years later. And if you're still making money with songs like those, for me, that's just unbelievable," he said.

Discography

"Commodores"
The Commodores
March 30, 1977

Side One

"Squeeze the Fruit" - (Walter Orange) 3:00

"Funny Feelings" - (Lionel Richie, Thomas McClary) 4:51

"Heaven Knows" - (Lionel Richie, Thomas McClary) 4:41

"Zoom" - (Lionel Richie, Ronald LaPread) 6:43

Side Two

"Won't You Come Dance with Me" - (Lionel Richie, Thomas McClary) 3:47

"Brick House" - (Shirley Hanna-King [uncredited], Lionel Richie, Milan Williams, Walter Orange, Ronald LaPread, Thomas McClary, William King) 3:27

"Funky Situation" - (William King) 3:39

"Patch It Up" - (Milan Williams) 3:58

"Easy" - (Lionel Richie) 4:16

Two tickets to rock stardom
Self-titled
Eddie Money

In the early 1970s, Eddie Money, mostly broke and trying to make it in the music business, was dating a woman who was a student at the University of California, Berkeley. But the woman's mother didn't like her daughter hanging out with the young musician.

"She was in a sorority and her mother didn't want her to be involved with a rock star, so to speak," said Money.

So Money wrote a song about the experience.

"It was about being broke and going with a rich girl at the time, which was good for me because she moved out of the sorority house and her mother didn't know it," he said. "She was living with me in North Oakland and paying my rent. And she was also bringing steaks home for the icebox, which was fantastic. So it all worked out great."

Oh, and the song worked out great, too. Money wrote the words and Jimmy Lyon wrote the music. They titled it "Baby Hold On" and it was the lead single off Money's self-titled debut album *Eddie Money*, released in late 1977.

After performing in various clubs around the Bay Area, Money had finally attracted the attention of rock impresario Bill Graham, who agreed to be Money's manager. Graham, a Holocaust survivor who was born Wulf Wolodia Grajonca in Berlin, Germany, had immigrated to the United States from Russia before the domination of Nazism. He eventually became known as a concert promoter in the psychedelic music scene of the late 1960s at the Fillmore Auditorium in San Francisco. The Fillmore turned out to be one of the proving ground venues for bands like the Grateful Dead,

Mike Morsch

Jefferson Airplane, and Big Brother and the Holding Company, which at the time featured Janis Joplin as its lead singer.

By the mid-1970s, Graham had become a promoter of large outdoor benefit concerts and a manager for some artists. And he liked Eddie Money.

"Bill Graham was a fantastic guy. He actually walked out of Germany to France with 500 kids and 250 of them died of starvation on the way to Paris," said Money. "He was really into the Grateful Dead and was friends with Janis Joplin. Jerry Garcia would always be on the couch sleeping in Bill's office. Bill was a big Dead freak."

According to Money, Graham liked living vicariously through Money and his life as a rock star, but wanted Money to tone it down a bit in the beginning.

"He wanted me to sit on a stool and sing cocktail songs, some bullshit like that. He didn't like my spins. But he liked me and knew I was a good writer and an entertainer," said Money.

When it came time to record the *Eddie Money* album in 1977, it would basically be a studio version of Money's live show at the time, which had been honed by the band's club performances in the Bay Area.

The album was recorded at the Record Plant in Los Angeles. Bruce Botnick produced, and Andy Johns was the engineer. Botnick had produced the *L.A. Woman* album for the Doors in 1970, the band's last album with Jim Morrison as lead singer. Johns had engineered several Rolling Stones albums, including *Sticky Fingers* in 1971, *Exile on Main Street* in 1972 and *Goats Head Soup* in 1973; and a series of Led Zeppelin albums including *Led Zeppelin II* in 1969, *Led Zeppelin III* in 1970, *Led Zeppelin IV* in 1971, *Houses of the Holy* in 1973 and *Physical Graffiti* in 1975.

In addition to Money and Lyon, the band for *Eddie Money* included saxophone player Tom Scott, who had played with George Harrison, Paul McCartney, the Beach

Boys, Rod Stewart, the Grateful Dead, and Steppenwolf, among others; and former Steve Miller Band members, bassist Lonnie Turner and drummer Gary Mallaber.

"It was a wonderful record to make at the Record Plant in L.A.," said Money. "When I was in the studio, Aretha Franklin was in there and Rod Stewart was in there, some really big people. Every time I turned around, Aretha Franklin was trying to get me to eat. 'C'mon honey, have some more of this cornbread.' It was a good time to be alive and the record was a lot of fun to make."

Not only was the single "Baby Hold On" featured on the album, but the record would also include another of what would become a classic rock single from the era, the Money-penned "Two Tickets to Paradise."

"I thought the first single off the album should have been 'Two Tickets to Paradise.' I wrote that song on Manilla Avenue, which was in North Oakland. I wrote it on a piano and it's a great song. I just sat down and wrote it. I knew that 'paradise' rhymed with 'tonight.' Who wouldn't want two tickets to paradise?" said Money. "It wasn't about anybody in particular, not really. It was about getting away. Two tickets to paradise can be taking a plane to Hawaii or a Greyhound bus up to the Redwoods. I didn't take a girl to Hawaii but I did take one up to the Redwoods back in 1976. A girl I'm very happy I didn't end up with, by the way."

Despite "Baby Hold On" and "Two Tickets to Paradise" being the big hits off the album, neither one of them was the first song to be recorded when the sessions started at the Record Plant.

Money thought it was a good idea, and Graham and Botnick agreed, that the album should have a song that was recognizable to audiences. So the band recorded its version of "You've Really Got a Hold on Me," written by Smokey Robinson, which was a Top 10 hit for the Miracles in 1962. The Beatles also covered it on their second album, *With the Beatles* in 1963.

"I wanted to do something that was more of a cover tune than to dig right into my material. I wanted to throw something to the wolves," said Money. "So we did 'You've Really Got a Hold on Me' and I took out the 'hold me, squeeze me, please me' lines. I did it different than the Beatles and I did it different than Smokey Robinson. I ran into Smokey four years later and he said he liked my version better than the Beatles'. And I said, 'I like my version better than your version.'"

Another song included on the album, also co-written by Money and Lyon, was called "Jealousys" and was about Money's early struggles when he first moved to California.

"I was in a group called the Rockets. All these guys lived at home and they drove their parents' cars. They all lived at home like I did when I was living on Long Island with my parents," said Money. "I was living in North Oakland, borrowing everyone else's car and living on canned ravioli and fuckin' powdered milk. I had nothing. That song was all about how tough it was coming up."

When it came time to shoot the photo for the album cover, Money decided to wear a suit that he had purchased at a thrift store because it was a "dead guy" suit from the 1940s and he liked the way it looked.

But it was a long photo shoot and Money eventually ran out of patience.

"They took a million pictures. But I got so tired of taking pictures," said Money. "I finally said, 'Here's your fuckin' album cover. I lit up a cigarette and bang, sure enough, that was the album cover they picked. If you look at all my early album covers, I've got a cigarette in my hand."

Eddie Money was released in December 1977. Three singles were released from the album: "You've Really Got a Hold on Me," which got good airplay, but failed to crack the Top 20 singles chart; "Two Tickets to Paradise," which reached No. 22 on the U.S. Billboard Hot 100 Singles and No. 14 on the Canadian RPM Top Singles; and "Baby Hold

On," which ended up doing the best, reaching No. 11 on the U.S. Billboard Hot 100 Singles, No. 5 on the U.S. Cashbox Top 100 Singles, No. 4 on the Canadian RPM Singles and No. 41 on the Single Top 100 in the Netherlands.

The album itself peaked at No. 37 on the Billboard 200 Albums chart and No. 24 on the Canadian RPM Albums chart.

Part of the success of the *Eddie Money* album — and for some subsequent Money albums — was because Money was admittedly "the poster child for promotion" of his own records.

"There was nothing that I wouldn't do to get on the radio," said Money. "In fact, there was a female DJ out of Pittsburgh and she was thinking about adding 'Baby Hold On' to the playlist in that market. I went there and she was good looking, so we got a little thing going. That's how I got on the radio there. She was cute, I was young and handsome. She liked the record, I liked her, and the next thing you know — bang, it was number seventeen in that market."

While the fans appeared to like his music, the critics, however, weren't crazy about it, according to Money. Part of it, he believes, was that he was living the rock and roll lifestyle and burning a lot of bridges while doing it.

"I never did shows drunk. I wish I could have because I was such an alcoholic in those days. But Bill Graham put the fear of God into me. I did one show drunk with the Marshall Tucker Band and Bill just reamed me out. So I never drank before work, but after work, I'd be drinking like crazy," said Money. "Then I'd be getting up in the morning with a really bad hangover, calling them [the critics] up and saying, 'I'm going to blow up your car, I'm going to fuck your wife.'"

Another reason, Money believes, he had difficulties finding a solid niche in the late 1970s, was because he was trying to serve two different audiences.

On weekdays, he'd be in San Jose or Fremont, California, playing disco bars and then on the weekends, he'd play his original compositions in venues that were more rock and roll oriented. He thinks maybe the weekday gigs might have affected his rock and roll fans by the time he recorded his second album, *Life For the Taking* in 1979, featuring the single "Maybe I'm a Fool," which reached No. 22 on the Billboard Hot 100 Singles early that year.

"That song, 'Maybe I'm a Fool,' it alienated a lot of my rock fans. 'Eddie is going disco.' But I knew it was going to be a hit. I was chasing the radio," said Money. "It had a disco beat and it had disco strings and a lot of my fans were going, 'What the fuck happened to Eddie Money? He's got 'Life For the Taking,' which is a great song, and then he's got 'Maybe I'm a Fool.' But you know what, it was the same thing. Back in the 1970s, on the weekdays, Sundays through Thursdays, I'd be playing disco bars and then I'd be playing rock gigs on the weekends.

"So when I put the second record out, it had a couple of disco songs on it. Am I supposed to apologize for that? No. I was chasing FM radio with 'Life For the Taking' and I was chasing AM radio with 'Maybe I'm a Fool,'" he said. "I remember when I was number one in airplay on both AM and FM. I did good."

These days, Money still tries to perform on the weekends. He's been married since 1989 and has five children. He is working on a possible television show idea, planning a new album, writing a book, and working on a theme song for the National Basketball Association's Los Angeles Clippers, which he hopes the team will adopt. He also helps raise money for the Intrepid Fallen Heroes Fund, a nonprofit organization that provides support to U.S. military personnel and their families.

He's sober now, but if he has any regrets about his early rock and roll days of the 1970s, he isn't sharing them.

"I've been to jail, I've been to college and I've been to rehab. What the fuck haven't I done?" he said. "It was an amazing time. I was a rock star. I had a fuckin' blast."

Discography

"Eddie Money"
Eddie Money
December 1977

"Two Tickets to Paradise" (Money) 3:58

"You've Really Got a Hold on Me" (Smokey Robinson)............ 3:45

"Wanna Be a Rock 'n' Roll Star" (Money, Chris Solberg) 4:02

"Save a Little Room in Your Heart for Me" (Money) 4:57

"So Good to Be in Love Again" (Money, Jimmy Lyon) 4:12

"Baby Hold On" (Money, Lyon) 3:31

"Don't Worry" (Money, Lyon) 3:45

"Jealousys" (Money, Lyon) 3:59

"Got to Get Another Girl" (Money, Lyon) 3:26

"Gamblin' Man" (Money, Dan Alexander, Lyon) 4:02

They wanted to see the old card trick first
Works Volume I
Emerson, Lake and Palmer

In the early- to mid-1970s, Carl Palmer believed his band, Emerson, Lake and Palmer, was legitimately breathing the same rarified air as the top bands of the era, like the Rolling Stones and Pink Floyd. Not necessarily musically, but in the area of fame.

ELP — which included Keith Emerson, Greg Lake, and Palmer — had three albums, *Tarkus* in 1971, *Trilogy* in 1972, and *Brain Salad Surgery* in 1973 that were No. 1, 1 and 2 in the United Kingdom and No. 9, 5 and 11 in the United States on the charts. The band had come out of the blocks strong.

"For three years we were at the top end and obviously setting the pace. Prog rock is an English invention and we were one of the first bands to come out with concept albums," said Palmer. "Pink Floyd did it a lot better than us with *The Wall*, but nevertheless, *Tarkus* is a monumental piece of music. So ELP was way up there, albeit for a very short period of time. It was a keyboard-driven band; it wasn't guitar-driven. So that put it in a different area straightaway. Lake wasn't a blues singer; he was almost a choirboy, soprano-esque in a way. And that put us in another area of the game as well."

And then in 1974, the band decided to take an extended hiatus.

Mike Morsch

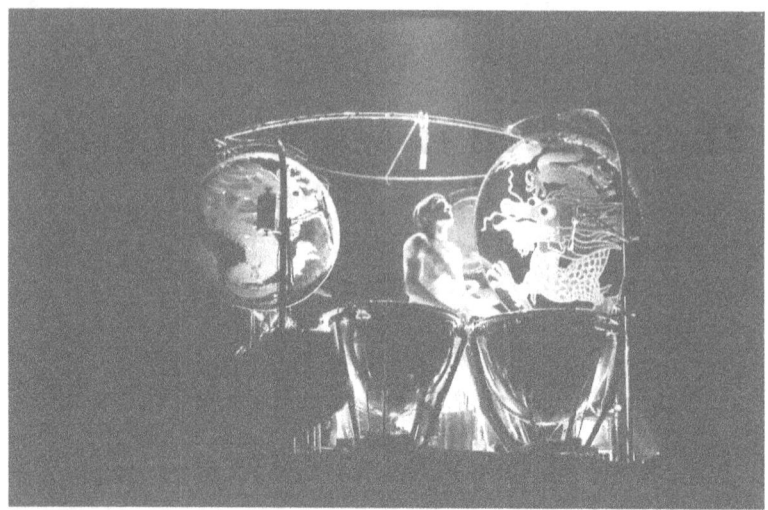

Carl Palmer's side of the "Works Volume I" album included two covers of classical pieces of Russian composer Sergei Prokofiev and German composer Johann Sebastian Bach. (Photo by Phil McAuliffe)

"Unfortunately, the band didn't work as much as it should have. We did work an awful lot, but only for a very short period of time. Possibly we burned ourselves out within the first four years and then the rest of the time was kind of just sitting around and not making too many albums," said Palmer.

The band regrouped in 1976 and started work on its next studio album, *Works Volume I* at Mountain Studios in Montreux, Switzerland, and EMI Studios in Paris, France. It was to be a concept double album, with each member of the band doing solo work on three sides, with the fourth side featuring material from the entire group.

Emerson's side included an 18-minute piece, the three movement, "Piano Concerto #1"; Lake's side included five songs he co-wrote with Peter Sinfield, lyricist and co-founding member of King Crimson; and Palmer's side included covers of two classical pieces, one by Russian composer Sergei Prokofiev and one by German composer

Johann Sebastian Bach. And one of the group tracks was "Fanfare for the Common Man," which was the cover of an Aaron Copland piece that Copland had given the band permission to record.

Palmer also enlisted the help of Joe Walsh for the song "L.A. Nights" on his side of the double album.

"Joe Walsh is a lovely man and a gentleman. I met him somewhere — I can't remember where. I told him I was in the studio. He was in L.A. I said. 'Why don't you come down? I've got an idea for an intro and we could take it into kind of a bluesy thing.' And he said, yes, he'd love to. He came down and we did it straightaway," said Palmer.

It would be the only time in their careers that Palmer and Walsh would work together on a song.

Works Volume I was released in March 1977 and made it to No. 9 on the U.K. and No. 12 on the U.S. Billboard 200 Albums chart. The single "Fanfare for the Common Man" got to No. 2 on the U.K. singles chart and became the band's highest-charting U.K. single.

According to Palmer, the chart success belied the reality of what was happening with the band at the time.

"I think that album was the beginning of the end. And by the time *Works Volume II* came out, the band was completely finished," said Palmer.

"During the making of *Works*, it was just a nightmare, really. Nothing seemed to work for us. 'Fanfare for the Common Man' was just one of those things that we recorded the first time, straightaway, just sat down and played. It was basically just a jam with each other for a while. And the engineer that we had was clever enough to switch on the recorder. That was kind of nice," he said. "We never managed to capture that same kind of excitement again on that particular piece of music. But there were a lot of things going on."

Palmer attributes part of the band's initial demise to the long down time between studio albums, which also may explain why both fans and reviewers were lukewarm to *Works Volume I* when it was released, despite its chart success.

And that reaction, in turn, was drawing fewer people to the band's live performances in support of the album. "Unfortunately, it was a situation that if we didn't fill every seat, we lost money. And we lost money. What we did is we used an orchestra for three weeks [of live shows], then we laid them off and then came back out as a trio and we played to sold-out crowds. And that's what we should have done first of all, come out as a three-piece band first and then come out with the orchestra after that and carry on from there," he said. "But after a three-year absence, it was too much for the people to sort of understand. They wanted to see the old card trick first. That basically is *Works Volume I* in a nutshell."

Emerson, Lake and Palmer would disband for the first time in 1979. By the beginning of the 1980s, Palmer would reboot his career by joining a new British prog rock band called Asia, which was then being billed as a 'supergroup.' It would include Palmer, bassist John Wetton — who had been with several bands, including King Crimson, Uriah Heep and Wishbone Ash — and Steve Howe and Geoff Downes, guitarist and keyboardist respectively, of the band Yes under the newly formed Geffen Records. Geffen Records was headed by music-industry businessman, David Geffen, who had founded Asylum Records in the early 1970s.

"It was at the beginning of MTV, so we had all of that new social media on our side. There was an awful lot that David Geffen needed to prove and he realized that he could do it with a great band if they had great songs," said Palmer. "And he decided to choose prog rock English musicians, which he did. We all came from great backgrounds."

Asia's eponymous debut album was released in March 1982 and it was a hit, enjoying enormous commercial success. The album itself got to No. 1 on the U.S. Billboard

200 Albums chart and ended up becoming the No. 1 album of the year on both Billboard and Cash Box charts for 1982.

The album contained two Top 20 singles: "Heat of the Moment," which would become the band's biggest hit and signature song, and would reach No. 4 on the Billboard Hot 100 Singles charts; and "Only Time Will Tell," which would get to No. 17 in the U.S.

"We did incredibly well. That was a kind of era that Asia managed to thrive in at the time. It was corporate rock, when intros had to be twenty seconds long because DJs couldn't talk any longer. It was all that kind of stuff. The second line of every chorus had to rhyme. The corporates and the record company executives were trying to work this out — how do you get a hit?" said Palmer.

Palmer maintains that Emerson, Lake, and Palmer could have had a similar success if they had just stuck with it.

"That's exactly what ELP could have carried on and done. We could have gone through the 1980s that way if we'd just been a little more selective in what we were trying to do," said Palmer. "Because radio was no longer an art form, radio was not playing the longer pieces, ten-minute or fifteen-minute pieces like it was in the 1970s. We had to adjust and people [in the band] didn't understand that."

Palmer said that the whole essence of the music industry business was understanding how to work with and manage the media. It was something that Asia seemed to understand in the 1980s, but something that ELP didn't seem to be able to grasp to move forward from the 1970s.

"You've got to play what you want to play, you got to play the way you want to play it and you've got to present the music the way you want to present it. But, you've got to bear in mind what the mechanics are around you and what the machinery is you're dealing with," said Palmer. "And if radio won't play you in drive time because your songs are too long or this or that, then you say, hey, we need to adjust. ELP could have crossed that boundary, but we weren't clever enough to realize it at the time. But I was fortunate enough to be in Asia in that period and I took the bull by the horns and I rode with it."

ELP would give it another shot in the 1990s, reforming as a trio in 1991 and releasing a comeback album called *Black Moon* on the Victory Records label. The world tours in 1992 and 1993 followed and were successful, but ELP never did approach its mega-success of the early 1970s.

"ELP was up there with the biggest of names. Unfortunately, it didn't sustain its presence. It lost its posting, it lost its position in general. And when we came back in the 1990s, it wasn't as big. It didn't really ring the bell," said Palmer. "By the time we came back, radio had changed, the climate had changed. The corporates were already in. I had already had an incredible amount of success with Asia. So basically, when ELP got back together again, it had fallen in between the cracks a little bit. It still did OK, but it would have been better if we hadn't broken up and just carried on. The band would have climbed very slowly, but gotten bigger and bigger."

But Palmer has few complaints about how his career has progressed and evolved over the decades and he is secure in the legacy of ELP.

He still performs the music of ELP at his solo shows, albeit with a fresher approach, while still maintaining the integrity of the original music.

"ELP music can be played in many ways. I've heard it played with an orchestra, I've heard it played with a synthesizer band as in ELP, and now we're playing it in a metal sort of instrumental guitar way," said Palmer. "So the music had many facets to it. There is a lot of light and shade in there. And this is just another way of presenting it. Obviously, there is no reason to try and copy what ELP did because we did that so well. I just want to bring the music back in a different format where maybe we can attract some newer fans and some younger fans."

Palmer still plays 80 to 90 shows a year. But he still looks to those early ELP years fondly.

"We [ELP] did have four great years, so I can't complain. I would say it was up there in the top of the A category and then after that, it was kind of in the B section, as it were. That's fine, it's not a problem," he said. "We sold close to fifty million albums, which is not a helluva lot these days. Some artists do that with one album. But nevertheless, you have to understand that prog rock is a minority market and always will be. It's like jazz and that's the way it goes. If you pick that type of music, you pay your price and you take your chances."

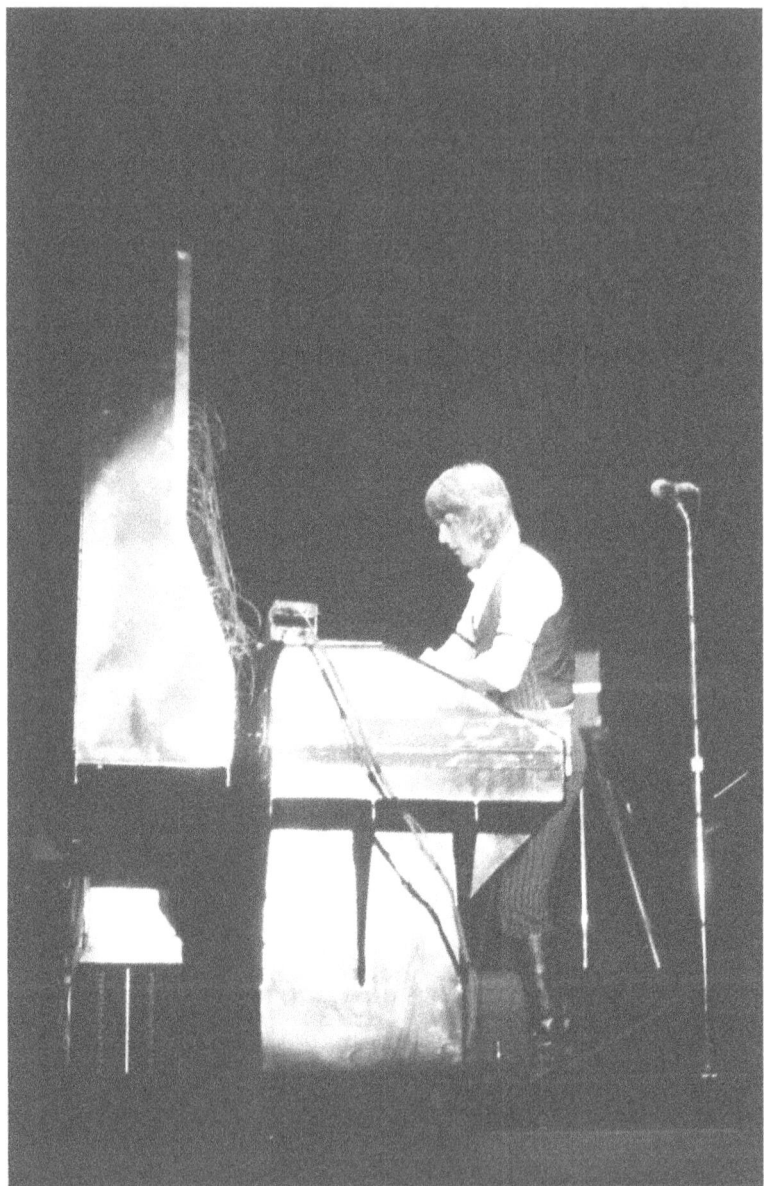

Keith Emerson's side of the "Works Volume I" album included an 18-minute, three movement "Piano Concerto No.1." (Photo by Phil McAuliffe)

Stacks of Wax

Greg Lake's side of the "Works Volume I" album included five songs he co-wrote with Peter Sinfield, lyricist and co-founding member of King Crimson. (Photo by Phil McAuliffe)

Discography

"Works Volume I"
Emerson, Lake and Palmer
March 17, 1977

Side one: Keith Emerson
"Piano Concerto No. 1" (Keith Emerson) 18:18
• I. First Movement: Allegro giojoso
• II. Second Movement: Andante molto cantabile
• III. Third Movement: Toccata con fuoco)
Side two: Greg Lake
"Lend Your Love to Me Tonight" (Greg Lake, Peter Sinfield)..4:01
"C'est la Vie" (Lake, Sinfield)...4:16
"Hallowed Be Thy Name" (Lake, Sinfield)................................. 4:35
"Nobody Loves You Like I Do" (Lake, Sinfield)......................... 3:56
"Closer to Believing" (Lake, Sinfield) 5:33
Side three: Carl Palmer
"The Enemy God Dances with the Black Spirits" (Sergei Prokofiev, arr. Emerson, Lake, Carl Palmer) 3:20
"L.A. Nights" (Palmer; features Joe Walsh on guitars and scat vocal and Keith Emerson on keyboards).. 5:42
"New Orleans" (Palmer)... 2:45
"Two Part Invention in D Minor" (J. S. Bach, arr. Palmer)...... 1:54
"Food for Your Soul" (Palmer)...3:57
"Tank" (Emerson, Palmer) 5:08
Side four: Emerson, Lake and Palmer
"Fanfare for the Common Man" (Aaron Copland, arr. Emerson, Lake, Palmer)... 9:40
"Pirates" (Emerson, Lake, Sinfield) 13:18

The hush surrounding a blond-haired soul brother
Self-titled
Bobby Caldwell

Bobby Caldwell had spent several years beating around the streets of Los Angeles in the early to mid-1970s, looking for a recording deal with a major record label.

He was in a band that was doing Top 40 hits performing five nights a week in the Los Angeles clubs making a decent living. But that wasn't what he wanted out of life. Caldwell thought there was more for him out there in the world of music.

So during his afternoons, he started writing music, singing into a cassette recorder, and then taking those tapes around to all the major labels, hoping to impress recording executives.

After about four years of knocking on doors and not getting noticed, Caldwell was beaten down.

"I was tempted to go back home and go into business with my dad. He wanted to start a real estate company. So I kind of went home with my tail between my legs," said Caldwell.

While sitting around his parents' home one day after his return to Miami, Caldwell's mother pointed out an article to him in the *Miami Herald*. It was about Harry Wayne Casey, whose band, KC and The Sunshine Band, had become a huge success in the mid-1970s.

Casey himself was one of Miami's favorite sons in the music industry. He had formed the band in 1973 in Hialeah, Florida, while working in the warehouse for TK Records, which was started by record distributor Henry Stone that same year.

TK Records would become closely associated with the rise of disco music, and KC and The Sunshine Band was the label's biggest stars.

By 1978, TK Records was still at the top of its game, despite the fact that disco was entering what would become the later stages of its popularity.

After bringing the article in the *Miami Herald* about KC and The Sunshine Band to her son's attention, Caldwell's mother suggested he visit TK Records.

"She worked on me and worked on me and I did — I went down to TK Records," said Caldwell.

There he got a meeting with Stone and his then-partner, Steve Alaimo, a teen idol in the early 1960s. Alaimo had been an artist on one of Stone's early labels in the late 1950s, and had gone on to co-produce Dick Clark's *Where the Action Is* television show, which ran from 1965 to 1967. The house band for the show its first year was Paul Revere and the Raiders.

After the show ended, Alaimo became a record producer for Atlantic Records through the early 1970s, eventually reuniting with Stone to form TK Records in 1973.

Within two days of the meeting with Stone and Alaimo, Caldwell finally had his record deal.

"It was all in my own backyard to begin with," said Caldwell. "After four years of beating the L.A. streets, I was surprised I got signed so quickly."

Within weeks, Caldwell was recording his self-titled debut album, *Bobby Caldwell*.

"They gave me carte blanche in the studio. We had a great facility there at TK Records. I'd go in pretty much in the dead of night and work until six in the morning," said Caldwell.

Stacks of Wax

When Bobby Caldwell finished writing and recording his self-titled debut album, it didn't have a breakout single that record company officials were expecting. So he went back and wrote and recorded "What You Won't Do For Love" in three days. (Photo by Mike Morsch)

Caldwell poured his heart and soul into the album, and when it was done, he presented it to the higher ups and TK Records.

They were not all that impressed.

"The general consensus was, 'We really love the album, but we're not hearing a breakout single.' So they made me go back into the studio and see what I could come up with," said Caldwell.

He had a concept for a song, which at the time he called "a blue-eyed soul song." But there was something else at play according to Caldwell: Since it was his debut album for the label, he really needed to make a mark with it.

And the pressure was on.

In three days he had written and recorded "What You Won't Do for Love." It would become the breakout single that record company officials were looking for.

"And I didn't give it much thought after giving this brilliant album a whole lot of thought," said Caldwell. "The moral of this story is, don't get too close to your own stuff. I got so into the music [on the album] that I couldn't see the forest through the trees. And I missed out on the immediacy of a song like 'What You Won't Do for Love.' Those things happen when you let go. And it's a lesson I learned then and have used ever since."

The song reached the Top 10 on three different charts. It was No. 9 on the Billboard Pop Chart, No. 6 on the R&B chart and No. 10 on the Adult Contemporary chart.

"At that point, I didn't claim to even have an opinion [about the song]. I was just glad that everyone was excited about 'What You Won't Do for Love,' and what was about to happen was pretty amazing. It took the world by storm," said Caldwell.

The single was released before the album, and since it had become so popular, TK Records decided on a specific strategy when it came time to determine what the cover art would be for the album.

TK Records took full advantage of the similarities between Boz Scaggs, above, and Bobby Caldwell. (Photo by Mike Morsch)

TK Records' main springboard at the time for its artists was R&B radio. Once the company decided to call the album *Bobby Caldwell* and once the soulful "What You Won't Do for Love" had become popular among R&B radio listeners, TK was in no hurry to reveal that Caldwell was a white singer.

And they weren't about to give that little secret away with the album cover art. So they decided to use a silhouette image of Caldwell wearing a hat, sitting on a park bench, under a full moon.

"I looked very British at the time, with my blond hair down to my shoulders. And the record company didn't want to reveal that quite yet," said Caldwell. "So the album came out and I found myself in all of these strange situations where people were seeing me live for the first time and trying to associate the visual with the sound on the record."

One of those strange situations occurred early in Caldwell's touring career, courtesy of Natalie Cole.

Cole, daughter of legendary crooner Nat "King" Cole, had burst onto the music scene in 1975 with her debut album *Inseparable*. That album included the hits "This Will Be (An Everlasting Love)," that became a No. 1 hit on the U.S. Billboard Hot Soul Singles chart and reached No. 6 on the Billboard Hot 100 Singles chart; and the title track "Inseparable," which also reached No. 1 on the Billboard Hot Soul Singles chart and No. 32 on the Billboard Hot 100 Singles chart. The strength of those two singles propelled the album to No. 1 on the Billboard Top Soul LPs chart and No. 18 on the Billboard Top LPs chart.

By 1978, Natalie Cole was at the top of her game. She was looking for somebody as an opener for her major tour of 1978 and she wanted Bobby Caldwell to do about 40 dates with her.

"She was a huge fan and very well aware of the fact that I was white. But she loved the idea that people would see me for the first time and not know I was white," said Caldwell.

The first concert where Caldwell opened for Cole was in Cleveland. And Caldwell's "What You Won't Do for Love" was a Top 5 song at the time, although not many fans of the song had laid eyes on him.

"So I opened the show and they introduced me as 'soul brother Bobby Caldwell.' I come out and a hush came over the audience. You could have heard a pin drop. That was the night I became a man," said Caldwell.

Caldwell calls his initial success with his debut album a situation of "being in the right place at the right time."

"Disco was burning out. But don't forget, three years prior to me releasing my first album, Boz Scaggs had the *Silk Degrees* album. That kind of like almost ushered in that type of path for me. And TK Records took full advantage of that," said Caldwell. "I did recognize that there were some similarities between myself and Boz. Especially in the music we grew up on."

Scaggs and Caldwell finally met in 1980 and Caldwell ended up co-writing two songs on Skaggs' 1988 album *Other Roads*.

Caldwell's second album, *Cat in the Hat* in 1980, reached No. 46 on the U.S. Billboard R&B chart. Along with his third album, *Carry On* in 1982, both albums were considered artistic improvements over his first album, but neither did as well commercially in the U.S.

In the mid-1980s, Caldwell moved back to Los Angeles and started writing songs with some of the people who wrote songs for Toto. Also during that period, he and Paul Gordon wrote "The Next Time I Fall," which was a No. 1 hit for Peter Cetera and Amy Grant in 1986. Cetera, one of the original members of the band Chicago, had left the group to embark on what would become a successful solo career.

In addition, Caldwell wrote songs for the Commodores, Chicago, and Al Jarreau.

"It was only four years, but it was a great learning experience," said Caldwell of transitioning from being a performer to primarily being a songwriter. "I became better at the craft."

During the rest of the 1980s, he also contributed songs to the soundtracks of the movies including *Back to School* in 1986 and *Ghostbusters II* in 1989, among others.

Today, he still writes and performs, and he accepts the reality that he'll always sing "What You Won't Do for Love" for his audiences.

"I've had some great peaks and a few valleys in my career. But more peaks than valleys," said Caldwell. "A lot of people think it would bother me to sing 'What You Won't Do for Love' every show. But every time I do it, the crowd makes it feel like it's the first time. So you get past the feeling of, 'Oh, not this again' very quickly.

"But I'm still very fortunate to be working, still playing to sold-out crowds. The venues may be smaller now and I have to work twice as hard to make the same kind of money I made thirty years ago, but I still enjoy it as long as the people are enjoying it," he said.

Discography

"Bobby Caldwell"
Bobby Caldwell
1978

"Special To Me" - (Bobby Caldwell, Marsha Radcliffe) 4:00

"My Flame" - (Bobby Caldwell) 4:12

"Love Won't Wait" - (Bobby Caldwell) 4:00

"Can't Say Goodbye" - (Bobby Caldwell, George "Chocolate" Perry) 5:20

"Come To Me" - (Bobby Caldwell, Kari) 2:52

"What You Won't Do For Love" - (Bobby Caldwell, Alfons Kettner) 4:45

"Kalimba Song" - (Bobby Caldwell) 2:00

"Take Me Back To Then" - (Bobby Caldwell) 3:30

"Down For The Third Time" - (Bobby Caldwell) 3:30

A bottle of Jack to complement My Fair Lady
Kenny
Kenny Rogers

Billy Edd Wheeler reached for the bottle of Jack Daniels. He and fellow songwriter Roger Bowling had sequestered themselves in Wheeler's rural Kentucky cabin in the late 1970s with the intention of writing a song together, and both agreed that a little Tennessee whiskey might be just the thing to get the creative process started.

Wheeler recalled Bowling asking, "'Have you got any ideas?' And I told him, 'Not really, have you got any?' And he said, 'Well, I've got a title I've been thinking about called "The Promise."' I said, 'Do you know who is promising what?' He said, 'No, it's just the title.'"

Wheeler and Bowling were part of a group of songwriters working in Nashville in the 1970s. Wheeler had co-written and recorded the single "Jackson" in 1963 that was made into a country hit single by Johnny Cash and June Carter in 1967. Bowling had co-written "Lucille," which became the first solo hit in 1977 for Kenny Rogers after he had left the country rock group The First Edition.

Both songwriters had gotten tired of being in Nashville and had left - Wheeler moving to North Carolina and Bowling settling just across the border in Georgia — but they kept in touch.

Roger Bowling, left, and Billy Edd Wheeler, co-wrote the song "Coward of the County," which became a hit for Kenny Rogers. The song reached No. 1 on the Billboard Hot Country Singles, No. 1 on the Cash Box Top 100 Singles, and crossed over to reach No. 3 on the Billboard Hot 100 singles and No. 5 on the Billboard Hot Adult Contemporary Singles. (Photo courtesy of Billy Edd Wheeler)

Wheeler had been commissioned by National Geographic to write a folk opera about Daniel Boone and there was a theater group in Kentucky near Wheeler's cabin that was making the folk opera into an outdoor drama.

That's where Bowling, Wheeler, and Jack Daniels started brainstorming for a new song.

As the two songwriters kicked around ideas, Wheeler started to think that he wanted to write a song about somebody who comes from behind — like Daniel Boone.

"Like nobody would expect this person to do anything," said Wheeler. "Maybe he was considered a loser, but damn if he doesn't come from behind and prove them all wrong."

That idea for some reason — and he doesn't know exactly why — made Wheeler think of *My Fair Lady*, a musical based on George Bernard Shaw's *Pygmalion*. The story centers around a Cockney flower seller who takes speech lessons from a professor so that she could pass as a lady.

The original 1956 Broadway production of *My Fair Lady* starred Rex Harrison as Professor Henry Higgins and Julie Andrews as Eliza Doolittle. The 1964 film adaptation starred Harrison and Audrey Hepburn.

"Well, I kind of felt sorry for that girl," said Wheeler. "I didn't think he was showing too much respect for her. And then at the end, she's in control of him because he's fallen in love with her. She came from behind. That's a far-fetched idea for country music, but that's what went through my mind."

So Bowling had a title called "The Promise" and Wheeler was drawing inspiration from *My Fair Lady*. From that, Bowling had written the first line of a song: "Everyone considered him the coward of the county."

But they still didn't have a song.

"I thought at one point that we might write it about a black man that everybody looked down on who became the hero and did something really great to prove everybody wrong," said Wheeler. "But that didn't work."

The song really started to come together, though, when Bowling and Wheeler determined what "the promise" would be. And that happened with the line, "Promise me, son, not to do the things I've done."

They wrote the rest of the lyrics and changed the title of the song to "Coward of the County."

Now all they had to do was convince somebody to record the song.

Bowling happened to be close friends with producer Larry Butler, who had joined United Artists Records in 1973 as the head of its Nashville division. Under Butler's leadership, the label signed country artists Crystal Gayle, Dottie West, the Kendalls . . . and Kenny Rogers.

Butler liked to play poker. Unfortunately, he was a lot better at signing talented artists to the UAR label than he was at cards. And the beneficiary of Butler's misfortune oftentimes was Bowling.

"Roger told me that Larry was not a good poker player," said Wheeler. "At one point, Larry owed Roger ten grand. Larry had a money manager and he was fussing at him all the time because he wasn't going to give him any money to pay off Larry's gambling debts."

That wasn't lost on Bowling. According to Wheeler, Bowling would ask Butler for $500 and call the rest of the debt even, knowing that in order to satisfy the difference, Butler would pitch Bowling's songs to the artists that he knew.

That's how Bowling's song, "Blanket on the Ground" got recorded by country singer Billie Jo Spears. The song reached No. 1 on Billboard's Hot Country Singles chart and even crossed over to No. 78 on the Billboard Hot 100 Pop chart in 1975.

And now Butler was going to put "Coward of the County" in front of Kenny Rogers.

"I loved it, I loved the concept of it," said Rogers about the first time he heard "Coward of the County" in mid-1979. "I thought it was very cleverly written. It was a very powerful message, saying that even though there are times some things are wrong, there may be times when you have to do them. That's what the story is about."

Rogers was on a roll by 1979. Bowling had already scored a hit with Rogers in 1977 with the single "Lucille," which had propelled the self-titled *Kenny Rogers* album to No. 1 on the Billboard Country Albums chart that same year.

But Rogers had bested that — and sent his career even higher into the stratosphere — in 1978 with the release of *The Gambler* album, which would be another No. 1 record on the Billboard Top Country Albums chart.

And the string of success would continue into 1979 with the release of the *Kenny* album, featuring "Coward of the County," which blew away all of the charts, reaching No. 1 on the Billboard Hot Country Singles, No. 1 on the Cash Box Top 100 Singles, and crossing over to reach No. 3 on the Billboard Hot 100 Singles and No. 5 on the Billboard Hot Adult Contemporary Singles.

There was, however, some controversy about the song, and it had to do with another country group that was having success in the 1970s — Larry Gatlin and the Gatlin Brothers.

In the lyrics of "Coward of the County," the "Gatlin boys" play a critical role in the song's story. They are, in essence the "bad guys" who commit unspeakable acts with the girlfriend of the song's main character.

For his part, Rogers said that Larry Gatlin and his brothers had no issues with the lyrics.

"No, they loved it. They were good friends of mine and they viewed it as promotion for them," said Rogers. "There was no criticism about it, there was just a lot of hoopla because of the coincidence of the names."

Wheeler tells a similar story. Sort of.

"I just liked the sound of the name Gatlin," said Wheeler about why he and Bowling decided to use the surname in the song. "It's a really good name. We tried other names and just kept coming back to Gatlin."

But it was certainly on the minds of the songwriters when they were writing the song that they were using the name of a popular country artist of the 1970s in the lyrics to "Coward of the County."

"I said to Roger, 'What if Larry Gatlin thinks we're writing about him and his brothers?'" said Wheeler. "And Roger said, 'Well, who gives a damn?' I don't think he was in love with Larry Gatlin.'"

Wheeler suggested that may have had to do with a time earlier in the 1970s when Gatlin and Bowling just happened to cross paths in the recording studio while in the presence of Larry Butler, who introduced the two.

"And Butler said to Gatlin, 'I guess you know Roger Bowling?' And Gatlin said, 'No, but I'm sure he knows me.' Roger was pretty quick. He said, 'Gatlin? Gatlin? Is your family in guns?' And I think that pissed off Larry Gatlin," said Wheeler.

"Coward of the County" wasn't the only memorable hit to come off the *Kenny* album.

"You Decorated My Life," written by Debbie Hupp and Bob Morrison, became the second No. 1 and the second crossover hit off the album. In addition to its No. 1 standing on the Billboard Hot Country Singles chart, it was No. 2 on the Billboard Hot Adult Contemporary chart and No. 7 on the Billboard Hot 100 Singles chart.

Even though it wasn't a "story song" like those that Rogers had become associated with at that point in his career, he liked the fact that it also crossed over from country to pop.

"It was a little less preachy and a little more personal and I liked the fact that it was successful," said Rogers. "It was an unusual song. If you get away from the other side of those that were more story songs, this was just a statement. This was more of a song that said what everybody would like to say and that every woman would like to hear. You really cover everyone if you can do that."

Rogers believes that his crossover appeal in the 1970s was due in part because more people were being exposed to non-traditional country music.

"There just seemed to be a demand at the time for something other than traditional country music. I think there were a lot of people in New York who had never listened to country music because they didn't relate to it. I'm using New York specifically, but in the North. When you do a song that people can relate to, they sometimes don't realize it's considered country," said Rogers. "Country music is one of those contagious genres of music. Once you get in, you don't leave. It's so hard to go anywhere else after you've done good country music."

It was, Rogers said, a way for an artist to survive in the music business of the late 1970s going into the 1980s. And it was a big part of helping the *Kenny* album become the success it became.

"There are only two ways you can survive in this business: You can do what everybody else is doing and do it better, or you can do something nobody else is doing and you don't invite comparison," said Rogers. "That's kind of always the road I've taken, to just find songs that say something that I enjoy singing, and then see what happens. I've been extremely lucky from that standpoint."

Rogers said he was always surprised when his songs or his albums crossed over from country to pop and are popular with both audiences.

"Only because I don't take myself that seriously. We've had some great production companies and some great people to do the promotion. They have to believe in it more than I do. And they seemed to kind of get on my bandwagon for some reason and we had a great period there," he said.

Rogers also is still a little puzzled why his songs have stood the test of time and are still talked about today.

"I had no idea. I was always flattered and thrilled and I was always as surprised as everyone else was," said Rogers about the lasting success of his music. "I think the secret has been that between myself and my producers, I've always picked really good songs. I don't think it's my voice that does it as much as the songs themselves. It really boils down to what I'd like to hear on the radio and then I try to find those songs and do them. And I assume and hope that other people would like to hear them as well."

The *Kenny* album, and the singles "You Decorated My Life" and "Coward of the County" are examples of Rogers' lasting legacy.

Mike Morsch

As for Wheeler, "Coward of the Country" became one of his biggest hits. And he believes Rogers was just the artist to sing it.

"I was tickled to death that it was a hit because I knew that Kenny sold a lot of records. He was really hot at the time," said Wheeler. "As I've told many people, to me, Kenny is the greatest country music singer. He's the master of story songs."

Discography

"Kenny"
Kenny Rogers
September 1979

"You Turn the Light On" (Louis Anderson, Stephen Geyer).... 3:03

"You Decorated My Life" (Deborah Kay Hupp, Robert E. Morrison).. 3:38

"She's a Mystery" (Larry Keith, Steve Pippin).......................... 2:54

"Goodbye Marie" (Dennis Linde, Mel McDaniel) 2:47

"Tulsa Turnaround" (Larry Collins, Paul Cotton, Alex Harvey) 2:52

"I Want to Make You Smile" 3:20

"Santiago Midnight Moonlight" (John Porter McMeans) 3:14

"One Man's Woman" (Steve Glassmeyer)...................................3:45

"In and Out of Your Heart" (Thomas Cain, Randy Cullers, Dennis Linde, Alan Rush).. 3:23

"Old Folks" (Willard Robison) 2:44

"Coward of the County" (Roger D. Bowling, Billy Ed Wheeler)....... .... 4:22

The success just spread like wildfire
Lost in Love
Air Supply

Russell Hitchcock thought his band had arrived. Air Supply had spent part of late 1977 touring 60 cities with Rod Stewart in support of his eighth studio album, *Foot Loose & Fancy Free*.

It was pretty cool for the Australian band, which had released its self-titled debut album in December 1976 and had just released its second album, *The Whole Thing's Started* in July 1977, to perform with Stewart at many of the big venues in the United States: Madison Square Garden in New York, Three Rivers Stadium in Pittsburgh, Candlestick Park in San Francisco, and a host of others across the country.

After the Stewart tour ended, Hitchcock and his band mates returned home to Australia in late December 1977.

"I was going through customs and I heard all these girls screaming outside the doors. I thought, 'Wow, this is pretty cool,'" said Hitchcock. "I grabbed my bags and went through the doors and I realized that the girls were there for another band and not us. I really had to hit the side door and go out with my tail between my legs."

Turns out that Air Supply had not yet arrived after all.

"For about a year after that, we couldn't get arrested," said Hitchcock. "We had six or seven people in the band then and we were getting offers to play for a couple hundred dollars a night. Obviously if you do the math, you can't afford to be on the road."

Hitchcock ended up going to Melbourne and staying with his sister while another co-founder of Air Supply, Graham Russell, settled back in Adelaide.

While in Melbourne, Hitchcock reconnected with an old friend, Les Gock, who had been in a band called Hush.

Hush formed in 1971 and had eventually become famous due to frequent appearances on *Countdown*, a weekly Australian music television show. It became an important springboard for Australian artists, helping the careers of many of them, including Olivia Newton-John, AC/DC, Men at Work, and Little River Band.

By 1977, Hush had disbanded and Gock became a jingles producer. Fortunately for Hitchcock, Gock was able to offer him a job writing jingles.

Twelve, maybe fourteen months, had passed and Air Supply was all but dead. Despite that, Hitchcock and Russell had stayed in touch and still harbored dreams of being rock stars.

"I said to Graham on the phone during that time period, 'I don't know whether we can keep doing this.' And he said, 'Let's just stick with it. We've got the songs; we've got the talent. It's going to happen,'" Hitchcock recalled Russell saying.

One day, Russell called Hitchcock to say he had written some songs and he wondered if Hitchcock would travel to Adelaide to listen to them.

"He said, 'I think we've got something here,' so I went out there," said Hitchcock. "One of the first songs he played me was 'Lost in Love.' As soon as I heard it, I said, 'This is a hit song, man.' There was no doubt in my mind. I would have bet the farm on it."

Another one of the songs that Russell played for Hitchcock that day in Adelaide was called "All Out of Love."

Graham Russell, left, reassured Russell Hitchcock in the late 1970s that Air Supply would eventually be successful. "Let's just stick with it. We've got the songs, we've got the talent. It's going to happen,'" Russell told Hitchcock. (Photo by Kiley Shetler)

Hitchcock and Russell were able to get a small record label in Australia called Wizard to record the song "Lost in Love" as a single and it became a huge hit in Australia.

"But we still couldn't afford to do too much as far as playing live was concerned," said Hitchcock.

By now, Russell and Hitchcock were backed by Ralph Taylor on drums, Brian Hamilton on bass, and David Moyse on guitar.

In April 1979, Air Supply released its fourth studio album, *Life Support*, which included a longer, five-and-a-half minute version of "Lost in Love." The album was recorded at Trafalgar Studios in Sydney, Australia. The single "Lost in Love" made it to No. 13 on the charts in both Australia and New Zealand.

Fate was about to intercede.

Somehow — Hitchcock isn't quite sure to this day how — the single "Lost in Love" found its way to the United States and to Clive Davis, former president of Columbia Records. Davis had left Columbia in 1975 to form his own label, Arista Records.

Davis heard "Lost in Love" and loved the song. And because of that, life was about to drastically change for the members of Air Supply.

"As soon as Clive heard the song he called Graham and he said, 'We want to sign you guys. This is going to be epic.' Once you had Clive in your corner, with the support of Arista and the people he had there at the time, as they say, the rest is history," said Hitchcock.

Davis confirmed in his autobiography *The Soundtrack of My Life* that he did immediately think "Lost in Love" was a hit.

"I was not aware of the group's background as a moderately well-known duo in their home country, that they'd released a 1977 album on Columbia in the States that flopped, or that 'Lost in Love' had been passed on by at least ten American record companies," Davis wrote in his book.

"I felt the song had true potential, that the vocal sound was unique, and that there is always a market for a well-crafted love song," wrote Davis.

"Lost in Love" was re-recorded and remixed and served as the focal point of Air Supply's fifth studio album of the same name. The album was released in March 1980 and featured three hit singles: the title track, which got to No. 3 on the U.S. Billboard Hot 100 Singles chart; "All Out of

Love," which reached No. 2 on the U.S. Billboard Hot 100 Singles chart; and "Every Woman in the World," which got to No. 5 on the Singles chart.

Hitchcock said that Russell's original intent on "All Out of Love" was for Hitchcock to sing both the verses and the chorus. But it didn't turn out that way.

"Typically to me, he'll say, 'I just wrote a new song, do you want to hear it? I'm not sure if it's any good,' or he'll say, 'This is your song to sing.' We just figure it out as we go," said Hitchcock. "In fact, with 'All Out of Love,' I was supposed to sing the verses as well as the chorus. And I just couldn't get it, so he ended up singing the verses and I sang the choruses. It couldn't have been any more well-planned if we tried. So those things are kind of lucky as well."

When it was released, the *Lost in Love* album hit big in the U.S. and worldwide.

"The success of the *Lost in Love* album just spread like wildfire," said Hitchcock. "We were one of the first bands ever to go to Seoul, South Korea; we played in Japan at the Budokan. We went everywhere."

The *Lost in Love* album itself reached No. 22 on the U.S. Billboard 200 Albums chart. It also reached No. 22 in New Zealand and No. 21 in Australia.

The album was the beginning of a handful of successful albums for Air Supply through the middle of the 1980s, including *The One That You Love* in 1981, *Now and Forever* in 1982, a *Greatest Hits* album in 1983 and the self-titled *Air Supply* in 1985.

In addition, during that same time period, the band had several Top 5 singles on the U.S. Billboard Hot 100 chart and the U.S. Adult Contemporary chart, including "The One that You Love," "Here I Am," "Sweet Dreams," "Even the Nights Are Better" and "Making Love Out of Nothing at All."

The constant for Air Supply through the 1970s, 1980s, and still today, has been Russell and Hitchcock.

"Graham is an amazing songwriter to me. I think he's very underrated and underappreciated to some degree because he's never been nominated for a Grammy. I think that's a bit of a tragedy," said Hitchcock. "It's always been about the music, and we've said this many times — in the beginning, especially when we hit in America to the degree that we did, we didn't know what we were doing so we couldn't make any mistakes."

The two have maintained a good relationship over the years, through both the tough times and the successes.

"I'm really very lucky. I have a great relationship with Graham. I love him to death. I don't have any brothers and neither does he, so we've kind of formed that bond over the years," said Hitchcock. "We're very supportive of each other, in our music and our private lives. It couldn't have worked out better for me. We get along at every level. It's quite amazing to me."

That relationship has also translated well to onstage performances.

"You always know that the guy beside you on stage is going to be there for you, vocally and musically. He's going to do the best job he can for Air Supply and the song at that particular time," said Hitchcock. "And we've kind of instilled that in the guys in the band today, who have been with us now anywhere from fifteen years to about three or four years. I always say to them, 'You only get one chance to do this tonight and that's right now. Have lots of energy. Be respectful of the music. Most of all, have fun and project something that's very positive because that's what we're all about.'"

Although life on the road can be challenging, particularly the traveling aspect, Hitchcock said he doesn't have any plans on hanging it up anytime soon. Air Supply still draws crowds wherever it performs.

"We love being on the road; touring is everything to us. Forty years is a long time. You can count the bands on one hand that are still together and the other bands that don't have any original members left," said Hitchcock.

"Sometimes I think to myself, 'How am I going to do this today?' Get to the theater, get ready, get changed. But as soon as you put the stage clothes on, that kind of clicks the switch for you. Getting together with all the guys in the band and the crew, it's just a lot of fun. I really wouldn't do it if I wasn't enjoying it because the rest of it is hard enough as it is."

As for the *Lost in Love* album, that's the one that thrust Air Supply on the fast track to stardom, a ride that's lasted for more than four decades.

"From day one, the songs have touched everybody that's listened to them. Like a lot of songs that Graham writes, lyrically I think they just go straight to your heart and, melodically, they are just exceptional songs, in my opinion," said Hitchcock. "People just heard them and they wanted more and more. It's very important to us that we make an emotional connection with people."

Discography

"Lost in Love"
Air Supply
March 1980

"Lost in Love" (Graham Russell) 3:51

"Every Woman in the World" (Dominic Bugatti, Frank Musker).... .... 3:33

"Just Another Woman" (Graham Russell)................................. 3:51

"Having You Near Me" (Graham Russell, Rex Goh, Clive Davis).... .... 3:50

"American Hearts" (Graham Russell, Frank Musker, Clive Davis) 3:13

"Chances" (Graham Russell) 3:31

"Old Habits Die Hard" (Criston Barker, David Moyse) 3:03

"I Can't Get Excited" (Graham Russell) 5:01

"All Out of Love" (Graham Russell, Clive Davis)....................... 3:59

"My Best Friend" (Graham Russell).. 2:32

Finding the lost skins and laying the foundation
On Through the Night
Def Leppard

At the ripe old age of 14, Rick Allen was ready to give up his career as a musician. He was fed up with being in local bands that just played cover songs in and around Sheffield, England.

So in a fit of frustration one evening, he threw his drum kit down the outside steps of his parents' house and it rolled into the street.

"It wasn't very smart of me," said Allen. "But it made a great sound as it was going down the steps."

His parents, however, didn't believe the youngster's music career was over. They were avid readers of *The Star*, the daily newspaper published in Sheffield. One day, Allen's mother was reading an article by reporter Keith Strong titled "Leppard loses skins." It was about a local band looking to replace its drummer, Tony Kenning.

"Why don't we call?" Allen recalled his parents saying to him. "I was too scared to call. But my mother called up and within days of talking to Keith Strong, he put us in touch with Joe Elliot and Steve Clark."

Allen met Elliot and Clark at one of the local clubs in Sheffield and realized that they had all crossed paths while playing the local club scene.

Def Leppard had a new drummer.

"It was just a natural fit. We were instantly friends because we had common ground in our music," said Allen. "Tony Kenning, the original drummer, came around and wanted his job back. But fortunately, I knew the parts really well and I got the job."

It was November 1978 and Allen was just 15 years old.

For much of 1979, Def Leppard developed a loyal following and was considered the leaders of the new wave of British heavy metal by its fans. That popularity got the band noticed by the Phonogram/Vertigo record label, which in the United States was known as Mercury Records.

The band began recording its debut album, *On Through the Night*, in late 1979 at Startling Studios in Ascot, Berkshire, England.

Startling Studios wasn't just any old recording studio. By late 1979, it already had quite a history. It was originally called Ascot Sound Studios and was a tape-based, analog recording studio built in 1970 by John Lennon and Yoko Ono, on their estate, Tittenhurst Park, in Berkshire.

The final photo session for the Beatles as a band was shot at Tittenhurst Park on August 22, 1969, and those photos were used for both the front and back covers of their 1970 album *Hey Jude*.

In September 1973 when Lennon and Ono moved to New York City, they sold Tittenhurst Park to Ringo Starr, who renamed the studio "Startling Studios" and made it available to other recording artists to use. Lennon's video for his "Imagine" video was shot there.

Tom Allom, who had worked with Judas Priest and Black Sabbath, would produce Def Leppard's *On Through the Night* album. Because the band had spent all of 1979 playing in clubs, it had honed all the songs that were going to be recorded for the album.

"The songs really didn't have to be written or rewritten or rearranged; they were all there. So all that Tom had to do was really just capture a performance. We did very few overdubs," said Allen.

Lead vocalist Elliot, guitarists Clark and Willis, and bass player Rick Savage wrote or co-wrote all the songs that would appear on the album.

"We were all into glam rock. We loved David Bowie, we loved Roxy Music, we loved Slade, we loved Queen, all these different bands, Mott the Hoople, Ian Hunter," said Allen. "Those were really our influences. It wasn't what a lot of people think. Our influences were quite diverse and we were very fortunate to have grown up in the 1970s, and be exposed to so many different kinds of music."

Four singles were released from *On Through the Night*, including "Rocks Off," "Wasted," "Hello America," and "Rock Brigade." The singles versions of "Rocks Off," "Wasted" and "Hello America" ended up being different recorded versions of the ones used on the album. But the singles versions of those songs have never been released on CD, because the band's management didn't like the production aspects of the singles.

The album itself made it to No. 51 on the U.S. Billboard 200 Albums chart, but did substantially better in the band's home country, getting to No. 15 on the U.K. Albums chart. None of the singles charted in the U.S., but "Hello America" made it to No. 45 and "Wasted" got to No. 61 on the U.K. Singles chart.

By the time *On Through the Night* was released in March 1980, Allen was now a 16-year-old drummer in a rock and roll band that had just made its first album.

"I didn't really look very far into the future at that point. For me, making that album was the endeavor of doing something that I loved to do. You just try to have fun," said Allen. "I knew that I was working in a situation where there was a bunch of talented people around me. Maybe we all had a different perspective on what it was that we were actually doing. Joe is really driven. Maybe his thought process was different. But for me, I was just happy to be where I was and doing what I loved to do."

After the album was released, there was a perception among U.K. fans that *On Through the Night* was the band's attempt to appeal to U.S. audiences. The song "Hello America" particularly, and the fact that Def Leppard was touring more in the U.S. in support of bands like Ted Nugent, Pat Travers and AC/DC, helped fuel that perception.

There was also a time that Allen thought the music on *On Through the Night* didn't hold up well as the band's career progressed through the 1980s and beyond. But he has softened his stance on that over the years.

"Going back to it, it's almost like music that we grew up listening to. Even if you didn't like it in the particular time period that it happened, you find yourself actually liking it now," said Allen. "Maybe it's because it's in your DNA and it's just something that after so much time passes, you go, 'Oh, that was really good and I'm really proud that I did that.'"

Def Leppard continued to evolve and hit its stride through much of the 1980s. Its next album, *High 'n' Dry* in 1981, reached No. 38 on the U.S. Billboard 200 Albums chart and No. 26 on the U.K. Albums chart.

But it was the band's third studio album, *Pyromania,* released in January 1983 and produced by Robert John "Mutt" Lange, who had also produced for AC/DC, that helped elevate Def Leppard's heavy metal chops. It would reach No. 2 on the U.S. Billboard 200 Albums chart and No. 18 on the U.K. Albums chart.

Allen said that the music and the experience of making the *On Through the Night* album laid the groundwork for what the band would achieve through the 1980s.

"If I didn't do that, [*On Through the Night*], I wouldn't have gotten to do '*High 'n Dry* and I wouldn't have gotten to do *Pyromania* and I wouldn't have eventually gotten to do *Hysteria*. So I think it's a process, it's a journey, and I'm just happy to be doing what I'm doing now. Without all that in the early days, I'm not sure I would be in the same place."

Def Leppard's lead vocalist Joe Elliot is on the record as saying that drummer Rick Allen eventually became "a better drummer than he was when he had two arms." (Photo by Tom Curley)

But Allen just about didn't get to do the band's fourth studio album, *Hysteria,* which wasn't released until August 1987. It took more than three years to record and release the follow-up album to *Pyromania* because of a tragedy.

According to media accounts at the time, Allen was involved in a car accident on December 31, 1984. While trying to pass another car at a high speed, Allen lost control of his Corvette and hit a stone wall. Because he had improperly fastened his seatbelt, Allen was thrown from the car, and the ejection severed Allen's left arm. Doctors tried to reattach his arm, but it eventually had to be amputated due to infection.

Allen's long road to recovery contributed to the delay of the recording and release of *Hysteria* in 1987. He eventually recovered and ended up, through hard work and determination, redefining what could be done on the drums with new techniques and technology using only one arm and his feet.

"The accident and everything at the time was devastating. But over time, it's actually become a blessing. It's nice that I can share my life experiences and inspire others. That, to me, is a huge gift," said Allen.

Over the years, Allen has continued to play with Def Leppard and eventually became "a better drummer than he was when he had two arms," according to Joe Elliott.

In addition to his duties with the band, Allen has become an artist as well. His fine art exhibit, titled *Rick Allen: Angels and Icons*, has been on display at various art galleries in the U.S.

Working in a mixed media process that fuses photography, LED light art, and painting, Allen's creations began with the filming of him playing with the use of LED lights attached to the tip of his drumsticks. Using long exposures, the lights created abstract patterns corresponding to the song performed.

Stacks of Wax

Rick Allen was just 15 years old when he joined Def Leppard as its drummer in 1978. (Photo by Mike Morsch)

"In essence, what you do is capture huge chunks of a song," said Allen. "I'd be sitting there playing 'Hysteria,' or any other song, for that matter. The idea is to capture that with the light sticks in a dark room, and it having a unique sort of footprint as that relates to the song that you're playing. A lot of times the imagery would really capture the emotion and the essence of the song. It was a long process of picking the pieces that conjured up the right sort of emotion. But most of the time, it was pretty obvious."

But it all started in the late 1970s for a teenager who would be behind the drum kit when Def Leppard recorded its first album, *On Through the Night*.

"When I first started out, I was into big band, into all kinds of different music, music that my dad was listening to at the time - Elton John, Deep Purple. It was fantastic. It was a great time for music," said Allen. "I think naturally what happens is that you take that on; it becomes part of your influenced me, that really lit a fire under my backside.

Bass player Rick Savage co-wrote all of the songs that would appear on Def Leppard's 1979 album "On Through the Night." (Photo by Tom Curley)

Discography

"On Through the Night"
Def Leppard

Side one

"Rock Brigade" (Rick Savage, Steve Clark, Joe Elliott) 3:09

"Hello America" (Savage, Clark, Elliott) 3:27

"Sorrow Is a Woman" (Savage, Clark, Pete Willis, Elliott) 3:54

"It Could Be You" (Willis, Elliott) 2:33

"Satellite" (Savage, Clark, Willis, Elliott) 4:28

"When the Walls Came Tumbling Down" (Clark, Elliott, Andrew Smith) 4:44

Side two

"Wasted" (Clark, Elliott) 3:45

"Rocks Off" (Willis, Savage, Clark, Elliott) 3:42

"It Don't Matter" (Willis, Elliott, Clark) 3:21

"Answer to the Master" (Willis, Clark, Savage, Elliott) 3:13

"Overture" (Savage, Clark, Willis, Elliott) 7:44

Acknowledgements

Once again, *The Vinyl Dialogues* series features a talented group of professionals who collaborated to produce the best book possible.

Leading the way, as has been the case since the inception of the series, is my friend and mentor Frank D. Quattrone. He and I have worked together for a long time and he has always helped me to be a better writer. He's the one who gets the first look at the copy, and his reactions, suggestions, and edits are important to the process. His continued support and encouragement, and endless enthusiasm for the subject matter, are invaluable assets. The fact that Frank is a longtime friend with whom I enjoy working, makes a fun project even more so.

Much the same can be said for designer Ron Dacanay, who took the photo of, and designed, the front cover as well as provided the creative design for the back cover. Ron and I have worked together for years in the newspaper business and I've never seen a design of his that I didn't like. He knows what I want from a visual standpoint and he delivers an attractive presentation.

A lot of the fine-tuning of the copy was done by editors Ann Stolinsky and Ruth Littner of Gemini Wordsmiths (www.geminiwordsmiths.com). They took the final look at all three books in *The Vinyl Dialogues* series, and their skills help establish the credibility of the information presented here. It's critical to have good editors and these two are among the best.

Several colleagues and friends contributed photographs to this volume: Phil McAuliffe, newspaper colleague and great photographer, provided some vintage shots of

Mike Morsch

Emerson, Lake and Palmer and the Pointer Sisters; Tom Curley, director of Wentworth Gallery in King of Prussia, Pennsylvania, contributed some shots of Def Leppard; Patti Myers, the "webmistress" for the band Player, offered some great shots of the late Natalie Cole; my daughter Kiley Shetler, who filled in for me at the Air Supply concert and got some photos for me; Jim Messina, of Loggins and Messina, who offered me the use of a few shots from his personal collection; and songwriter Billy Edd Wheeler, who supplied a photo from his personal collection.

I could not document the history of these albums without the artists who lived those experiences and made the music. They were all gracious with their interview time and their recollections. My goal has always been to get the stories documented accurately through their eyes. And it's been an added bonus — in all three volumes of this series — to get a personal walk through the soundtrack of my life, courtesy of these artists.

I dealt directly with several of them, including Ray Dorset, a.k.a Mungo Jerry; Walter "Bunny" Sigler, a songwriter and performer with Philadelphia International Records; Michael Stanley; Jim Messina of Buffalo Springfield and Loggins and Messina; Kent LaVoie, a.k.a. Lobo; and producer Christopher Bond.

I also dealt with publicists who helped me gain access to the artists who I could not reach on my own.

At the top of the list for the past 10 years has been Jonathan Wolfson of Wolfson Entertainment. He is the manager for Daryl Hall and John Oates and I've known him for a long time. Hall and Oates are the only artists who have appeared in all three volumes of *The Vinyl Dialogues*. I have interviewed both John and Daryl many times and Jonathan has always provided me with access to them when I've asked for interviews. I appreciate that he has that much confidence in my writing.

Other publicists who provided access to the artists include Randy Alexander of Randex Communications; Taylor Page of Barn Party Productions, who represents Fito de la Parra of Canned Heat; Amanda French Clark of Webster Public Relations, who represents Kenny Rogers and Harry Wayne Casey, a.k.a. KC, of KC and The Sunshine Band; Michela DellaMonica of Autonomic Media, who represents Mark Lindsay of Paul Revere and the Raiders; Acela Cortese Burkhardt, who represents Pat Vegas of Redbone; Ravi Dabiesingh of 21st Century Artists, Inc., who represents Walter Williams of the O'Jays; Jack White of Bobby Caldwell Entertainment, Ltd., who represents Bobby Caldwell; Chloe Newline of Tag/The Awareness Group, who represents Peter Wolf of the J. Geils Band; Allison Zucker-Perelman, President of Relevant Communications, Inc., who represents Rick Allen of Def Leppard; Jaclyn Burgess, who represents Henry Fambrough of the Spinners; Doug Weber of New Ocean Media, who represents Brad Whitford, and Derek St. Holmes of Whitford St. Holmes; Bruce Pilato, who represents Carl Palmer of Emerson, Lake and Palmer; Lee Beverly, who represents Eddie Money; Cleve Hattersley, who represents Kinky Friedman; Andy Gilmartin, who represents Liberty DeVitto of the Billy Joel Band; Waldemar "Wally" Dents, who represents Howard Bellamy of the Bellamy Brothers; Rob Cotto, who represents Neil Sedaka; Steve Levesque, President of Luck Media and Marketing, who represent Russell Hitchcock of Air Supply; and Todd Brodginski of Reckoning PR, who represents Art Garfunkel. I thank all of them for their help in securing interviews with the artists.

Special thanks to Aubrey Huston, my boss at Packet Media LLC in Princeton N.J., and Anthony Stoeckert, entertainment editor at Packet Media LLC, for allowing me to write music stories; and my publisher, Bob Sims of Biblio Publishing of Columbus, Ohio, who has continued to have

Mike Morsch

faith in my writing through four books now, including three in *The Vinyl Dialogues* series.

And finally, my books would not be possible without the love and support of my family: my wife Judy, daughter and son-in-law Kiley and Mat Shetler, daughter Lexi Morsch, stepdaughter Kaitie Hughes, and stepson Kevin Hughes.

Sources

Author interview with Natalie Cole on March 10, 2015; *Angel on My Shoulder* by Natalie Cole and Digby Diehl, published in 2000.

Author interview with Fito de la Parra of Canned Heat on June 10, 2015.

Author interview with Kenny Rogers on July 3, 2015; author interview with Billy Edd Wheeler on November 4, 2015.

Author interview with Mark Lindsay of Paul Revere and the Raiders on July 13, 2015.

Author interview with Ray Dorset of Mungo Jerry on July 14, 2015.

Author interview with Harry Wayne Casey of KC and The Sunshine Band on July 16, 2015.

Author interview with Pat Vegas of Redbone on July 31, 2015.

Author interview with Walter Williams of the O'Jays on August 6, 2015; author interview with Walter "Bunny" Sigler on October 26, 2015.

Author interview with Bobby Caldwell on August 7, 2015.

Author interview with Peter Wolf of the J. Geils Band on August 12, 2015.

Author interview with Rick Allen of Def Leppard on August 27, 2015.

Author interview with Henry Fambrough of the Spinners on September 21, 2015; author interview with Dionne Warwick on October 26, 2015; Henry Fambrough YouTube interview with Tom Meros.

Author interview with Michael Stanley on September 21, 2015.

Author interview with Sandy Yaguda of Jay and the Americans on September 23, 2015.

Author interview with Kinky Friedman on September 28, 2015.

Author interview with Eddie Money on October 20, 2015.

Author interview with Carl Palmer of Emerson, Lake and Palmer on October 29, 2015.

Author interview with Derek St. Holmes of the Ted Nugent band on November 6, 2015.

Author interview with Ruth Pointer of the Pointer Sisters on November 16, 2015.

Author interview with Jim Messina of Loggins and Messina on November 19, 2015.

Author interview with Liberty DeVitto of the Billy Joel band on January 6, 2016; interview with Billy Joel by Bill DeMain, *Performing Songwriter Magazine*, 2008.

Author interview with Howard Bellamy of the Bellamy Brothers on January 11, 2016.

Author interview with Neil Sedaka on January 19, 2016.

Author interview with Russell Hitchcock of Air Supply on January 19, 2016; *The Soundtrack of My Life* by Clive Davis with Anthony DeCurtis.

Author interview with Kent LaVoie, a.k.a. Lobo, on January 25, 2016.

Author interview with Daryl Hall of Hall & Oates on February 11, 2016; author interview with John Oates of Hall & Oates on March 11, 2016; author interview with Barry Rudolph on February 22, 2016; author interview with Christopher Bond on March 28, 2016; 2014 *Philadelphia Magazine* interview with *Rocky* director John Avildsen.

Author interview with William A. King of the Commodores on March 1, 2016.

Author interview with Art Garfunkel on April 25, 2016.
Author interview with Bruce Johnston, October 2014.

About the author

Mike Morsch has been a reporter, editor, and columnist for nearly 40 years at newspapers in Iowa, Illinois, Pennsylvania, and New Jersey.

He has earned numerous awards for his writing from the Illinois Press Association, the Pennsylvania Newspaper Association, the Philadelphia Press Association, the Local Media Association, and the New Jersey Press Association.

This is Mike's fourth book for Biblio Publishing, which includes three volumes of *The Vinyl Dialogues* series, and a

Mike Morsch

memoir titled *Dancing in My Underwear: The Soundtrack of My Life.*

    A 1982 graduate of the University of Iowa, he earned a bachelor of science degree in journalism and was a two-year letterman on the Hawkeyes' baseball team.

    Mike is currently the executive editor and digital news director of Packet Media LLC in Princeton, New Jersey. You can reach him by email at msquared35@yahoo.com.

Index

1

10cc, 141

A

Abandoned Luncheonette, 151, 152, 155, 156, 157, 162, 163
ABC Records, 111, 135
AC/DC, 272, 282
Aerosmith, 192, 193
AIR Studios, 165
Air Supply, vii, 271, 272, 273, 274, 275, 276, 277, 278, 290, 291, 295
Al Perkins, 109, 113
Alan Freed, 10
Alan Jackson, 136
Alex Kazanegras, 21
All Out of Love, 272, 275, 278
Allen Collins Band, 64
Amy Grant, 257
Andrew Gold, 170
Andy Williams, 17, 18
Angel on My Shoulder, 180, 182, 183, 293
Anne Murray, 22
Aretha Franklin, 82, 103, 177, 179, 216, 235
Arif Mardin, 155, 163
Arista Records, 274
Art Garfunkel, v, 165, 167, 170, 171, 175, 291, 295
Artie Butler, 42
Asia, 244, 245, 246
Atlantic Records, 60, 79, 82, 100, 151, 163, 252
Audrey Hepburn, 263

B

B.B. King, 101, 111
Baby Hold On, 233, 235, 237, 239
Baby, Don't Get Hooked on Me, 62
Back Stabbers, iv, 67, 69, 72, 74, 75, 76, 77, 79, 83
Badfinger, 62
Barry Bailey, 61
Barry Manilow, 45
Barry Mann, 47, 140
Barry McGuire, 44
Barry Rudolph, 156, 295
Beach Boys, 39, 40, 166, 170, 171, 207, 235
Ben E. King, 9
Bernie Taupin, 141
Berry Gordy, 80, 82, 228
Big Brother and the Holding Company, 234
Big Tree Records, 57, 58, 60
Bill Conti, 150
Bill Graham, 233, 234, 237
Bill Szymczyk, 101, 109, 111
Billie Holiday, 122, 137
Billy Edd Wheeler, 261, 262, 290, 293
Billy Henderson, 80
Billy Joel, vi, 213, 215, 221, 222, 291, 294
Billy Paul, 70, 75, 83
Black Sabbath, 30, 193, 280
Bloodshot, iv, 99, 100, 101, 102, 103, 104, 107, 115
Blue Thumb Records, 122, 123
Bob Dylan, 35, 99, 135, 136, 207, 216

Bobby Caldwell, vii, 251, 252, 253, 255, 256, 259, 291, 293
Bobby Goldsboro, 46
Bobby Hart, 139
Bobby Smith, 80
Boogie Shoes, 201
Boz Scaggs, 255, 256
Brad Whitford, 192, 291
Brain Salad Surgery, 241
Breakaway, v, 165, 166, 167, 168, 170, 171, 172, 173, 175
Breaking Up is Hard to Do, 146
Brick House, 225, 230, 231
Bridge Over Troubled Water, 168, 220
Bridge Over Troubled Waters, 168
Brill Building, 139, 140, 145
Bruce Botnick, 234
Bruce Johnston, 39, 166, 170, 171, 175, 295
Bruce Springsteen, 99, 127
Bryan Garafalo, 117
Buddy Holly, 144
Buffalo Springfield, 15, 18, 19, 21, 114, 290
Burt Bacharach, 139
Butch Rillera, 93

C

C.P. Spencer, 80
Caddyshack, 25
Calendar Girl, 140, 146
Camellia, 153, 154, 155, 156, 157, 158, 164
Candido "Lolly" Vegas, 91
Canned Heat, iii, 49, 50, 51, 53, 54, 55, 291, 293
Capitol Records, 177, 181, 182
Cara Mia, 8

Caribou Ranch, 114, 115
Carl Palmer, 241, 242, 250, 291, 294
Carol Burnett, 126
Carole King, 139, 140
CBS Records, 70, 93
Celine Dion, 160
Charles "Cholly" Atkins, 75, 87
Chateau Marmont Hotel, 173
Christopher Bond, 155, 290, 295
Chuck Berry, 104
Chuck Glazer, 131
Chuck Jackson, 177, 185
Cliff Davies, 188, 191
Cliff Richard, 141
Clive Davis, 19, 24, 45, 170, 274, 278, 295
Colin Earl, 29, 30, 34
Columbia Records, 15, 17, 19, 23, 24, 39, 42, 45, 165, 170, 215, 219, 220, 274
Come and Get Your Love, 92, 96, 97, 98
Connie Francis, 140
Could It Be I'm Falling in Love, 83, 84
Coward of the County, 262, 263, 264, 265, 266, 267, 269
Cream, 104
Crystal Gayle, 263
Curb Records, 207, 208, 210
Curtis Mayfield, 10, 13, 20, 182
Curtom Records, 182
Cynthia Weil, 47, 140

D

Dan Fogelberg, 109, 114
Dan Tana's Restaurant, 172
Daryl Hall, v, 149, 151, 152, 164, 290, 295

David Bellamy, 205, 206, 209, 212
David Bowie, 1, 161, 281
David Gahr, 99
David Geffen, 244
David Rubinson, 121, 127
David Spero, 116
Dawn Records, 30
Deep Purple, 285
Def Leppard, vii, 279, 280, 282, 283, 284, 285, 286, 287, 290, 291, 294
Denny Carmassi, 192
Derek St. Holmes, 187, 189, 191, 194, 195, 291, 294
Diana Ross, 122
Dick Clark, 41, 144, 252
Dionne Warwick, 85, 86, 294
Disco Duck, 210
Doc Pomus, 9, 13
Dolly Parton, 132
Don Fardon, 42
Don Kirshner, 109, 117
Doobie Brothers, 207
Dottie West, 263
Doug Morris, 60
Doug Stegmeyer, 213, 214, 221

E

Earl Young, 72
Easy, 63, 66, 143, 166, 226, 227, 230, 231
Ed Greene, 156
Ed Sullivan, 4
Eddie Levert, 67
Eddie Money, vi, 233, 234, 236, 237, 238, 239, 291, 294
Electric Lady Studios, 60
Electronically Tested, iii, 29, 31, 33, 34, 35, 37

Elton John, 141, 144, 285
Elvis Presley, 7
Eric Carmen, 112
Every Woman in the World, 275, 278

F

Faces, 33
Faye Dunaway, 101, 115, 144
Fito de la Parra, 49, 291, 293
Five Easy Pieces, 172
Flip Wilson, 126
Flying Burrito Brothers, 132
Foot Loose & Fancy Free, 271
Footloose, 25
Four Tops, 82, 87, 227, 228
Frank Sinatra, 137, 216
Friends and Legends, iv, 109, 110, 111, 113, 115, 116, 117, 118, 119

G

G.C. Cameron, 82
Gary Coleman, 156
Gary Mallaber, 235
Gary Puckett, 42, 46
Geffen Records, 244
Gene Cotton, 208
Gene McFadden, 72, 77
Geoff Downes, 244
George Harrison, 234
George McCrae, 199
Gerry Goffin, 140
Ginger Baker, 30
Gladys Knight and the Pips, 87, 228
Glen Campbell, 134
Going Up the Country, 50, 54
Gonna Fly Now, 150, 151

Graham Russell, 272, 273, 278
Gram Parsons, 132
Grateful Dead, 30, 104, 233, 234, 235
Greg Lake, 241, 249, 250

H

Hal Blaine, 42
Hal David, 139, 175
Hall & Oates, v, 149, 150, 151, 153, 155, 156, 159, 162, 164, 295
Happy Birthday Sweet 16, 140
Harold Melvin & the Blue Notes, 70, 83
Harry Wayne Casey, 197, 198, 203, 251, 291, 293
Harvey Fuqua, 80, 87
Heat of the Moment, 245
Helen Reddy, 126
Helena Kallianiotes, 172
Henry Fambrough, 79, 81, 291, 294
Hey Little Cobra, 39, 40
Honky Chateau, 141
Hoodoo Rhythm Devils, 123
Hooker 'n Heat, iii, 49, 50, 52, 53, 54, 55
House at Pooh Corner, 16, 20, 22, 27
How Could I Let You Get Away, 83, 84, 90
Howard Bellamy, 205, 206, 207, 208, 209, 212, 291, 295
Howard Emerson, 213
Howard Greenfield, 140, 142, 147
Howard Kane, 7
Hysteria, 282, 284, 285

I

I Feel the Earth Move, 139
I Only Have Eyes for You, 166, 175
I'll Be Around, 83, 84
Ian Hunter, 281
Ike and Tina Turner, 109
In the Summertime, 29, 30, 31, 32, 33, 34, 35, 37
Inseparable, v, 177, 178, 180, 181, 182, 183, 185, 256

J

J. Geils Band, iv, 99, 100, 101, 104, 105, 106, 111, 115, 291, 293
Jack Gold, 42
Jack Nicholson, 172
Jailhouse Rock, 7
James Carmichael, 225, 227
James Edwards, 80
James Taylor, 103, 111, 139, 207
Janis Ian, 43
Janis Joplin, 99, 104, 234
Jay and the Americans, iii, 4, 5, 6, 7, 8, 9, 10, 11, 12, 13, 294
Jay Black, 5, 8, 10
Jefferson Airplane, 1, 104, 234
Jenny Sullivan, 16
Jerry Butler, 179
Jerry Fuller, 41, 45
Jerry Garcia, 234
Jerry Leiber, 7, 139
Jerry Ragovoy, 101
Jesus Christ, Superstar, 117
Jim Gordon, 156
Jim Messina, 15, 19, 20, 23, 26, 27, 290, 294
Jim Morrison, 234

Jim Stafford, 206, 209, 212
Jimi Hendrix, 60, 93
Jimmy Lyon, 233, 239
Joe Elliot, 279, 283, 284, 287
Joe Guercio, 114
Joe Lala, 109, 113
Joe Osborn, 170
Joe Vitale, 109, 113, 119
Joe Walsh, 101, 109, 110, 111, 119, 243, 250
John, 7
John Avildsen, 150, 295
John Godfrey, 30
John Lee Hooker, iii, 49, 50, 51, 55, 103
John Lennon, 115, 119, 142, 280
John Loudermilk, 42
John Oates, v, 149, 151, 152, 155, 164, 290, 295
John Wetton, 244
Johnny Cash, 261
Johnny Mathis, 42
Johnny Rivers, 207
Johnny Winter, 34
Judas Priest, 280
Judy Garland, 144
Julie Andrews, 263
June Carter, 261
Just the Way You Are, 219, 222

K

KC and The Sunshine Band, 197, 198, 199, 201, 202, 203, 251, 252, 291, 293
Keith Emerson, 2, 241, 248, 250
Kenny Gamble, 67, 68, 79, 179
Kenny Loggins, 15, 20, 23, 25, 26, 27
Kenny Passarelli, 113, 117, 119

Kenny Rogers, vii, 261, 262, 263, 264, 269, 291, 293
Kenny Vance, 7
Kent LaVoie, 57, 290, 295
Kiki Dee, 141
Kim Carnes, 208
King Crimson, 33, 242, 244, 249
Kinky Friedman, v, 131, 132, 134, 135, 136, 138, 291, 294
KISS, 161
Kris Kristofferson, 136

L

Lady Sings the Blues, 122
Larkin Arnold, 180
Larrabee Sound Studios, 154, 155
Larry Butler, 263, 266
Larry E. Williams, 207, 212
Larry Gatlin, 265, 266
Larry Sims, 18
Larry Taylor, 53
Las Vegas Turnaround, 152
Laurie Bird, 172, 173
Led Zeppelin, 54, 193, 227, 234
Lee Dorsey, 123
Leland Sklar, 156
Leo Gallagher, 207
Leon Huff, 67, 77, 79, 179
Leon Russell, 44
Lester, 18
Let Your Love Flow, vi, 205, 207, 208, 209, 210, 211, 212
Levon Helm, 135
Liberty DeVitto, 213, 291, 294
Liberty Records, 50, 52
Lionel Richie, 223, 224, 225, 226, 228, 229, 230, 231
Little River Band, 272
Lobo, iv, 57, 58, 59, 60, 61, 64, 65, 66, 290, 295

Loggins and Messina, iii, 15, 18, 22, 23, 25, 27, 207, 290, 294
Lonnie Turner, 235
Lost in Love, vii, 271, 272, 273, 274, 275, 277, 278
Lou Rawls, 70
Louie Louie, 39
Louis Armstrong, 137
Love Train, 69, 75, 76, 77
Love Will Keep Us Together, 140, 142, 143, 147
Lynyrd Skynyrd, 64

M

Manassas, 109, 113, 117
Marc Bolan, 33
Mariah Carey, 160
Mark Lindsay, 39, 42, 47, 291, 293
Marshall Tucker Band, 237
Martha Reeves, 228
Marvin Gaye, 82, 87, 228
Marvin Hamlisch, 140
Marvin Yancy, 177, 185
Mary Jo Webster, 95
McFadden and Whitehead, 73
Men at Work, 272
Mercury Records, 280
Merel Bregante, 18
MFSB, 72, 83, 84
Michael Baird, 156
Michael Stanley, iv, 101, 109, 110, 112, 118, 119, 290, 294
Mick Jagger, 128, 161
Mike Cole, 30
Mike Stoller, 7, 139
Milan Williams, 223, 224, 225, 231
Milt Holland, 21
Monterey Pop Festival, 49

Mort Shuman, 9, 13
Motown, 80, 82, 87, 180, 182, 223, 226, 228
Motown Studios, 226
Mott the Hoople, 33, 281
Mountain Studios, 242
Mud Slide Slim, 139
Muddy Waters, 103
Mungo Jerry, iii, 29, 30, 33, 34, 35, 37, 290, 293
Muskrat Love, 209
My Fair Lady, vii, 261, 262, 263
My Little Town, 167, 168, 175

N

Nat, 177, 256
Natalie Cole, v, 1, 177, 178, 182, 183, 184, 185, 256, 290, 293
Neil Diamond, 140, 207
Neil Sedaka, v, 139, 140, 147, 291, 295
Neil Young, 15, 25, 35
Nelson Mandela, 131
New York State of Mind, 215
Nils Lofgren, 91
Nitty Gritty Dirt Band, 22
Norman Harris, 72
Norman Seeff, 172

O

Of A Simple Man, 66
Olivia Newton-John, 272
On Through the Night, vii, 279, 280, 281, 282, 285, 286, 287
One of a Kind, 83, 84, 90
Only the Good Die Young, 218, 219, 222

P

P.F. Sloan, 44, 47
Paragon Studios, 182
Pat Vegas, 91, 92, 93, 94, 96, 97, 291, 293
Paul Harris, 109, 113, 119
Paul King, 30, 33, 34
Paul McCartney, 115, 119, 234
Paul Revere and the Raiders, 39, 40, 41, 42, 252, 291, 293
Paul Simon, 135, 140, 167, 168, 175, 216
Pervis Jackson, 80
Pete DePoe, 92, 93, 98
Pete Ham, 62
Pete Willis, 287
Peter Cetera, 257
Peter Finch, 197
Peter Sinfield, 242, 249, 250
Peter Wolf, 99, 107, 115, 291, 293
Phil Cody, 142, 147
Phil Gernhard, 57, 207
Phil Nicholson, 189
Phil Ramone, 170, 216, 221
Phil Spector, 140
Philadelphia International Records, 67, 69, 70, 79, 83, 179, 290
Philippe Wynne, 82
Phonogram/Vertigo, 280
Piano Man, 213, 214, 215
Pierre LaRoche, 161
Pink Floyd, 34, 241
Planet Records, 126
Poco, 15, 19, 21, 25, 207
Pye Records, 30
Pyromania, 282, 284

Q

Queen, 82, 195, 281

R

Raquel Welch, 172
Ray Charles, 216
Ray Dorset, 29, 35, 37, 290, 293
RCA Records, 151
Redbone, iv, 91, 93, 95, 96, 97, 98, 109, 291, 293
Rex Harrison, 263
Richard, 99
Richard Perry, 165, 170
Richie Cannata, 214
Richie Furay, 15, 25, 114, 115
Rick Allen, 279, 283, 284, 285, 291, 294
Rick Dees & His Cast of Idiots, 210
Rick Derringer, 112
Rick Savage, 281, 286, 287
Righteous Brothers, 4, 5, 163
Ringo Starr, 6, 280
Rip Chords, 39, 40
Ritchie Valens, 144
Rob Grange, 188, 191
Rock Your Baby, 199
Rocket Records, 141, 144
Rocky, 150, 161, 295
Rod Stewart, 33, 235, 271
Roger Bowling, 261, 262, 266
Roger Miller, 136
Rolling Stones, 101, 104, 105, 144, 234, 241
Ronald LaPread, 223, 231
Ronnie Baker, 72
Rossington Collins Band, 64
Roxy Music, 281
Russ Kunkel, 170

Russell Hitchcock, 271, 273, 291, 295
Ruth Pointer, 121, 127, 294

S

Sands of Time, iii, 9, 10, 11, 13
Sandy Baron, 94
Sandy Yaguda, 3, 6, 294
Santana, 34, 60
Sara Allen, 151
Sara Smile, 153, 157, 159, 160, 162, 164
Saturday Night Fever, 201, 219, 221
Scotty Edwards, 156
Seth Justman, 99, 101, 107
Shake Your Booty, 197, 198, 203
Shirley Hanna-King, 224, 229, 231
Sigma Sound Studios, 67, 71, 75, 83
Simon and Garfunkel, 168, 173, 220
Sir George Martin, 2, 215
Skip Taylor, 51, 52
Slade, 281
Sold American, v, 131, 132, 133, 134, 137, 138
Sonny Bono, 140
Sony Music Entertainment, 160
Soul Survivors, 214
Specialty Records, 50
Stephen Bishop, 166, 175
Stephen Stills, 15, 25, 109
Steppenwolf, 235
Steve Alaimo, 252
Steve Clark, 279, 287
Steve Earle, 136
Steve Howe, 244
Steve Miller Band, 91, 235

Stevie Wonder, 44, 69, 82, 170, 175
Still, 4, 42, 46, 96, 159, 167, 168, 189, 190, 210, 216, 227, 229
Still Crazy After All These Years, 167, 168, 216
Stranglehold, 190, 195
Streetlife Serenade, 213, 214, 215
Sylvester Stallone, 149

T

Take Good Care of My Baby, 140
Tapestry, 139, 140
Tarkus, 241
Ted Nugent, vi, 187, 188, 189, 190, 191, 192, 193, 194, 195, 282, 294
Teddie Neeley, 117
Teddy Pendergrass, 70
Terry Melcher, 39, 47
Terry O'Neill, 144
The Amboy Dukes, 187, 188
The Ballad of Charles Whitman, 131, 133
The Beach Boys, 10, 11
The Beatles, 4, 6, 235
The Captain & Tennille, 143
The Commodores, 226, 228, 229, 231
The Dells, 158
The First Edition, 261
The Four Tops, 82, 87, 227, 228
The Hit Factory, 101
The Immigrant, 142, 143, 147
The O'Jays, 67, 68, 69, 70, 71, 72, 73, 75, 76, 79, 83, 87, 291, 293
The Pointer Sisters, v, 121, 124, 130
The Rubberband Man, 81, 87

The Silver Album, v, 149, 151, 152, 153, 154, 155, 156, 158, 159, 160, 161, 162, 163, 164
The Spinners, 79, 80, 81, 82, 83, 84, 85, 86, 87, 88, 291, 294
The Stranger, vi, 213, 215, 217, 218, 219, 220, 221, 222
The Stylistics, 79
The Supremes, 82, 87, 228
The Temptations, 82, 87, 227, 228
The Three Degrees, 70
The Three Musketeers, 101, 115
The Wrecking Crew, 156
Then Came You, 85, 86, 87
This Magic Moment, 9, 10, 13
Thom Bell, 72, 79, 81, 82, 90
Thomas McClary, 223, 224, 231
Three Dog Night, 227
Three Times a Lady, 227, 229
Tittenhurst Park, 280
TK Records, 199, 251, 252, 254, 255, 256
Todd Rundgren, 151, 161
Tokyo Sexwale, 131
Tom Allom, 280
Tom Evans, 62
Tom Scott, 234
Tommy Boyce, 139
Tommy Mottola, 149, 160
Tommy Roe, 4
Tony Bellamy, 93, 97
Tony Peluso, 44
Tower of Power, 121
T-Rex, 33
Trilogy, 27, 241
Tri-Phi Records, 80
Turnstiles, 213, 214, 215, 216, 217, 218
Two Tickets to Paradise, 235, 236, 239

U

United Artists, 7, 8, 11, 45, 50, 172, 263
United Artists Records, 45, 50, 172, 263
Universal Recording Studios, 182
Uriah Heep, 244

V

Van Morrison, 103, 207
Vanilla Fudge, 214
Victory Records, 246

W

Wally Heider Studios, 123
Walter, 73, 74, 290, 293
Walter Orange, 223, 231
Walter Williams, 67, 68, 291, 293
Wang Dang Doodle, 124, 129, 130
War Babies, 151, 157, 162
Warner Brothers Records, 207, 210
Warren Beatty, 101
Washington Coliseum, 4
We Were All Wounded at Wounded Knee, 93, 94, 95, 96, 98
West Side Story, 7
What You Won't Do For Love, 253
Will You Love Me Tomorrow, 140
William A. King, 223, 224, 295
William Powell, 67
Willie Nelson, 135, 136, 137
Wishbone Ash, 244
WLS, 58, 59
Woodie Guthrie, 32
Woodstock, 50, 54, 115

Works Volume I, vii, 241, 242, 243, 244, 248, 249, 250
Works Volume II, 243
Wovoka, iv, 91, 92, 93, 95, 96, 97, 98

Y

Yes, 43, 92, 123, 124, 129, 130, 203, 228, 244

Yes We Can Can, 123, 124, 129, 130
Yoko Ono, 280
You Decorated My Life, 266, 267, 269
Your Mama Don't Dance, 25

Z

Ziggy Stardust, 161

www.ingramcontent.com/pod-product-compliance
Lightning Source LLC
Chambersburg PA
CBHW052013070526
44584CB00016B/1730